Design Patterns in .NET

Mastering design patterns to write dynamic and effective .NET Code

Timur Yaroshenko

www.bpbonline.com

FIRST EDITION 2024

ISBN: 978-93-55517-821

LIMITS OF LIABILITY AND DISCLAIMER OF WARRANTY

Distributors:

BPB PUBLICATIONS
20, Ansari Road, Darya Ganj
New Delhi-110002
Ph: 23254990/23254991

DECCAN AGENCIES
4-3-329, Bank Street,
Hyderabad-500195
Ph: 24756967/24756400

MICRO MEDIA
Shop No. 5, Mahendra Chambers,
150 DN Rd. Next to Capital Cinema,
V.T. (C.S.T.) Station, MUMBAI-400 001
Ph: 22078296/22078297

To View Complete BPB Publications Catalogue Scan the QR Code:

Published by Manish Jain for BPB Publications, 20 Ansari Road, Darya Ganj, New Delhi-110002 and Printed by him at Manipal Technologies, Manipal

www.bpbonline.com

Dedicated to

My beloved cat:

Kuzja

About the Author

Timur Yaroshenko, started his journey in programming at the age of eight by writing his first line of code at school. In 2003, he started his professional career in software development: developing, designing, and architecting web/distributed applications. After working for a software outsourcing company for a couple of years, he became an independent consultant and has participated in many projects. He is now an independent consultant in the Senior Software Developer position at C.T.Co Latvia. Timur is passionate about .NET Core, C#, software architecture, and the cloud. His love for sharing knowledge led him to write his first book, the one you now hold in your hands.

About the Reviewer

Anton Tereshko, a seasoned, certified software developer, holds a degree in Computer Software Engineering. His extensive career, spanning over eight years in the software development sector, includes three years of demonstrated leadership. He has proficiently led and streamlined the development processes for application services across numerous large-scale businesses operating in complex sectors such as medicine, transport and logistics, and insurance, utilizing his expert knowledge of MAUI, Xamarin, .NET, Flutter, and Microsoft Azure technologies.

Embracing the rise of AI/ML technologies, Anton is actively engaged in the development of applications featuring artificial intelligence. He holds a certificate in Azure Cognitive Service and continues to advance in this direction. In addition to his software development accomplishments, Anton is a serial entrepreneur, having co-founded multiple technology startups.

Acknowledgement

I want to express my deepest gratitude to the owner of the computer club in which I fell in love with gaming and became interested in computer technology.

I am also grateful to BPB Publications for their guidance and expertise in bringing this book to fruition. It was a long journey of revising this book, with valuable participation and collaboration of reviewers, technical experts, and editors.

I would also like to acknowledge the valuable contributions of my colleagues and co-workers during many years of working in the tech industry, who have taught me so much and provided valuable feedback on my work.

Finally, I would like to thank all the readers who have taken an interest in my book and for their support in making it a reality. Your encouragement has been invaluable.

Preface

.NET. This small and simple word is already known in the world of software development for 20 years. Each year, the evolution of this platform has been enormous.

Microsoft invested a significant effort to modernize and make this platform competitive in our rapidly changing world. Now, after 20 years, it has become one of the leading platforms for developing software in many areas, including enterprise and distributed systems, mobile, games, home pages, IoT systems, AI, etc. However, to use it efficiently, it is not enough to just learn the language and libraries. You need to start thinking from a new perspective. This book can help you take your first step on the path of writing efficient, concise code that will be understandable by your colleagues and executed quickly by your devices.

Chapter by chapter, you will learn how to structure your code to make it concise. The first few chapters will cover the history, evolution, and concepts of design patterns. You will be introduced to the **Gangs of Four** (**GoF**) and SOLID approaches. Next, we will explore the most famous and usable patterns that help software developers simplify their everyday work and solve complex problems. In the end, you will see how modern .NET Core platform supports and uses many of these patterns in its standard libraries and packages.

This book can give you insights into how modern software is written, the problems that software developers face in their daily work, and how they solve the design and structure of the code. After reading this book, you will become a better developer who can communicate effectively with experienced colleagues and solve complex tasks with minimum effort.Parte superior do formulárioParte inferior do formulário

Chapter 1: Main OOP Standpoints - In this chapter, we will learn about the OOP paradigm and see how .NET Core implements it. To better understand the purpose of Design patterns and principles, you need to grasp the fundamental blocks of OOP, including Inheritance, Encapsulation, and Polymorphism. Also, we will review the additional capabilities that .NET Core and C# provide to developers: generic, extension methods, and interfaces.

Chapter 2: Creational Design Patterns: Factory and Builder - This chapter explores object creation using the Factory, Abstract Factory, and Builder Design patterns. These are some of the most used design patterns. They provide the best ways to create an object without exposing the creation logic to the caller and allow access to newly created objects using a standard interface.

Chapter 3: Creational Design Patterns: Singleton and Prototype - This chapter explores object creation using Singleton and Prototype Design patterns. These are some of the simplest design patterns from GoF.

Chapter 4: Structural Design Patterns: Adapter, Composite, and Flyweight - This chapter explores object composition using Adapter, Composite, and Flyweight design patterns.

These three patterns provide three cornerstones of structural decomposition: interface to the outside world, encapsulation of a group of objects, and sharing a common state between a group of objects.

Chapter 5: Structural Design Patterns: Object Composition - This chapter explores object composition using Proxy, Facade, Bridge, and Decorator design patterns.

These patterns provide the possibility to conceal the actual implementation of the object while remaining interconnected and being able to interact with it.

Chapter 6: Object Behavioral Design Patterns- This chapter explores object behaviors using the Template method, Strategy, and Chain of responsibility design patterns.

These three patterns are basic for our processing pipeline. With them, we can redefine our pipelines modularly, so it will be easy to add new pipelines for different events.

Chapter 7: Behavioral Design Patterns: Observer, Visitor, and State - This chapter explores object behaviors using the Observer, Visitor, and State design patterns.

These design patterns provide the possibility to react and modify the state of objects in reaction to changes in other objects.

Chapter 8: Behavioral Design Patterns: Mediator and Command - This chapter explores object behaviors using Mediator and Command design patterns.

These two patterns provide the possibility to achieve loose coupling between objects that need to communicate with each other.

Chapter 9: Behavioral Design Patterns: Interpreter, Iterator, and Memento - This chapter explores object behaviors using three different design patterns. These objects are not often used, so we will review them together.

Chapter 10: The SOLID Principles - Here, we will discuss SOLID architectural principles, their history, and structure.

Chapter 11: Inversion of Control in .NET Core - In this chapter, we will see how we can use the SOLID principles in .NET Core with its dependency injection support.

Code Bundle and Coloured Images

Please follow the link to download the
Code Bundle and the *Coloured Images* of the book:

https://rebrand.ly/9edcm5m

The code bundle for the book is also hosted on GitHub at **https://github.com/bpbpublications/Design-Patterns-in-.NET**. In case there's an update to the code, it will be updated on the existing GitHub repository.

We have code bundles from our rich catalogue of books and videos available at **https://github.com/bpbpublications**. Check them out!

Errata

We take immense pride in our work at BPB Publications and follow best practices to ensure the accuracy of our content to provide with an indulging reading experience to our subscribers. Our readers are our mirrors, and we use their inputs to reflect and improve upon human errors, if any, that may have occurred during the publishing processes involved. To let us maintain the quality and help us reach out to any readers who might be having difficulties due to any unforeseen errors, please write to us at :

errata@bpbonline.com

Your support, suggestions and feedbacks are highly appreciated by the BPB Publications' Family.

Piracy

If you come across any illegal copies of our works in any form on the internet, we would be grateful if you would provide us with the location address or website name. Please contact us at **business@bpbonline.com** with a link to the material.

If you are interested in becoming an author

If there is a topic that you have expertise in, and you are interested in either writing or contributing to a book, please visit **www.bpbonline.com**. We have worked with thousands of developers and tech professionals, just like you, to help them share their insights with the global tech community. You can make a general application, apply for a specific hot topic that we are recruiting an author for, or submit your own idea.

Reviews

Please leave a review. Once you have read and used this book, why not leave a review on the site that you purchased it from? Potential readers can then see and use your unbiased opinion to make purchase decisions. We at BPB can understand what you think about our products, and our authors can see your feedback on their book. Thank you!

For more information about BPB, please visit **www.bpbonline.com**.

Join our book's Discord space

Join the book's Discord Workspace for Latest updates, Offers, Tech happenings around the world, New Release and Sessions with the Authors:

https://discord.bpbonline.com

Table of Contents

Chapter 1
Main OOP Standpoints

Introduction

This chapter of the book will cover the main standpoints of OOP, along with their meaning and usage.

We would start identifying the fundament of the OOP paradigm.

Structure

The chapter covers the following topics:

- Inheritance
- Polymorphism
- Encapsulation
- Main OOP standpoints in .NET
- Interfaces
- Abstract classes
- Generics

- Extensions methods
- Partial classes

Objectives

By the end of this chapter, you will be able to understand what OOP is, why it is important, and how to apply basic tricks to make a good code structure.

Also, you will understand the constraints .NET OOP implementation has and how .NET enriches OOP with special types and approaches.

We will see how our basic structure can be transformed using .NET specific approach with Interfaces, Generics, and Extension methods.

Inheritance

One of the core concepts of object-oriented programming language is inheritance. This mechanism allows you to derive a class from another class and share a set of attributes and methods.

You can use it to add custom logic to existing classes/libraries/frameworks, extend or change the behavior of a class, and so on.

The main meaning of inheritance is to add existing functionality of the superclass to your subclass, and it allows you to overwrite their implementation. This technique is called *polymorphism,* which we will cover later.

In the following code example, we will show you basic inheritance mechanics. We will create a base pipeline class and derive from it to create a new extended pipeline:

```
public class BasicPipeline
{
        public void Process(BasicEvent basicEvent)
        {
            WriteLog($"Starting processing of event {basicEvent.Id}");
            Validate(basicEvent);
            WriteLog($"Processing {basicEvent.Id}");
            ProcessEvent(basicEvent);
            WriteLog($"Processing successfully completed for event
                    {basicEvent.Id}");
        }
```

```
        private void ProcessEvent(BasicEvent basicEvent)
        {
            // Do processing stuff ..
        }

        protected void WriteLog(string message)
        {
            Console.WriteLine(message);
        }

        protected void Validate(BasicEvent basicEvent)
        {
            if(basicEvent == null)
            {
              throw new ArgumentNullException("Event object cannot be null");
            }
            if (string.IsNullOrWhiteSpace(basicEvent.Data))
            {
                throw new ArgumentException($"Event {basicEvent.Id} is invalid");
            }
        }
}
public class BasicEvent
{
        public Guid Id { get; set; }
        public string Data { get; set; }
}
```

In the preceding code example, you can see that we have created a new class called **BasicPipeline**. It provides one public method **Process** that accepts the **BasicEvent** object, contains a few protected methods that provide additional functionality like validation and logging, and one private method that processes the event. This can include mail sending, math calculations, 3rd party services execution, and so on.

For example, we want to create a new pipeline which will accept an extended event and provide some additional functionality with preprocessing and postprocessing actions. However, the core of processing should stay the same.

Code copy-pasting leads to buggy, unmaintainable code, so we should derive existing functionality from the existing **BasicPipeline** class and extend it with two new methods that can be called outside of the class.

In the next code example, we will create new classes for **EventData** and Pipeline, which will contain extension code:

```
public class ExtendedPipeline: BasicPipeline
{
        public void PreProcessing(ExtendedEvent extendedEvent)
        {
            WriteLog($"Preprocessing event: {extendedEvent.Id} from
                    {extendedEvent.Source}");
        }

        public void PostProcessing(ExtendedEvent extendedEvent)
        {
            WriteLog($"Postprocessing event: {extendedEvent.Id} from
                    {extendedEvent.Source}");
        }
}
public class ExtendedEvent: BasicEvent
{
        public string Source { get; set; }
}
```

In the preceding code example, you can see that we have created two new classes: first for a new extended pipeline and second for a new extended event.

Each of them contains new members. In the case of an extended pipeline, there are two new methods, and in the case of an extended event, it is a new property called **source**.

The rest of the classes are derived from their source. Now you can use new classes to process events with extended data and to call pre-processing and post-processing functionality:

```
BasicPipeline pipeline = new BasicPipeline();
ExtendedPipeline extendedPipeline = new ExtendedPipeline();

BasicEvent basicEvent = new BasicEvent
{
   Id = Guid.NewGuid(),
   Data = "Some Event data"
};
```

```
ExtendedEvent extEvent = new ExtendedEvent
{
    Id = Guid.NewGuid(),
    Data = "Some extended event data",
    Source = "Email"
};

pipeline.Process(basicEvent);
Console.WriteLine();
extendedPipeline.PreProcessing(extEvent);
extendedPipeline.Process(extEvent);
extendedPipeline.PostProcessing(extEvent);
```

In this code example, we have created two instances of **Basic** and **Extended** pipelines and two events. Then, we passed those events to corresponding pipelines to be processed.

In the result of the preceding code example execution, you will receive the following result, as shown in *Figure 1.1*:

```
Microsoft Visual Studio Debug Console
Starting processing of event 781e5400-c66f-4c5b-bea7-0f282683fb1d
Processing 781e5400-c66f-4c5b-bea7-0f282683fb1d
Processing successfully completed for event 781e5400-c66f-4c5b-bea7-0f282683fb1d

Preprocessing event: 3fcb3f89-8928-4a7f-879f-dd03aac7b600 from Email
Starting processing of event 3fcb3f89-8928-4a7f-879f-dd03aac7b600
Processing 3fcb3f89-8928-4a7f-879f-dd03aac7b600
Processing successfully completed for event 3fcb3f89-8928-4a7f-879f-dd03aac7b600
Postprocessing event: 3fcb3f89-8928-4a7f-879f-dd03aac7b600 from Email
```

Figure 1.1: *Basic and Extended pipelines execution example*

So, as you can see in *Figure 1.1*, the same functionality is executed for Basic and Extended events by **Basic** and **Extended Pipelines**. Also, we were able to call additional functionality from **ExtendedPipeline** class for post- and pre- processing.

Polymorphism

The most interesting part of the inheritance is coming with polymorphism.

It can be described as situations in which something occurs in several different forms. In computer science, polymorphism describes the case when a type behaves differently depending on the object which hides under the cover. It is possible because of inheritance and methods overriding.

Let us look at a simple example of polymorphism:

```
public class ExtendedPipeline: BasicPipeline
{
        public void PreProcessing(ExtendedEvent extendedEvent)
        {
            WriteLog($"Preprocessing event: {extendedEvent.Id} from
                    {extendedEvent.Source}");
        }

        public void PostProcessing(ExtendedEvent extendedEvent)
        {
            WriteLog($"Postprocessing event: {extendedEvent.Id} from
                    {extendedEvent.Source}");
        }

        protected override void Validate(BasicEvent basicEvent)
        {
            var extendedEvent = basicEvent as ExtendedEvent;
            if (extendedEvent == null)
                throw new ArgumentException("This pipeline can process only
                                extended events");

            if (string.IsNullOrWhiteSpace(extendedEvent.Source))
            {
                throw new ArgumentException($"Event {basicEvent.Id} is
                                invalid. Source cannot be null.");
            }

            base.Validate(basicEvent);
        }
}
```

As you can see, it is an extended pipeline from the previous section. But now we have added a new member called method **`Validate`**. It has the same signature as in **`BasicPipeline`** class, but we have supplemented it with an **`override`** keyword.

What does it mean? At runtime, the method of **`ExtendedPipeline`** will be selected to be executed to process event object by **`ExtendedPipeline`** instance. If you want to process

BasicEvent object by **ExtendedPipeline**, you will receive an exception telling you that this pipeline cannot process such types of object.

The following code example will show how you can use the polymorphic method:

```
BasicPipeline pipeline = new BasicPipeline();
BasicPipeline extendedPipeline = new ExtendedPipeline();

BasicEvent basicEvent = new BasicEvent
{
    Id = Guid.NewGuid(),
    Data = "Some data"
};

ExtendedEvent extendedEvent = new ExtendedEvent
{
    Data = "Some data",
    Id = Guid.NewGuid(),
    Source = "Console App"
};

pipeline.Process(basicEvent);
extendedPipeline.Process(extendedEvent);
extendedPipeline.Process(basicEvent);
```

In the preceding code example, we are creating two pipelines and two event objects. The first two execution of Process method works fine, and the third throws an exception because the validation of object was not successful. Refer to the following *Figure 1.2:*

***Figure 1.2:** Example of polymorphism for function Validate*

The preceding code is also an interesting creation and assignment of the **ExtendedPipeline** variable. As you can notice, we are assigning **ExtendedPipeline** to **BasicPipeline** variable.

In this case, you may think that we are calling **Process** method of **BasicPipeline** class. However, runtime always knows what is covered under the hood and will execute the correct method.

From the design perspective, our class diagram does not look very serious, however, later we will extend and deepen it. Refer to the following *Figure 1.3*:

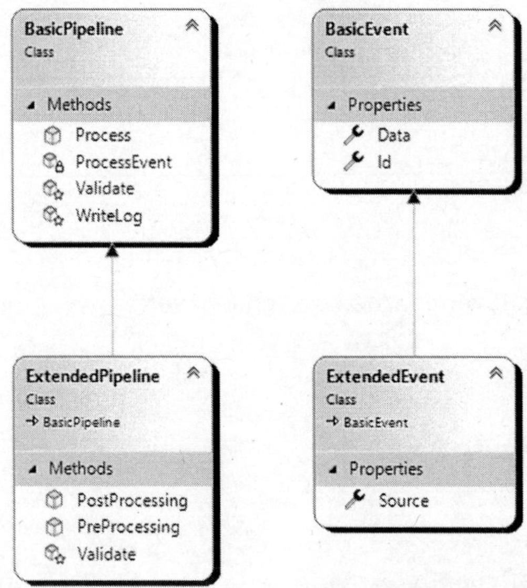

Figure 1.3: *Class diagram for Basic and Extended Pipelines*

Encapsulation

Encapsulation is the third pillar of OOP. Let us see how it helps and supplements the other two: *inheritance* and *polymorphism*.

The main goal of encapsulation is to hide an internal state and functionality from the outside world. For example, you have some attributes of the class that cannot be lower than 10 and more than 100. In the constructor, you assign a default value of 10 to it. But, you want to control what values could be assigned to it and how. To achieve this, you mark the variable as private and create two methods: getter and setter.

Let us look at the following code example:

```
public class ExtendedEvent : BasicEvent
{
	private string source;

	public ExtendedEvent()
	{
```

```
            this.source = "EMAIL";
        }

        public string GetSource()
        {
            return this.source;
        }

        public void SetSource(string strValue)
        {
            if (!string.IsNullOrWhiteSpace(strValue))
            {
                if (strValue == "EMAIL" || strValue == "MSG")
                {
                    this.source = strValue;
                }
            }
        }
}
```

As you can see, we have created a pair of methods to get and set source variable. In set methods, we have added validation to restrict the possibility to set invalid values in the source variable. The get method returns the value of variable.

The second reason why we need encapsulation is to control access to members of the superclass using access modifiers like **private**, **protected**, **internal**, and **public**. They allow you to control access to internal variables and methods. You can mark your methods as **protected virtual**, and it will be possible to overwrite them in subclasses or use them in the same class. No other class will have a possibility to call it from outside of the class. It allows you to make a clear separation from the public API that your class provides to the outside world and internal structure, which can be overwritten and called inside the class or its subclasses. In our previous code example, we had a class called **BasicPipeline**:

```
public class BasicPipeline
{
        public void Process(BasicEvent basicEvent)
        {
            WriteLog($"Starting processing of event {basicEvent.Id}");
            Validate(basicEvent);
            WriteLog($"Processing {basicEvent.Id}");
            ProcessEvent(basicEvent);
```

```
        WriteLog($"Processing successfully completed for event
              {basicEvent.Id}");
    }

    private void ProcessEvent(BasicEvent basicEvent)
    {
        // Do processing stuff ..
    }

    protected void WriteLog(string message)
    {
        Console.WriteLine(message);
    }
    protected virtual void Validate(BasicEvent basicEvent)
    {
        if(basicEvent == null)
        {
            throw new ArgumentNullException("Event object cannot be null");
        }
        if (string.IsNullOrWhiteSpace(basicEvent.Data))
        {
            throw new ArgumentException($"Event {basicEvent.Id} is invalid");
        }
    }
}
```

There is a method called **Validate**. It is marked as **protected virtual**, so it is possible to use it inside the superclass subclasses, and override it as we did in the **ExtendedPipeline** example:

```
public class ExtendedPipeline: BasicPipeline, IPipeline, IPostProcessing
{
        protected sealed override void Validate(BasicEvent basicEvent)
        {
            var extendedEvent = basicEvent as ExtendedEvent;
            if (extendedEvent == null)
                throw new ArgumentException("This pipeline can process only
                                     extended events");
```

```
            if (string.IsNullOrWhiteSpace(extendedEvent.Source))
            {
                throw new ArgumentException($"Event {basicEvent.Id} is invalid.
                                            Source cannot be null.");
            }
            base.Validate(basicEvent);
        }

        public void PostProcessing(BasicEvent basicEvent)
        {
            Console.WriteLine($"Postprocessing of event: {basicEvent.Id}");
        }
}
```

Ultimately, we can say that these three core components make OOP a favorable choice when you choose the language and platform to develop your next big project. It allows you to granularly restrict access to fields and methods using *encapsulation*, avoid copy-pasting code using *inheritance*, and customize subclasses behavior using the polymorphism technique. All these three components are extensively used in our everyday programmer's life, in every tiny library written by enthusiasts, and in every big framework written by hundreds of programmers in offices of big technological companies.

In our next step, we will review how C# language implements the OOP paradigm and the instruments it provides to make our lives easier while trying to construct our own unique hierarchy of classes.

Main OOP standpoints in .NET

The main goal of .NET from the beginning was to provide the public with easy-to-use instruments to construct software. And the brilliant of the infrastructure provided was C# language.

It has a great syntax and many capabilities, including OOP, functional paradigm, dynamic programming concept, AOP, and more.

Here, we will stop on the OOP side of this beautiful language and see how it supports and enriches the OOP paradigm.

First of all, we will start with encapsulation and access modifiers.

As you remember, encapsulation provides capabilities to control access to fields and methods of the class granularly.

C# language provides the following access modifiers:

- **Public:** Objects with public access modifiers are accessible everywhere in and outside the project. There are no accessibility restrictions at all.
- **Protected:** Objects with protected access modifiers are accessible inside the class it defines and in all subclasses.
- **Private:** Objects implementing a private access modifier are accessible only inside a class or a structure. The outside code cannot directly execute/access them.
- **Internal:** Objects implementing an internal access modifier are accessible only inside the project. It is not possible to execute/access them from other projects/ assemblies.
- **Protected-internal:** Objects that implement protected internal access modifiers are accessible inside the assembly or in subclasses in other assembly.
- **Private-protected:** Objects implementing private protected access modifiers are accessible inside the class it defines or in subclasses in the same assembly.

We can summarize the preceding list in the following *Table 1.1*:

Called from	Public	Protected	Private	Internal	Protected internal	Private protected
Within the class	X	x	x	x	x	x
Derived class (same assembly)	x	x	x	x	x	
Non-derived class (same assembly)	x	x		x		
Derived class (different assembly)	x	x	x			
Non-derived class (different assembly)	x					

***Table 1.1:** Access modifiers summary table*

Structures and classes can have only two access modifiers: public and internal. Public objects can be accessed everywhere, and internal can be accessed only in the assembly in which the object is defined.

Also, C# eases the definition of getters and setters functions for us. As you can remember, to restrict access to a variable in the class or structure from outside, you should define it as private and provide functions like **getVariable** and **setVariable** to be able to access and set its value from the outside of the class.

C# allows us to shorten the definition and declare all needed functionality in one code block called **property**:

```
public class ExtendedEvent : BasicEvent
{
        private string source;
        public ExtendedEvent()
        {
            this.source = "EMAIL";
        }

        public string Source
        {
            get
            {
                return this.source;
            }
            set
            {
                if (!string.IsNullOrWhiteSpace(value))
                {
                    if (value == "EMAIL" || value == "MSG")
                    {
                        this.source = value;
                    }
                }
            }
        }
}
```

As you can see in the preceding code example, we have defined a new property called **Source**, in which you can define get or set code blocks or both.

To talk further about access modifiers, C# allows you to set access modifiers to get/set accessors. They are obeying the same rules as functions in the class.

The next theme that we will review is inheritance in C#.

C# and .NET support single inheritance only for classes. It means that any class can be derived only from one class. However, you can make an inheritance hierarchy because inheritance is transitive. So, you can derive **`type B`** from **`type A`** and **`type C`** from **`type B`**. In **`type C`**, you will have access to all the accessible variables/properties/functions from **`type A`** and all preceding mentioned from **`type B`**.

Variables, properties, and functions can be derived and overridden. Static, instance constructors (you can call them directly), and finalizers could not be derived. Only polymorphism has been left undescribed. So, let us see what .NET offers in this area.

We will start reviewing how polymorphism works in .NET under the hood.

At runtime, subclasses may be treated as base class objects, for example, in function parameters. It means that you can pass any derived type of a superclass to a function that accepts base class as a parameter. However, when a call of the function occurs, the declared type and run-time type will be different.

To use a polymorphic function, first of all, you need to define a virtual method in a base class, and the derived class should override it and provide its own implementation. At runtime, when client code calls the method, the CLR looks up the runtime type of the object and executes that override of the virtual method. In your source code, it will look like the client calls the function of the base class, but in actuality, the derived class's version of the method will be executed.

As an example of polymorphism, we can look at **`ExtendedPipeline`**:

```
public class ExtendedPipeline: BasicPipeline
{
        public void PreProcessing(ExtendedEvent extendedEvent)
        {
            WriteLog($"Preprocessing event: {extendedEvent.Id} from
                   {extendedEvent.Source}");
        }

        public void PostProcessing(ExtendedEvent extendedEvent)
        {
            WriteLog($"Postprocessing event: {extendedEvent.Id} from
                   {extendedEvent.Source}");
        }

        protected override void Validate(BasicEvent basicEvent)
        {
            var extendedEvent = basicEvent as ExtendedEvent;
            if (extendedEvent == null)
```

```
            throw new ArgumentException("This pipeline can process only
                                  extended events");

        if (string.IsNullOrWhiteSpace(extendedEvent.Source))
        {
         throw new ArgumentException($"Event {basicEvent.Id} is invalid.
                          Source cannot be null.");
        }

        base.Validate(basicEvent);
    }
}
```

As you can see, we have defined an override of the **`Validate`** method, extended its functionality, and called the base class method at the end.

C# provides the following mechanisms to implement and use polymorphic methods:

- **Virtual methods:** Virtual methods can be overridden in the subclass. A subclass can define its own implementation of the method.
- **Sealed methods:** When creating an inheritance hierarchy, sometimes you want to deny the possibility to override a method in the subclass of subclass. In this case, you can override a base class method and mark it as sealed.
- **Override methods:** When a virtual method in the base class is marked as override in subclass, it will be selected and executed instead of the base class's method.
- **Base functions execution:** It is possible to call a base class method from overridden method using **`base`** keyword. You should type **`base.MethodName()`** to execute the base function.
- **New methods:** When you do not want to override a method but add your own implementation in a subclass, you can mark your method as **`new`**. The behavior of such a method will be different from overridden method. When object is cast to a base class, base function will be executed, otherwise, new function will be called.

We have already seen virtual methods definition, overriding, and base class function called inside an overridden method. Let us see how we can deny overriding of the function:

```
public class ExtendedPipeline: BasicPipeline
{
        // Pre/Post processing …

        protected sealed override void Validate(BasicEvent basicEvent)
```

```
        {
            var extendedEvent = basicEvent as ExtendedEvent;
            if (extendedEvent == null)
                throw new ArgumentException("This pipeline can process only
                                extended events");

            if (string.IsNullOrWhiteSpace(extendedEvent.Source))
            {
             throw new ArgumentException($"Event {basicEvent.Id} is invalid.
                                Source cannot be null.");
            }

            base.Validate(basicEvent);
        }
}
public class ExtendedPipelineVersion2: ExtendedPipeline
{
        public override void Validate(BasicEvent basicEvent1)
        {
        }
}
```

When you try to compile this code, you will receive a compile time error saying, **cannot override inherited member 'ExtendedPipeline.Validate(BasicEvent)' because it is sealed**.

The new keyword, as mentioned previously, allows you to keep the possibility to execute the base class's function by casting an object to the base class.

Imagine a situation when you cannot override the main **`Processing`** function. Still, you should because new types of events are coming in, requiring a different pipeline to be executed. For this, extend the pipeline, make a new **`Process`** function, and make a new pipeline inside the derived class. Let us see an example:

```
public class ExtendedPipelineVer3: BasicPipeline
{
        public new void Process(BasicEvent basicEvent)
        {
            if(basicEvent is ExtendedEvent)
            {
                ProcessExtendedEvent(basicEvent as ExtendedEvent);
            }
```

```
            else
            {
                base.Process(basicEvent);
            }
        }

        private void ProcessExtendedEvent(ExtendedEvent extendedEvent)
        {
            Console.WriteLine("Processing extended event");
        }

        protected sealed override void Validate(BasicEvent basicEvent)
        {
            var extendedEvent = basicEvent as ExtendedEvent;
            if (extendedEvent == null)
                throw new ArgumentException("This pipeline can process only
                                        extended events");

            if (string.IsNullOrWhiteSpace(extendedEvent.Source))
            {
             throw new ArgumentException($"Event {basicEvent.Id} is invalid.
                                     Source cannot be null.");
            }

            base.Validate(basicEvent);
        }
}
```

As you can see in the preceding code, we have added a function **Process** with a new keyword.

We have also added a check on the type of event parameter to select the function that should be called for processing.

The following code shows how we can process an event object by a new pipeline:

```
ExtendedPipelineVer3 extendedPipelineVer3 = new ExtendedPipelineVer3();

BasicEvent basicEvent = new BasicEvent
{
    Id = Guid.NewGuid(),
    Data = "Some data"
};
```

```
ExtendedEvent extendedEvent = new ExtendedEvent
{
    Data = "Some data",
    Id = Guid.NewGuid(),
    Source = "Console App"
};

extendedPipelineVer3.Process(basicEvent);
extendedPipelineVer3.Process(extendedEvent);
```

In the result of the preceding code example execution, we receive the following figure:

```
Select Microsoft Visual Studio Debug Console
Welcome to pipelines world!
Processing extended event
Starting processing of event e5e96564-7031-44b4-96bc-b1f702b9ea5e
Processing e5e96564-7031-44b4-96bc-b1f702b9ea5e
Processing successfully completed for event e5e96564-7031-44b4-96bc-b1f702b9ea5e
```

Figure 1.4: *The result of executing function with new keyword*

As you can see, both events are processed successfully, each using a different procedure.

BasicEvent is processed using a base class function and extended event– by extended pipelinefunction **ProcessExtendedEvent**. Both of them are validated through overridden Validate method, which in the end uses Validate method of Basic pipeline.

Interfaces

The next concept to discuss is interfaces. Since you cannot have multiple inheritance .NET, they decided to provide you with the possibility to have it in a different way.

When you are signing a contract with an employer or b2b, it means that both of you should behave as per the contract. In the same way, contracts in .NET determine the behavior of the classes derived from them. In C#, a derived class should implement the main contract the interface defines.

To create an interface in C#, mark an entity with the interface keyword. This entity can contain the declaration of properties, methods, etc. The limitations are that it cannot contain instance variables and constructors.

Let us have a look at simple interface definition:

```
public interface IPipeline
{
      void Process(BasicEvent basicEvent);
}
```

The preceding code example declares an interface named **`IPipeline`**. It contains only one method: **`Process(BasicEvent)`**.

To implement this interface, create a new class and derive it from the interface as shown in the following code example:

```
public class BasicPipeline: IPipeline
{
        public void Process(BasicEvent basicEvent)
        {
            WriteLog($"Starting processing of event {basicEvent.Id}");
            Validate(basicEvent);
            WriteLog($"Processing {basicEvent.Id}");
            ProcessEvent(basicEvent);
            WriteLog($"Processing successfully completed for event
                   {basicEvent.Id}");
        }
}
public class ExtendedPipelineVer3: BasicPipeline
    {
        public new void Process(BasicEvent basicEvent)
        {
            if(basicEvent is ExtendedEvent)
            {
                ProcessExtendedEvent(basicEvent as ExtendedEvent);
            }
            else
            {
                base.Process(basicEvent);
            }
        }
    // The rest of the code
}
```

From now, it does not matter which Pipeline you want to use while it implements the **`IPipeline`** interface. Every pipeline instance is possible to cast to **`IPipeline`** variable and execute **`Process(BasicEvent)`** method on instance, as shown in the following example:

```
IPipeline pipeline = new BasicPipeline();
IPipeline extendedPipeline = new ExtendedPipeline();
```

```
IPipeline extendedPipelineVer3 = new ExtendedPipelineVer3();

BasicEvent basicEvent = new BasicEvent
{
    Id = Guid.NewGuid(),
    Data = "Some data"
};

ExtendedEvent extendedEvent = new ExtendedEvent
{
    Data = "Some data",
    Id = Guid.NewGuid(),
    Source = "Console App"
};

pipeline.Process(basicEvent);
extendedPipeline.Process(basicEvent);
extendedPipelineVer3.Process(extendedEvent);
extendedPipelineVer3.Process(basicEvent);
```

In our case, we have derived **IPipeline** implementation from **BasicPipeline**. However, we can remove inheritance from **BasicPipeline** and derive it from **IPipeline** for all defined pipeline classes.

Also, we can implement multiple interfaces in one class.

Let us add a new interface **IPostProcessing**:

```
public interface IPostProcessing
{
        void PostProcessing(BasicEvent basicEvent);
}
```

Add an implementation of this interface to the **ExtendedPipeline** class:

```
public class ExtendedPipeline: BasicPipeline, IPipeline, IPostProcessing
    {
        protected sealed override void Validate(BasicEvent basicEvent)
        {
            var extendedEvent = basicEvent as ExtendedEvent;
            if (extendedEvent == null)
```

```
                throw new ArgumentException("This pipeline can process only
                                    extended events");

            if (string.IsNullOrWhiteSpace(extendedEvent.Source))
            {
                throw new ArgumentException($"Event {basicEvent.Id} is
                                    invalid. Source cannot be null.");
            }

            base.Validate(basicEvent);
        }

        public void PostProcessing(BasicEvent basicEvent)
        {
            Console.WriteLine($"Postprocessing of event: {basicEvent.Id}");
        }
    }
```

Also, we will extend **BasicPipeline** and **BasicEvent** types and add a property **Type**:

```
public class BasicPipeline: IPipeline
{
        public string Type { get; set; }
      // rest of the code goes here…
}
public class BasicEvent
{
        public string Type { get; set; }
      // rest of the code goes here …
}
```

From this moment, we can write a code for an event to be processed by pipeline selected based on type, and also call **PostProcessing** functionality if pipeline does provide it, as shown in the following code:

```
Console.WriteLine("Welcome to pipelines world!");

IPipeline pipeline = new BasicPipeline { Type="Basic"};
IPipeline extendedPipeline = new ExtendedPipeline { Type = "Extended" };
IPipeline extendedPipelineVer3 = new ExtendedPipelineVer3 { Type = "Ver3" };
```

```
List<IPipeline> pipelines = new List<IPipeline>
{
    pipeline, extendedPipeline, extendedPipelineVer3
};

BasicEvent basicEvent = new BasicEvent
{
    Id = Guid.NewGuid(),
    Data = "Some data",
    Type = "Basic"
};

ExtendedEvent extendedEvent = new ExtendedEvent
{
    Data = "Some data",
    Id = Guid.NewGuid(),
    Source = "Console App",
    Type = "Ver3"
};

List<BasicEvent> events = new List<BasicEvent> { basicEvent, extendedEvent };

events.ForEach(eventObj => {
    var selectedPipeline = pipelines. FirstOrDefault (x => x.Type ==
                                                        eventObj.Type);
    if (selectedPipeline == null)
        return;

    selectedPipeline.Process(eventObj);
    var postProcessing = selectedPipeline as IPostProcessing;
    if (postProcessing == null)
        return;

    postProcessing.PostProcessing(eventObj);
});
```

As you can see, we are processing events one by one selecting preferred pipeline. We are casting this pipeline to two interfaces: IPipeline and IPostProcessing, to execute different functionality on the same instance.

Refer to the following figure to see what the classes looks like:

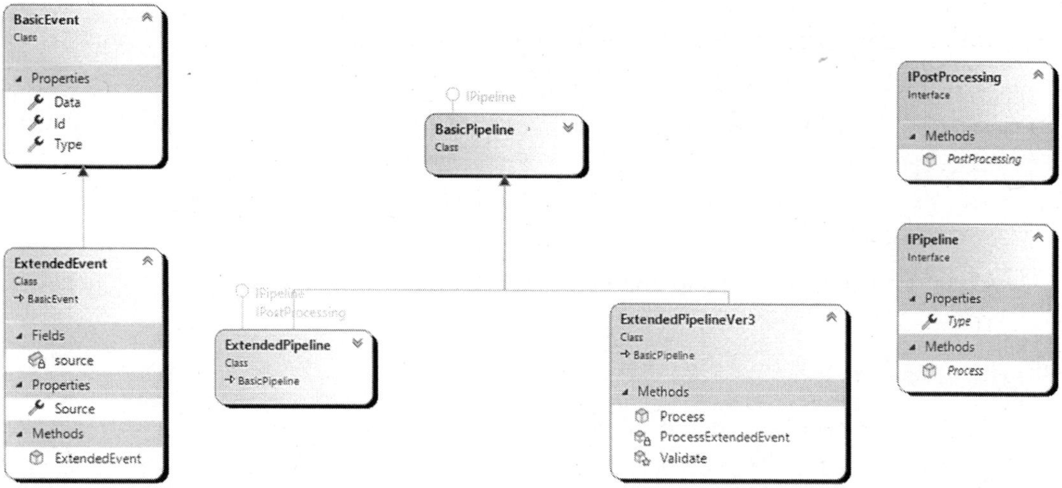

Figure 1.5: Class diagram

One more thing to describe is interface inheritance. A developer can combine different interfaces under one common interface. As an example, we can introduce a new interface called **IPostProcessingPipeline** which will combine **IPipeline** and **IPostProcessing** interfaces together:

```
public interface IPostProcessingPipeline: IPipeline, IPostProcessing
{
}
```

Add a new class called **ExtendedPipelineV2** to be derived from a newly created interface:

```
public class ExtendedPipelineV2: BasicPipeline, IPostProcessingPipeline
{
        public void PreProcessing(ExtendedEvent extendedEvent)
        {
                WriteLog($"Preprocessing event: {extendedEvent.Id} from
                        {extendedEvent.Source}");
        }

        public void PostProcessing(ExtendedEvent extendedEvent)
        {
                WriteLog($"Postprocessing event: {extendedEvent.Id} from
                        {extendedEvent.Source}");
        }
```

```
    protected sealed override void Validate(BasicEvent basicEvent)
    {
        var extendedEvent = basicEvent as ExtendedEvent;
        if (extendedEvent == null)
            throw new ArgumentException("This pipeline can process only
                                        extended events");
        if (string.IsNullOrWhiteSpace(extendedEvent.Source))
        {
          throw new ArgumentException($"Event {basicEvent.Id} is invalid.
                                     Source cannot be null.");
        }

        base.Validate(basicEvent);
    }

    public void PostProcessing(BasicEvent basicEvent)
    {
        Console.WriteLine($"Postprocessing of event: {basicEvent.Id}");
    }
}
```

It contains the same code as **ExtendedPipeline**, but instead of deriving two interfaces explicitly, it derives from the **IPostProcessingPipeline** interface.

In the preceding code example, we can use **ExtendedPipelinev2** instead of **ExtendedPipeline**. There will be no change as we can easily cast a new variable to any derived interfaces (**IPipeline** or **IPostProcessing**).

To summarize:

- Interface can contain declarations of methods, properties, indexers, and events.
- Interface cannot include private, protected, or internal members. All the members are public by default.
- Interface cannot contain fields.
- A class or a struct can implement one or more interfaces.
- An interface can inherit one or more interfaces.
- Interface can be derived from other interfaces and provide multiple inheritance capabilities.
- Interfaces can contain default implementation of functionality (C# 8.0 only).

Abstract classes

Abstract classes are different from standard classes. The main difference is that abstract classes cannot be instantiated directly. They provide the possibility to define a conceptual generalization of a piece of functionality.

We can define a basic pipeline as an abstract class that defines the standard flow of processing an event:

```
public abstract class AbstractBasicPipeline
{
        public bool IsPostProcessingEnabled { get; set; }
        public bool IsPreProcessingEnabled { get; set; }

        public virtual void Process(BasicEvent basicEvent)
        {
            try
            {
                WriteLog($"Starting processing of event {basicEvent.Id}");
                if (IsPreProcessingEnabled)
                    PreProcess(basicEvent);
                Validate(basicEvent);
                WriteLog($"Processing {basicEvent.Id}");
                ProcessEvent(basicEvent);

                if (IsPostProcessingEnabled)
                    PostProcess(basicEvent);
                    WriteLog($"Processing successfully completed for event
                       {basicEvent.Id}");
            }
            catch(Exception ex)
            {
              WriteLog($"Processing has failed for event: {basicEvent.Id}");
            }
        }
        protected abstract void ProcessEvent(BasicEvent basicEvent);
        protected virtual void WriteLog(string message)
        {
            Console.WriteLine($"[{DateTime.Now}]: {message}");
```

```
        }
        protected virtual void Validate(BasicEvent basicEvent)
        {
            if (basicEvent == null)
            {
                throw new ArgumentNullException("Event object cannot be null");
            }
            if (string.IsNullOrWhiteSpace(basicEvent.Data))
            {
                throw new ArgumentException($"Event {basicEvent.Id} is
                                            invalid");
            }
        }
        protected virtual void PostProcess(BasicEvent basicEvent)
        {
            throw new NotImplementedException("PostProcessing functionality
                                              is not implemented");
        }
        protected virtual void PreProcess(BasicEvent basicEvent)
        {
            throw new NotImplementedException("PreProcessing functionality
                                              is not implemented");
        }
}
```

In the preceding code example, we have defined an abstract class named **AbstractBasicPipeline**. Some methods like **WriteLog** are already implemented, some are marked as abstract and must be implemented in derived classes, and some are implemented with default functionality by throwing an exception.

The main goal of defining such a class is to make a standard execution flow for processing an event. We have defined this in the **AbstractBasicPipeline.Process** method.

From now on, each pipeline will be called through this method to process an event. We have left one point of customization, the **ProcessEvent** method, which stays abstract and should be implemented in each child separately.

In the following code example, we have defined a class that is a subclass of the **AbstractPipeline** class. The **BasicPipeline** class represents a simple pipeline without additional functionality like post-/pre- processing. It should implement only the **ProcessEvent** method, and it is ready to go:

```
public class BasicPipeline : AbstractBasicPipeline
{

        protected override void ProcessEvent(BasicEvent basicEvent)
        {
            WriteLog($"Processing of basic event: {basicEvent.Id}");
        }
}
```

On the other hand, we can define a more functional pipeline, which we will call **ExtendedPipeline**.

It also derives from **AbstractBasicPipeline** class, but in this case, we want to use it with pre and post-processing functionality. As we want to process different type of event (which is derived from BasicEvent), we should extend the **Validate** method functionality:

```
public class ExtendedPipeline : AbstractBasicPipeline
{
        protected override void ProcessEvent(BasicEvent basicEvent)
        {
            WriteLog($"Processing of extended event: {basicEvent.Id}");
        }

        protected override void Validate(BasicEvent basicEvent)
        {
            base.Validate(basicEvent);
            var extendedEvent = basicEvent as ExtendedEvent;
            if (extendedEvent != null)
            {
                if (string.IsNullOrWhiteSpace(extendedEvent.Source))
                {
                     throw new ArgumentException($"Event {basicEvent.Id} is
                                      invalid. Source cannot be null.");
                }
            }
        }
```

```
        protected override void PostProcess(BasicEvent basicEvent)
        {
              WriteLog($"Executing post processing functionality for event:
                    {basicEvent.Id}");
        }

        protected override void PreProcess(BasicEvent basicEvent)
        {
              WriteLog($"Executing pre processing functionality for event:
                    {basicEvent.Id}");
        }
}
```

The following list summarizes the abstract class in terms of its language and the capabilities it has:

- An abstract class cannot be instantiated directly.
- An abstract class may contain abstract methods.
- A concrete class derived from an abstract class must implement all inherited abstract members.
- Abstract method declarations are only permitted in abstract classes.
- It is not possible to use static or virtual methods in abstract classes.
- It is possible to define a concrete function in an abstract class that executes abstract methods in its body.

Interfaces and abstract classes have many differences and similarities that we can summarize in the following lists.

Similarities:

- Both interface and abstract class can have abstract and concrete members.
- Both the interface and abstract class can have different access modifiers like private, public, protected, and protected internals.
- Both interface and abstract class cannot be instantiated directly.
- Both interface and abstract class cannot be inherited from structures.
- Both interface and abstract class virtual members can be overridden in the inheriting class.
- Both interface and abstract class abstract members must be implemented in the inheriting class.

- Both interface and abstract class can be used only as a base for inheriting.

Differences:

- For the abstract class, it is necessary to have at least one abstract member, while an interface may not.
- An abstract class can have a constructor or destructor, while an interface cannot.
- An abstract class can contain instance fields and constants, but the interface cannot.
- A structure cannot be derived from abstract class but can derive from interfaces.
- It is not possible to derive an interface from abstract class, but the opposite is possible and used widely.
- The virtual interface methods are not inherited, but all concrete members of an abstract class are inherited.
- All abstract members of the abstract class must be overridden with an explicit override keyword, while interface virtual methods are not.

From my perspective, the main difference between abstract class and interface is that abstract class is a final conception of the process/class and its behavior/functionality. Interfaces define a piece of functionality. The class derived from multiple interfaces looks like an aggregator which can be used in different situations to provide different functionality.

Generics

Generic means no specific form. In C#, generics can work with a family of types, not a specific one. One of the biggest families is derived from type object.

You can use generics in classes, interfaces, abstract classes, fields, methods, static methods, properties, events, etc.

To define a generic type, a developer should specify the type parameter in angle brackets after type name, as you can see in the following example:

```
public class SimpleGenericType<T>
{
        private T value;
        public SimpleGenericType(T value)
        {
            this.value = value;
        }
```

```
        public T Value
        {
            get { return value; }
            set { this.value = value; }
        }
}
SimpleGenericType<int> simpleGenericType = new SimpleGenericType<int>(10);
Console.WriteLine(simpleGenericType.Value);
```

In the preceding code, we have defined a generic type with **type** parameter **T**.

This **type** parameter is accessible in the rest of the class. You can pass it as parameter in functions, define variables, and set it as return value of the functions and properties. In our current case, this type T represents the root object of the .NET class hierarchy. If you want to call a method on an instance of this type, you will be able to call only basic functions that are available for each of the .NET classes: **Equals**, **ToString**, **GetType**, and **GetHashCode**.

Sometimes, it is useful to indicate some constraint on a **type** parameter. Then, the developer will be able to use more specific methods of base class of indicated constraint.

Let us make our **AbstractPipeline** from our previous example to be more generic (we will remove post-/pre- processing functionality from this example as it can be a bit overloaded):

```
public abstract class GenericAbstractBasicPipeline<TEvent> where TEvent:
                                                                   BasicEvent
{

        public virtual void Process(TEvent basicEvent)
        {
                WriteLog($"Starting processing of event {basicEvent.Id}");
                if (IsPreProcessingEnabled)
                    PreProcess(basicEvent);

                Validate(basicEvent);
                WriteLog($"Processing {basicEvent.Id}");
                ProcessEvent(basicEvent);

                if (IsPostProcessingEnabled)
                    PostProcess(basicEvent);

                    WriteLog($"Processing successfully completed for event
                        {basicEvent.Id}");
```

```
        }
        protected abstract void ProcessEvent(TEvent basicEvent);
        protected virtual void WriteLog(string message)
        {
            Console.WriteLine($"[{DateTime.Now}]: {message}");
        }
        protected virtual void Validate(TEvent basicEvent)
        {
            if (basicEvent == null)
            {
                throw new ArgumentNullException("Event object cannot be null");
            }
            if (string.IsNullOrWhiteSpace(basicEvent.Data))
            {
                throw new ArgumentException($"Event {basicEvent.Id} is invalid");
            }
        }

}
```

As you can see, we have defined **GenericAbstractBasicPipeline** with generic type parameter **TEvent**, and now we have used it in all the places where **BasicEvent** was mentioned. Also, we indicated that this type parameter or some of its derived classes should be **BasicEvent**: **where TEvent: BasicEvent**.

So now, we can redefine our **Basic** and **Extended** pipeline classes with **type** parameter:

```
public class BasicPipeline: GenericAbstractBasicPipeline<BasicEvent>
{
        public BasicPipeline()
        {
            IsPostProcessingEnabled = false;
            IsPreProcessingEnabled = false;
        }
        protected override void ProcessEvent(BasicEvent basicEvent)
        {
            WriteLog($"Processing basic event: {basicEvent.Id}");
        }
}
```

```
public class ExtendedPipeline : GenericAbstractBasicPipeline<ExtendedEvent>
{
        protected override void ProcessEvent(ExtendedEvent extendedEvent)
        {
              WriteLog($"Processing extended event: {extendedEvent.Id} from
                      {extendedEvent.Source}");
        }

        protected override void Validate(ExtendedEvent extendedEvent)
        {
            base.Validate(extendedEvent);

            if (string.IsNullOrWhiteSpace(extendedEvent.Source))
            {
                  throw new ArgumentException($"Event {extendedEvent.Id} is
                                         invalid. Source cannot be null.");
            }
        }
        protected override void PostProcess(ExtendedEvent extendedEvent)
        {
              WriteLog($"Executing post processing functionality for event:
                 {extendedEvent.Id} from {extendedEvent.Source}");
        }

        protected override void PreProcess(ExtendedEvent extendedEvent)
        {
               WriteLog($"Executing pre processing functionality for event:
                 {extendedEvent.Id} from {extendedEvent.Source}");
        }
}
```

Generic parameter does not influence any change in **BasicPipeline** class except definition, but it means a lot for **ExtendedPipeline** class, which accepts **ExtendedEvent** class instance as a parameter.

From now on, you do not need to cast **BasicEvent** object to **ExtendedEvent** as your code already accepts **ExtendedEvent** as a function parameter. It is possible because we have defined it as a type parameter in the inherited class **GenericAbstractPipeline**. You can use additional properties defined in **ExtendedEvent** class without any restrictions.

Let us talk more about generic type constraints. C# allows you to use constraints to specify which types can be used as generic class type parameters. The compiler would give an error if the specified type passed as type argument does not satisfy these requirements.

The following *Table 1.2* summarizes type of constraints and possible values:

Constraint	Description
`class`	The `type` argument must be a class, an interface, a delegate, or an array type.
`class?`	Same as class and can be nullable
`struct`	The `type` argument must be non-nullable value types: int, char, bool, float, and so on.
`new()`	The `type` argument must be a reference type which has a public parameterless constructor.
`notnull`	Available C# 8.0. The `type` argument can be non-nullable reference types or value types.
`<base class name>`	The `type` argument must be or derive from the specified base class.
`<base class name>?`	The `type` argument must be or derive from the specified base class
`<interface name>`	The `type` argument must implement the specified interface.
`<interface name>?`	The `type` argument must implement the specified interface. It may be nullable
`where T: U`	The `type` argument supplied for `T` must be or derive from the argument supplied for `U`.

Table 1.2: *Generic type constraints*

The characteristics of generic class are as follows:

- The main idea of generics is to maintain reusability across families of types. It allows developers to shorten the code and avoid copy-pasting.
- A generic class can be a base class for other generic or non-generic classes or abstract classes.
- A generic class can be derived from other generic or non-generic interfaces, classes, or abstract classes.
- Generics are type-safe. You get compile-time errors if you try to use a different data type than the one specified in the definition.
- Generic has a performance advantage because it removes the possibilities of boxing and unboxing.

Extension methods

Imagine that you have a class that is sealed, so you cannot extend it to add additional functionality. To solve this issue, you could create a new class, pass an object of the class that you want to extend to a method of this new class, and do some magic with public fields methods. However, it does not work well when you need to extend 10 classes.

And on the scene appears **Extensions Methods**!

It allows a developer to extend the class without modifying, deriving, or recompiling the original class. Extension methods can be added to any type available in .NET, your or third-party library.

Let us see a simple example of extensions method in action:

```
public static class PipelinesExtensions
{
        public static void BatchProcessing<T>(
                            this GenericAbstractBasicPipeline<T> pipeline,
                            List<T> events) where T: BasicEvent
        {
            events.ForEach(eventObj =>
            {
                pipeline.Process(eventObj);
            });
        }
}
var extendedPipeline = new ExtendedPipeline();
ExtendedEvent basicEvent = new ExtendedEvent
{
       Id = Guid.NewGuid(),
       Data = "Some data",
       Type = "Ver3",
       Source = "Console App"
};

ExtendedEvent extendedEvent = new ExtendedEvent
{
Data = "Some data",
       Id = Guid.NewGuid(),
       Source = "Console App",
       Type = "Ver3"
};
```

```
List<ExtendedEvent> events = new List<ExtendedEvent> {basicEvent, extendedEvent};
extendedPipeline.BatchProcessing(events);
```

In this case, extension methods allow us to shorten the code in our main processing class, use more clear syntax, and extend existing class without deriving from it.

The key points of extension methods are:

- The main advantage of extension methods is the possibility to extend existing class without using inheritance.
- Extension methods are defined as static methods but used as instance methods.
- Extensions methods do not support methods overriding. You cannot override the method with the same signature.
- It is not possible to apply method extensions to fields, properties, or events.
- It must be defined in the top-level static class.
- It is not possible to bind the extensions method to multiple classes. For example, it does not support multiple binding parameters (with **`this`** keyword)
- It is possible to extend classes that are not possible to inherit (sealed).

Partial classes

Partial classes is not about OOP, it is more about structuring your code in terms of file structure. For example, it is useful when you want to extend some classes that are automatically generated, split overrides, and add new functionality.

Partial classes provide a possibility to split the definition of a class, a struct, an interface, or a method over two or more files. Each file contains some part of type or method definition, and at compile time, all files are combined together.

There are several situations when splitting a class definition is desirable:

- It is possible to work over the same class for multiple developers simultaneously when using partial classes.
- When using automatically generated code like in Windows Forms, Web Services, wrapper code, and so on, it is possible for the developer to add its own functionality in the generated code by using **`partial`** keyword.
- When generating additional functionality in a class using source generators.

To use partial classes functionality, use the partial keyword modified as shown in the next example:

```
public partial class PartialPipeline
{
    public void Log(string message)
    {
    }
}

public partial class PartialPipeline
{
    public void Process(BasicEvent event)
    {
    }
}
```

The partial keyword means that there are other parts of class in the same namespace. All the parts should use the partial keyword to be aggregated at the compile time and the same accessibility keyword (public, internal) should be applied to all parts of the class.

The main points of the keyword modifiers for partial class are:

- If any part is declared as sealed, then all parts are sealed.
- If any part is declared as abstract, then all parts are abstract.
- If any part derives from base type, then all parts are derived.
- Parts can implement different interfaces but the whole type should implement all derived interfaces.
- All parts have access of other's parts members.
- Class attributes, generic type parameters of any part of the partial class are merged.

Check the following code example:

```
partial class ExtendedPipeline : BasicPipeline, IValidate { }
partial class ExtendedPipeline : IPostProcessing { }
```

They are equivalent to the following declarations:

```
class ExtendedPipeline: BasicPipeline, IValidate, IPostProcessing { }
```

C# also allows to create partial methods. It should be included in partial class. One file of the class can contain the method definition, second file can contain method implementation. If the implementation of the method is not supplied, then definition and all calls to this method will be removed at compile time. Implementation is not required in the following cases:

- It does not have accessibility modifiers.
- It must return void.
- It does not have any out parameters.
- It cannot have any of the following modifiers: new, sealed, virtual, override, or extern

Any method that does not satisfy those restrictions must provide an implementation.

Partial methods are useful in the following scenarios:

- **Template code:** The template defines a method so that generated code can call the method. These methods satisfy the restrictions that enable developers to decide whether a method needs to be implemented.
- **Source generators:** Source generators generate an implementation for method. The developer can define the method and add the code that calls this method.
- Any partial method declaration starts with a **`partial`** keyword.
- Signatures of partial methods must match in both parts of the partial type.
- **`Static`** and `unsafe` modifiers are the only ones that partial method could have.
- It is possible to define generic partial method.

Conclusion

In this chapter, we have reviewed three pillars of OOP: encapsulation, inheritance, and polymorphism. These are the main fundamental basics on which OOP stands as a paradigm.

Encapsulation helps us to hide things, Inheritance allows us to reuse them, and Polymorphism enables us to change behavior. It is enough to make our code cleaner and more concise, which helps us in the future when we need to modify the existing code base.

Further, C# provides extended capabilities of OOP through interfaces, abstract classes, and generics, which help us to make our code maintainable. Later, we will look at the powerful capabilities of IoC provided by Microsoft integrated with their .NET Core framework. The next thing that we will review is how we can use the basics of OOP paradigms to construct complicated structures in a simple manner with the help of GoF patterns and SOLID principles.

Let us dive into the exciting world of software engineering!

Join our book's Discord space

Join the book's Discord Workspace for Latest updates, Offers, Tech happenings around the world, New Release and Sessions with the Authors:

https://discord.bpbonline.com

CHAPTER 2
Creational Design Patterns: Factory and Builder

Introduction

In this chapter, the basics of **Gang of Four** (**GoF**) patterns will be introduced. We will review object creation using Factory, Abstract Factory, and Builder design patterns. These are some of the most used design patterns. They provide better ways to create an object without exposing the creation logic to the caller and allow access to newly created objects using a standard interface.

Structure

The chapter covers the following topics:

- Factory
  - Designing the processing pipeline
  - Code
- Abstract Factory
  - Designing the processing event hub
  - Code

- Builder
  - o Designing the processing event hub
  - o Code
- Synergy of the patterns
  - o Code

Objectives

At the end of this chapter, you will be able to describe main GoF patterns like Factory, Abstract Factory, and Builder and apply them to real-world problems.

Together with C# and .NET Core capabilities of OOP, we will design a basic system that will be able to process different types of events in an intelligent manner, supporting clean structure and using methods of OOP paradigm like encapsulation, inheritance, and polymorphism.

Factory

We begin with the basic definition of Factory pattern. **Factory pattern** is a creational design pattern that provides an interface for creating objects in a superclass but allows subclasses to alter the type of objects that will be created.

The Factory design pattern is used for instantiating one of the subclasses. The selected type depends on some parameters. For example, when your system receives an event, it should decide which pipeline class should process it. In this case, Factory class decides which pipeline should be selected based on the event object properties. It provides decoupling and allows the code to work only with abstraction instead of concrete types.

In this chapter, we will continue the same way and extend the current code to make it more pattern-oriented.

Designing the processing pipeline

Let us start with the business. Imagine that we have the following process for all events that come into our system:

1. Preprocess the event and save metadata of the event processing.
2. A message should be sent to a Dashboard when event processing is started.
3. Validate the event (check if all data is set and has correct values).
4. The next step is to make a data preprocessing with the event (for example, download a file).

5. The fourth step is to process the downloaded data/action data.
6. The next step is to check the internal system/service/microservice to see if this data already exists. It will help us to decide if we should create or update it.
7. Then, we should create/update event entity in the target system.
8. Finally, update the metadata of the event.
9. A message should be sent to a Dashboard when event processing is finished.

In our case, we will have three types of events:

- **Type A:** It requires the file to be downloaded from source A. The target system is A.
- **Type B:** It requires the file to be downloaded from source B. The target system is B.
- **Type C**: It is self-contained. The target system is C.

Refer to the following *Figure 2.1*:

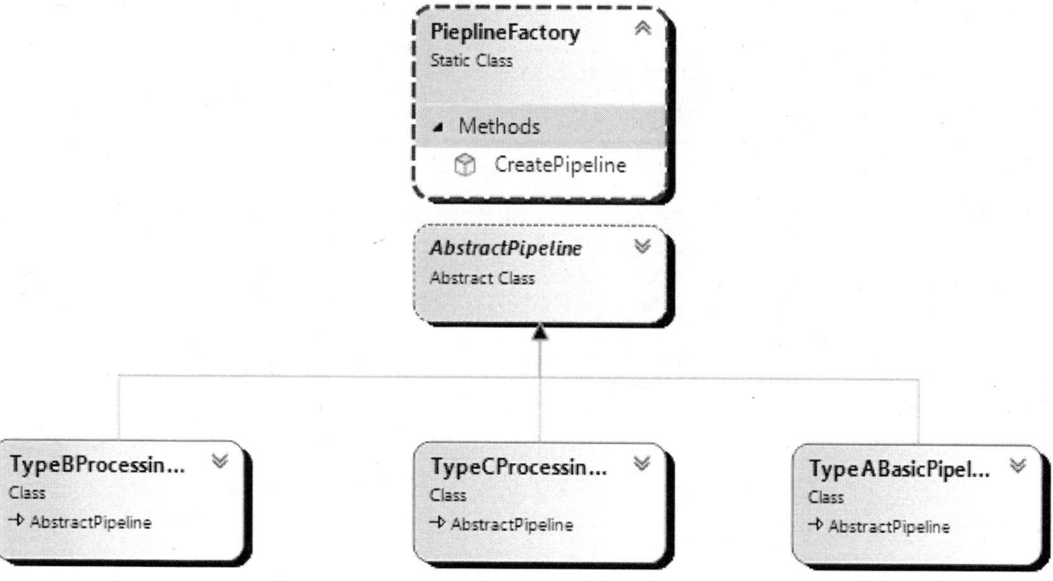

***Figure 2.1:** Factory basic design*

We have defined a **PipelineFactory**, which is responsible for pipelines creation based on the type of event. Further, we defined an **AbstractPipeline** class, which contains all the required pipeline functions. They are all abstract to support implementation in the derived classes. We have three different pipelines for each type of event.

Code

We should define a class to contain basic constants for event types identification. Right now, we should include two sources and three event types. We will use these constants later in Factory classes. Take a look at the following code:

```
public class Constants
{
        public const string IOT_EVENT_SOURCE = "IOT";
        public const string FILE_EVENT_SOURCE = "FILE";
        public const string A_EVENT_TYPE = "TypeA";
        public const string B_EVENT_TYPE = "TypeB";
        public const string C_EVENT_TYPE = "TypeC";
}
```

The basic event is defined in the following code example:

```
public class BasicEvent
{
        public Guid EventGuid { get; set; }
        public string EventType { get; set; }
}
```

In our case, **EventGuid** property will hold **Guid** of the event, and **EventType** will have three possible types, as mentioned above.

With this structure in mind, we can start defining our **AbstractPipeline** class:

```
public abstract class AbstractPipeline
{
        protected abstract Guid SaveMetadata(BasicEvent basicEvent);
        protected abstract void NotifyProcessingStarted(BasicEvent
                                              badicEvent, string message);
        protected abstract void Validate(BasicEvent basicEvent);
        protected abstract void Preprocess(BasicEvent basicEvent);
        protected abstract void ProcessEvent(BasicEvent basicEvent);
        protected abstract void Search(BasicEvent basicEvent);
        protected abstract void Store(BasicEvent basicEvent);
        protected abstract void UpdateMetadata(BasicEvent basicEvent);
}
```

In the above code example, we have defined a basic abstract pipeline that has all the required members.

However, we forgot about the main public method, which will be accessible to everyone and can be called from outside of the class. Let us define it:

```
public abstract class AbstractPipeline
{
        protected abstract Guid SaveMetadata(BasicEvent basicEvent);
        protected abstract void Notify(BasicEvent badicEvent, string message);
        protected abstract void Validate(BasicEvent basicEvent);
        protected abstract object Preprocess(BasicEvent basicEvent);
        protected abstract void ProcessEvent(BasicEvent basicEvent, object
                                               preprocessingResult);
        protected abstract object Search(BasicEvent basicEvent);
        protected abstract void Store(object existingObject, BasicEvent
                                      basicEvent);
        protected abstract void UpdateMetadata(Guid metadataGuid,
                                               BasicEvent basicEvent);

        public virtual void Process(BasicEvent basicEvent)
        {
            try
            {
                var metadataObjectGuid = SaveMetadata(basicEvent);
                Notify(basicEvent, "PROCESSING_STARTED");
                Validate(basicEvent);
                var proceprocessingResult = Preprocess(basicEvent);
                ProcessEvent(basicEvent, proceprocessingResult);
                var existingObject = Search(basicEvent);
                Store(existingObject, basicEvent);
                UpdateMetadata(metadataObjectGuid, basicEvent);
                Notify(basicEvent, "PROCESSING_FINISHED");
            }
            catch(Exception ex)
            {
                Notify(basicEvent, "PROCESSING_FAILED");
            }
        }
}
```

In the preceding code example, we have added the main function of **`AbstractPipeline`** class: **`public virtual void Process(BasicEvent basicEvent)`**. It defines the basic flow of event processing. Also, we have changed the signature of some methods to make them more logical.

The next step is to define the common methods for pipelines:

```
public abstract class AbstractPipeline
{
        protected abstract object Preprocess(BasicEvent basicEvent);
        protected abstract void ProcessEvent(BasicEvent basicEvent, object
                                             preprocessingResult);
        protected abstract object Search(BasicEvent basicEvent);
        protected abstract void Store(BasicEvent basicEvent, object
                                      existingObject);
        public virtual void Process(BasicEvent basicEvent)
        {
            try
            {
                var metadataObjectGuid = SaveMetadata(basicEvent);
                Notify(basicEvent, "PROCESSING_STARTED");
                Validate(basicEvent);
                var proceprocessingResult = Preprocess(basicEvent);
                ProcessEvent(basicEvent, proceprocessingResult);
                var existingObject = Search(basicEvent);
                Store(basicEvent, existingObject);
                UpdateMetadata(basicEvent, metadataObjectGuid);
                Notify(basicEvent, "PROCESSING_FINISHED");
            }
            catch(Exception ex)
            {
                Notify(basicEvent, "PROCESSING_FINISHED");
            }
        }
        protected virtual Guid SaveMetadata(BasicEvent basicEvent)
        {
            Notify(basicEvent, "Saving metadata");
            return Guid.NewGuid();
```

```
        }
        protected virtual void UpdateMetadata(BasicEvent basicEvent, Guid
                                              metadataGuid)
        {
            Notify(basicEvent, "Updating metdata");
        }
        protected virtual void Notify(BasicEvent badicEvent, string message)
        {
            Console.WriteLine($"Processing pipeline: {message}:
                              {badicEvent.EventGuid}");
        }
        protected virtual void Validate(BasicEvent basicEvent)
        {
            if (basicEvent == null)
                throw new ArgumentNullException("Event cannot be null");
            if (basicEvent.Data != null)
               throw new ArgumentException("Data of the event cannot be null");
        }
}
```

In the result of redefining our **AbstractPipeline** class, we have the following situation:

- Preprocess, Process, Search, and Store are defined as abstract classes because they are event specific.
- SaveMetadata, UpdateMetadata, Notify, and Validate are defined as virtual methods and have basic implementation.
- Process method defines our processing pipeline, which will be called for each event.

The next step is to define a basic pipeline for each type of events:

```
public class TypeABasicPipeline : AbstractPipeline
{
        private EventTypeAData data = null;
        private string targetSystemUploadUrl = "http://file.storage.com/
                                                systemA/upload";
        private string targetSystemApiIrl = "http://systemA.com/api";
        protected override object Preprocess(BasicEvent basicEvent)
        {
```

```
        this.data = JsonSerializer.Deserialize<EventTypeAData>(basicEvent.
                Data) ?? new EventTypeAData();
            Notify(basicEvent, "Preprocessing event");
            Notify(basicEvent, $"Downloading file {this.data.FileName} from
                {this.data.FileUrl}");
            return this.data;
        }
        protected override void ProcessEvent(BasicEvent basicEvent, object
                                    preprocessingResult)
        {
            Notify(basicEvent, "Processing event");
            Notify(basicEvent, $"Transfering file {this.data.FileName}
            downloaded from {this.data.FileUrl} to {this.
                                            targetSystemUrl}");
        }
        protected override object Search(BasicEvent basicEvent)
        {
            Notify(basicEvent, "Searching event in the target system");
            Notify(basicEvent, $"Calling {targetSystemApiIrl} to search for
                                            {this.data.FileName}");
            return null;
        }
        protected override void Store(BasicEvent basicEvent, object
                                                existingObject)
        {
            Notify(basicEvent, "Storing event in the target system");
           Notify(basicEvent, $"Calling {targetSystemApiIrl} api to save the
                                    data about transfered file");
        }
}
```

This is the basic pipeline for Type A event instance processing. We get console output, which will suffice our purposes.

Then, we define the same classes for Type B and C pipelines:

```
public class TypeBProcessingPipeline : AbstractPipeline
{
        protected override void Notify(BasicEvent badicEvent, string message)
        {
            Console.WriteLine($"Type B processing pipeline: {message}:
```

```
{badicEvent.EventGuid}");
        }
        protected override object Preprocess(BasicEvent basicEvent)
        {
            Notify(basicEvent, "Preprocessing event");
            return new object();
        }
        protected override void ProcessEvent(BasicEvent basicEvent, object
                                             preprocessingResult)
        {
            Notify(basicEvent, "Processing event");
        }
        protected override Guid SaveMetadata(BasicEvent basicEvent)
        {
            Notify(basicEvent, "Saving metadata");
            return Guid.NewGuid();
        }
        protected override object Search(BasicEvent basicEvent)
        {
            Notify(basicEvent, "Searching for event in target system");
            return null;
        }
        protected override void Store(object existingObject, BasicEvent
                                      basicEvent)
        {
            Notify(basicEvent, "Storing event B in the target system");
        }
        protected override void UpdateMetadata(Guid metadataGuid,
                                               BasicEvent basicEvent)
        {
            Notify(basicEvent, "Updating metdata for event B");
        }
        protected override void Validate(BasicEvent basicEvent)
        {
            if (basicEvent == null)
                throw new ArgumentNullException("Event cannot be null");
```

```
        if (string.IsNullOrEmpty(basicEvent.Data))
         throw new ArgumentException("Data of the event cannot be null");
    }
}
```

The Type C processing pipeline will be implemented differently as it does not need to download / process additional information:

```
public class TypeCProcessingPipeline : AbstractPipeline
{
        private EventTypeC data = null;
        private string targetSystemApiUrl = "http://systemC.com/api";
        private string targetSystemProcessingApiUel = "http://systemC.
                                            processing.com/api";
        protected override object Preprocess(BasicEvent basicEvent)
        {
             this.data = (basicEvent as EventTypeC) ?? new EventTypeC();
             Notify(basicEvent, "Preprocessing completed");
             return this.data;
        }
        protected override void ProcessEvent(BasicEvent basicEvent, object
                                        preprocessingResult)
        {
             Notify(basicEvent, "Processing event");
             Notify(basicEvent, $"Calling {this.
              targetSystemProcessingApiUel} to process a values of event:
              {this.data.Action} {this.data.Value}");
        }
        protected override object Search(BasicEvent basicEvent)
        {
             return null;
        }
        protected override void Store(BasicEvent basicEvent, object
                                    existingObject)
        {
             Notify(basicEvent, "Storing event in the target system");
             Notify(basicEvent, $"Calling {this.targetSystemApiUrl} api to
                                 save the data about transfered file");
        }
}
```

In the preceding code examples, we have defined three classes for processing different types of events. TypeA and TypeB processing pipelines differ only in Data property processing of an event and API variables that we use to define the URL of API and storage. TypeC, on the other hand, has a different event without the Data property filled in. It uses properties of **EventTypeC** class to keep the data of the event. Also, this type of event does not need to be checked for presence in the target system. These events should be registered in the appropriate system (A or B) for further processing.

For now, we need to define a class Factory to select and create the needed pipeline class for an incoming event.

We will define it in the following class:

```
public static class PieplineFactory
{
        public static AbstractPipeline CreatePipeline(BasicEvent basicEvent)
        {
            return basicEvent.Type switch
            {
 Constants.A_EVENT_TYPE => new TypeAProcessingPipeline(),
                Constants.B_EVENT_TYPE => new TypeBProcessingPipeline(),
                Constants.C_EVENT_TYPE => new TypeCProcessingPipeline(),
                  _ => throw new NotImplementedException("There is no such
                                        pipeline to process passed event")
            };
        }
}
```

It is one method that will return the required instance to process the event. It is simple because all functionalities are done by the **Console** class. Later, we will add some additional classes to imitate real actions.

In the following code example, we will create three events: one instance for each type, process them in the loop, and create pipelines on the fly:

```
EventTypeAData dataTypeA = new EventTypeAData
{
        FileName = "event_type_a.file",
        FileType = ".jpg",
        FileUrl = "http://event.type.a.file.url"
};
EventTypeBData dataTypeB = new EventTypeBData
```

```
{
        FileName = "event_type_b.file",
        FileType = ".png",
        FileUrl = "http://event.type.b.file.url"
};
BasicEvent basicEventA = new BasicEvent
{
        Data = JsonSerializer.Serialize(dataTypeA),
        EventGuid = Guid.NewGuid(),
        Type = Constants.A_EVENT_TYPE
};
BasicEvent basicEventB = new BasicEvent
{
        Data = JsonSerializer.Serialize(dataTypeB),
        EventGuid = Guid.NewGuid(),
        Type = Constants.B_EVENT_TYPE
};
EventTypeC eventTypeC = new EventTypeC
{
        EventGuid = Guid.NewGuid(),
        Action = "Update",
        Type = Constants.C_EVENT_TYPE
};
List<BasicEvent> basicEvents = new List<BasicEvent>
{
       basicEventA, basicEventB, eventTypeC
};
basicEvents.ForEach(eventObj =>
{
        Console.WriteLine("Processing new event!");
        var pipeline = PipelineFactory.CreatePipeline(eventObj);
        pipeline.Process(eventObj);
        Console.WriteLine();
});
```

The result of the execution is shown in *Figure 2.2*:

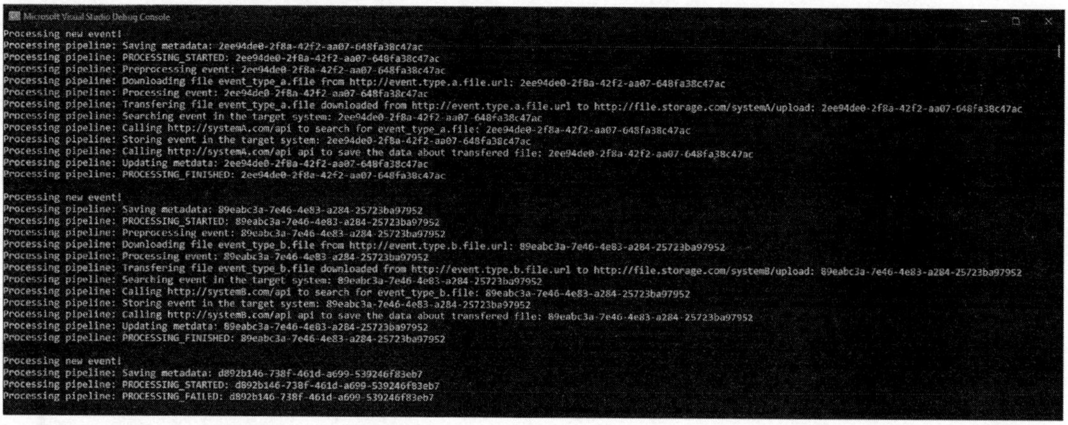

Figure 2.2: Processing events with the factory and failed TypeC event

As you can notice, the last event of TypeC is not processed and finished in the FAILED state. It happened because, in TypeCProcessingPipeline, we use the base **`Validate`** method to validate the existence of the Data in an event. For TypeC event class, we should override the base **`Validate`** method:

```
protected override void Validate(BasicEvent basicEvent)
{
            if (basicEvent == null)
                throw new ArgumentNullException("Event cannot be null");
}
```

In the end, we will be able to process any of the mentioned types of events. Refer to the following *Figure 2.3*:

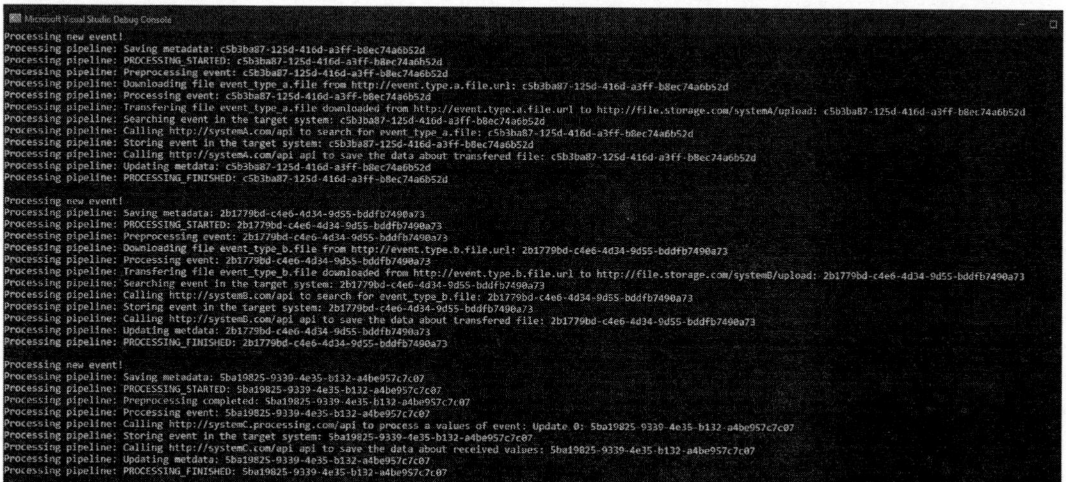

Figure 2.3: Factory basic design execution without any fault

The final class diagram is shown in *Figure 2.4*:

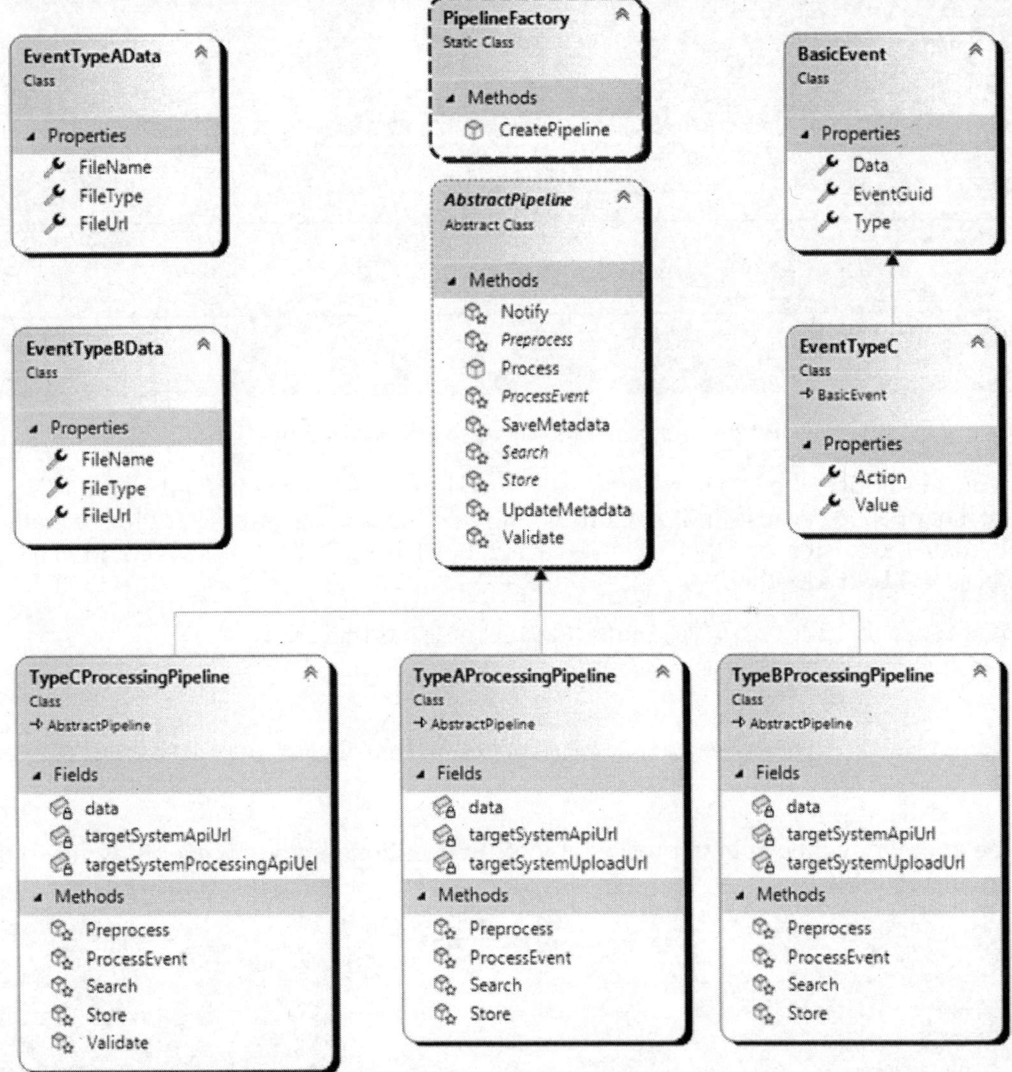

***Figure 2.4:** Factorydesign pattern final diagram*

`TypeCProcessingPipeline` has one additional member **`Validate`** if we compare it to the other two processing pipelines.

Factory design pattern is a practical choice for moving outside the initialization of a family of classes when they depend on some of the parameters.

In our case, it was easy to construct pipelines because we used only the **`Console`** class for functionality. However, there would be a problem if any of the pipelines required additional services that must be passed in the constructor, parameters that should be read from configuration or be set to properties of the initialized pipeline class. It could mess the event handler code which should select correct pipeline and initialize it.

Abstract Factory

In this section, we will continue to extend our processing pipelines with the help of Abstract Factory design pattern.

By definition, *the Abstract Factory design pattern is a creational design pattern that provides an interface for creating families of related or dependent objects without specifying their concrete classes. It allows you to create objects that belong to a specific family or group, ensuring that they are compatible and consistent.*

In other words, Abstract Factory design pattern provides a way to manage the creation of a family object with common parent class by using concrete factories which produce needed instances.

This pattern is useful in scenarios where we need to decouple business logic of creation from outside code. It allows us to incapsulate creation logic into separate Factories and unite them under one interface, which will be responsible for selecting correct Factory, its instantiation and execution.

Designing the processing event hub

In this section, we will create an event processing event hub. In the preceding section, we had three types of events and if TypeA and TypeB were similar, TypeC was different.

From a business perspective, we can separate them as:

- **FileUpload events:** We receive such events when our clients have uploaded documents.
- **Iot events:** We receive such events when something changes in an environment where IoT device is installed. For example, it can be temperature, humidity, amount of light, etc.

Each of the mentioned types of events should be processed by a specific pipeline and have its own factory. For this, we have a reason: each event type has its own format and data; therefore, each of them should be processed by a different algorithm.

Imagine building an event hub that can process any event that comes to the queue. To structure elements and support future maintenance, we want to separate their processing to smoothen the process.

As mentioned earlier, we will have two types of events. First, for document uploads to support our clients of web portals, and second, to support our IoT infrastructure.

In this case, we used the Abstract Factory pattern. It allows us to switch between factories responsible for creating a concrete pipeline to process an event.

In theory, an Abstract Factory is a super factory that creates a concrete Factory on request, which allows us to create a concrete object.

We will design one moving ahead. Refer to the following *Figure 2.5*:

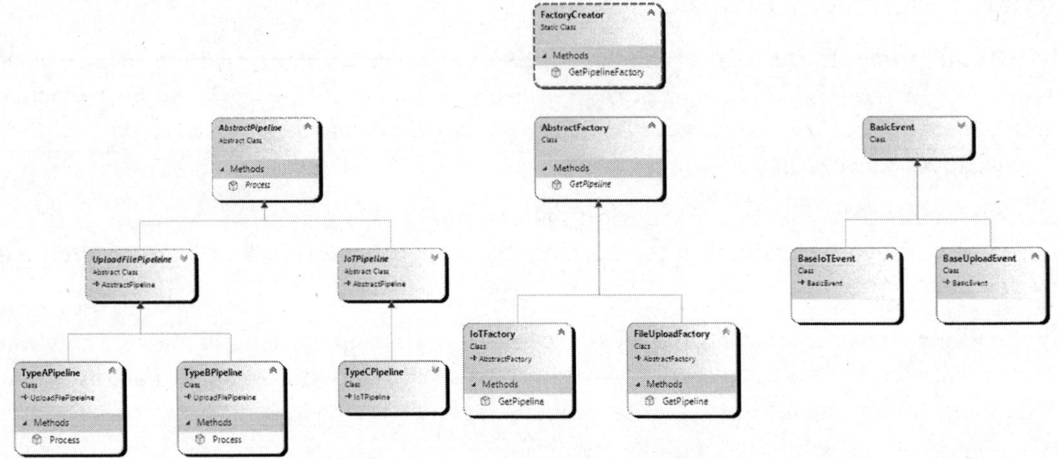

Figure 2.5: Abstract factory design pattern class hierarchy diagram

It is a basic design of our future structure of the event hub. It may appear complex as compared to the previous one. On the top, you can see a **FactoryCreator** class, which creates the required factory to select the correct pipeline for processing an incoming event. It has a **GetPipelineFactory** method, which will return an **AbstractFactory** class instance based on properties passed in the **BasicEvent** class instance. Further, you can call the **AbstractFactory** instance's **GetPipeline** method to get a pipeline to process the event.

It is a complex process. However, when you have many different types of events coming in, it is better to have a loosely coupled structure that can be distributed across classes and projects. This will help you in the future when you will need to change some processing logic.

Code

We will start coding exercises with the `BasicEvent` class. For now, the only requirement we have for the event is to have a `Source` property using which `FactoryCreator` will select the right factory in its turn. It will be able to supply the correct pipeline to process an event. Let us check the following code:

```
public class BasicEvent
{
    public Guid Id { get; set; }
```

```
    public string Type { get; set; }
    public string Source { get; set; }
}
```

Source property will be used to select a factory, and **Type** property will be used to select a pipeline.

The following are event classes specific to each type of pipeline: **BasicIoTEvent** and **BaseUploadEvent**, which derives from our **BasicEvent** class:

```
public class BaseIoTEvent: BasicEvent
{
        public string Action { get; set; }
        public string Value { get; set; }
}
public class BaseUploadEvent: BasicEvent
{
        public string FileName { get; set; }
        public string FileUrl { get; set; }
        public string FileType { get; set; }
}
```

For now, we define our **FactoryCreator** class, which will help us select an appropriate Factory to produce the correct pipeline:

```
public static class FactoryCreator
{
        public static AbstractFactory GetPipelineFactory(BasicEvent
                                                          basicEvent)
        {
            return basicEvent.Source switch
            {
                Constants.IOT_EVENT_SOURCE => new IoTFactory(),
             Constants.FILE_EVENT_SOURCE => new FileUploadFactory(),
             _ => throw new NotImplementedException("Cannot create a
             factory for non known source"),
            };
        }
}
```

We have defined a static **GetPipelineFactory** method. It selects a correct factory based on the **Source** property of the incoming event.

The next step is to define factories. First, we should define the **AbstractFactory** class:

```
public abstract class AbstractFactory
{
        public abstract AbstractPipeline GetPipeline(BasicEvent basicEvent);
}
```

It contains only one method, **GetPipeline**, which should produce **AbstractPipeline** instance to process the incoming event.

Next, we will define derived classes that have an implementation of the **GetPipeline** method:

```
public class FileUploadFactory: AbstractFactory
{
        public override AbstractPipeline GetPipeline(BasicEvent basicEvent)
        {
            return basicEvent.Type switch
            {

          Constants.A_EVENT_TYPE => new TypeAPipeline(),
                Constants.B_EVENT_TYPE => new TypeBPipeline(),
                _ => throw new NotImplementedException()
            };
        }
}
public class IoTFactory: AbstractFactory
{
        public AbstractPipeline GetPipeline(BasicEvent basicEvent)
        {
            return basicEvent.Type switch
            {
                Constants.C_EVENT_TYPE => new TypeCPipeline(),
                _ => throw new NotImplementedException()
            };
        }
}
```

As you can notice, Factories are not complicated. They simply return the correct pipeline selecting it by **Type** property.

Let us start with the most basic pipeline:

```
public abstract class AbstractPipeline
{
        public abstract void Process(BasicEvent basicEvent);
}
```

This pipeline has only one method: **Process**.

Further, we define **IoTPipeline** and **FileUploadPipelines**, the basic pipelines for our two types of events.

```
public abstract class IoTPipeline: AbstractPipeline
{
        protected abstract void ProcessEvent(BasicEvent basicEvent);
        protected abstract void Store(BasicEvent basicEvent);
        public override void Process(BasicEvent basicEvent)
        {
            try
            {
                var metadataObjectGuid = SaveMetadata(basicEvent);
                Notify(basicEvent, "PROCESSING_STARTED");
                Validate(basicEvent);
                ProcessEvent(basicEvent);
                UpdateMetadata(basicEvent, metadataObjectGuid);
                Notify(basicEvent, "PROCESSING_FINISHED");
            }
            catch (Exception ex)
            {
                Notify(basicEvent, "PROCESSING_FAILED");
            }
        }
        protected virtual Guid SaveMetadata(BasicEvent basicEvent)
        {
            Notify(basicEvent, "Saving metadata");
            return Guid.NewGuid();
        }
```

```
    protected virtual void UpdateMetadata(BasicEvent basicEvent, Guid
                                         metadataGuid)
    {
        Notify(basicEvent, "Updating metdata");
    }
    protected virtual void Notify(BasicEvent badicEvent, string message)
    {
        Console.WriteLine($"Processing pipeline: {message}: {badicEvent.Id}");
    }
    protected virtual void Validate(BasicEvent basicEvent)
    {
        if (basicEvent == null) throw new ArgumentNullException(
                                        "Event cannot be null");
        var iotEvent = basicEvent as BaseIoTEvent;
        if (iotEvent.Action == null) throw new ArgumentException(
                            "Filename of the event cannot be null");
        if (iotEvent.Value == null) throw new ArgumentException(
                            "Filename of the event cannot be null");
    }
}
```

In the preceding code example, we defined abstract **IoTPipeline**, which will be the foundation of IoT events processing pipelines.

UploadFilePipeline goes next and is demonstrated in the following code example:

```
public abstract class UploadFilePipeleine: AbstractPipeline
{
    protected abstract object Preprocess(BasicEvent basicEvent);
    protected abstract void ProcessEvent(BasicEvent basicEvent, object
                                        preprocessingResult);
    protected abstract object Search(BasicEvent basicEvent);
    protected abstract void Store(BasicEvent basicEvent, object
                                        existingObject);
    public override void Process(BasicEvent basicEvent)
    {
        try
        {
            var metadataObjectGuid = SaveMetadata(basicEvent);
            Notify(basicEvent, "PROCESSING_STARTED");
```

```
        Validate(basicEvent);
        var proceprocessingResult = Preprocess(basicEvent);
        ProcessEvent(basicEvent, proceprocessingResult);
        var existingObject = Search(basicEvent);
        Store(basicEvent, existingObject);
        UpdateMetadata(basicEvent, metadataObjectGuid);
        Notify(basicEvent, "PROCESSING_FINISHED");
    }
    catch (Exception ex)
    {
        Notify(basicEvent, "PROCESSING_FAILED");
    }
}
protected virtual Guid SaveMetadata(BasicEvent basicEvent)
{
    Notify(basicEvent, "Saving metadata");
    return Guid.NewGuid();
}
 protected virtual void UpdateMetadata(BasicEvent basicEvent, Guid
                                       metadataGuid)
{
    Notify(basicEvent, "Updating metdata");
}
protected virtual void Notify(BasicEvent badicEvent, string message)
{
    Console.WriteLine($"Processing pipeline: {message}:
                                             {badicEvent.Id}");
}
protected virtual void Validate(BasicEvent basicEvent)
{
    if (basicEvent == null)
        throw new ArgumentNullException("Event cannot be null");
    var baseUploadEvent = basicEvent as BaseUploadEvent;
    if (baseUploadEvent.FileName == null)
        throw new ArgumentException("Filename of the event cannot
                                    be null");
    if (baseUploadEvent.FileType == null)
```

```
            throw new ArgumentException("Filename of the event cannot
                                         be null");
        if (baseUploadEvent.FileUrl == null)
            throw new ArgumentException("Filename of the event cannot
                                         be null");
    }
}
```

These pipelines are similar but different. **UploadFilePipeline** defines more methods, for example, **Store** and **Preprocess** methods. They do not exist in **IoTPipeline** because simple IoT events need not be saved or preprocessed. However, **UploadFilePipeline** should download file in the preprocessing method and store information in the system.

The next step is the implementation of pipelines for concrete events. The first one is **TypeAPipeline**:

```
public class TypeAPipeline : UploadFilePipeleine
{
    private BaseUploadEvent data = null;
      private string targetSystemUploadUrl = "http://file.storage.test/
                                             systemA/upload";
    private string targetSystemApiUrl = "http://systemA.test/api";
    protected override object Preprocess(BasicEvent basicEvent)
    {
        this.data = basicEvent as BaseUploadEvent;
        Notify(basicEvent, "Preprocessing event");
         Notify(basicEvent, $"Downloading file {this.data.FileName} from
                                              {this.data.FileUrl}");
        return this.data;
    }
     protected override void ProcessEvent(BasicEvent basicEvent, object
                                              preprocessingResult)
    {
        Notify(basicEvent, "Processing event");
            Notify(basicEvent, $"Transfering file {this.data.FileName}
   downloaded from {this.data.FileUrl} to {this.targetSystemUploadUrl}");
    }
    protected override object Search(BasicEvent basicEvent)
    {
        Notify(basicEvent, "Searching event in the target system");
```

```
            Notify(basicEvent, $"Calling {this.targetSystemApiUrl} to search
                                              for {this.data.FileName}");

            return null;
        }
             protected override void Store(BasicEvent basicEvent, object
                                                       existingObject)
        {
            Notify(basicEvent, "Storing event in the target system");
              Notify(basicEvent, $"Calling {this.targetSystemApiUrl} api to
                                   save the data about transfered file");
        }
}
```

The next code example demonstrates **TypeCPipeline** for IoT events:

```
public class TypeCPipeline : IoTPipeline
{
        private string targetSystemApiUrl = "http://systemC.com/api";
            private string targetSystemProcessingApiUel = "http://systemC.
                                                   processing.com/api";
        protected override void ProcessEvent(BasicEvent basicEvent)
        {
            var iotEvent = basicEvent as BaseIoTEvent;
            Notify(basicEvent, "Processing event");
            Notify(basicEvent, $"Calling {this.targetSystemProcessingApiUel}
       to process a values of event: {iotEvent.Action} {iotEvent.Value}");
        }
        protected override void Store(BasicEvent basicEvent)
        {
            Notify(basicEvent, "Storing event in the target system");
              Notify(basicEvent, $"Calling {this.targetSystemApiUrl} api to
                                save the data about received values");
        }
}
```

The complete picture is shown in *Figure 2.6*:

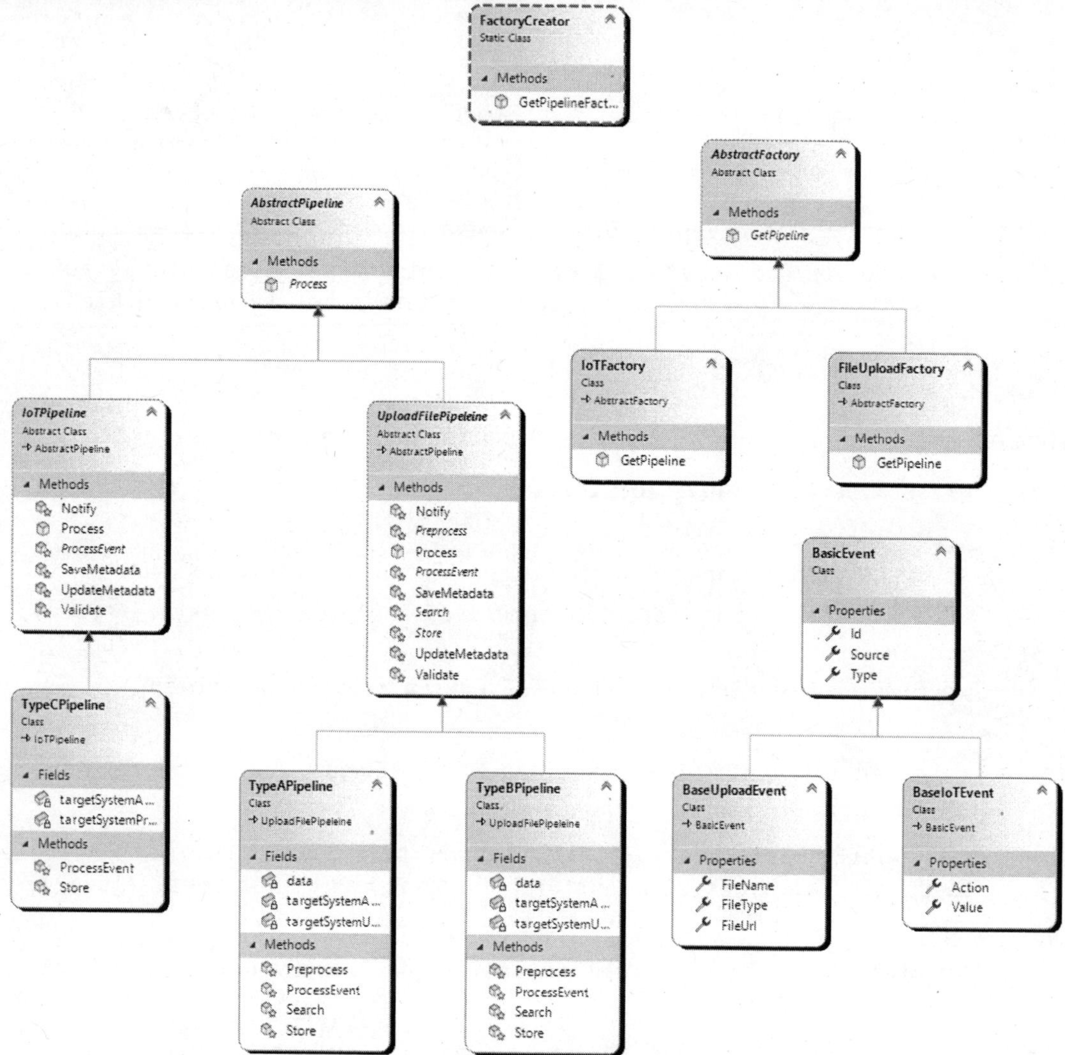

***Figure 2.6:** Abstract Factory final design*

AbstractFactory design pattern helps us in the management of different factories by incapsulating details of their creation. When you need to choose which factory to use, it is better to keep this type of code in one place, not distributing it across application. In general, this pattern allows you to incapsulate the details of the creation of the complex object and provide a simple API to use in the outside code. Use the Abstract Factory pattern when your code needs to instantiate an object which type depends on various parameters, however you want that selection logic to be hidden and distributed across your class hierarchy. This design pattern provides a great opportunity to hide complex logic of selection and instantiation inside Factory classes and supports extensibility.

The pros of Abstract Factory design pattern are as follows:

- Abstract Factory will always provide you with an object that implements a specific interface.
- It removes a tight coupling between the outside code and object's creation code.
- Object's creation code will be distributed across specific Factories, each of them provides a point of extensibility as Abstract Factory itself.
- Support and maintenance will be easier when the object's creation code is encapsulated inside concrete classes.

This pattern has only one visible con: a complication of class hierarchy as we are forced to add an additional layer of code which will be responsible for concrete factory selection.

Builder

In this section, we will introduce Builder design pattern to help us in pipelines creation.

The Builder design pattern alows you to construct complex objects using step-by-step instructions used by builder object. The goal is to separate construction of the object from its usage and hide the details of this object construction.

It is useful when a type has multiple properties or a complex initialization process.

Designing the processing event hub

The main part of this design pattern is Builder. It is the most crucial part of this pattern. From the beginning, you should define an object you want to build. In our example, it is a pipeline:

```
public abstract class AbstractPipeline
{
        public abstract void Process(BasicEvent basicEvent);
}
```

It is abstract, so we will have two more pipelines. One for the IoT pipeline:

```
public class IoTPipeline : AbstractPipeline
{
        public bool ShouldSaveMetadata {get;set;}
        public string ApiUrl { get; set; }
        public string TargetSystemApiUrl { get; set; }
        private Guid metadataGuid = Guid.Empty;
```

```
protected void ProcessEvent(BasicEvent basicEvent)
        {
            var iotEvent = basicEvent as BaseIoTEvent;
            Notify(basicEvent, "Processing event");
           Notify(basicEvent, $"Calling {this.TargetSystemApiUrl} to process
                a values of event: {iotEvent.Action} {iotEvent.Value}");
        }
        public override void Process(BasicEvent basicEvent)
        {
            try
            {
                if(ShouldSaveMetadata)
                    SaveMetadata(basicEvent);

                Notify(basicEvent, "PROCESSING_STARTED");
                Validate(basicEvent);
                ProcessEvent(basicEvent);

                if (ShouldSaveMetadata)
                    UpdateMetadata(basicEvent);

                Notify(basicEvent, "PROCESSING_FINISHED");
            }
            catch (Exception ex)
            {
                Notify(basicEvent, "PROCESSING_FAILED");
            }
        }
    // Other functionality goes here
}
```

The second is for the file upload pipeline:

```
public class FileUploadPipeline : AbstractPipeline
{
        public bool ShouldSaveMetadata { get; set; }
        public bool ShouldBeFilePreprocessed { get; set; }
        public bool ShouldBeEventStored { get; set; }
```

```
        public string TargetSystemUploadUrl { get; set; }
        public string TargetSystemApiUrl { get; set; }
        public override void Process(BasicEvent basicEvent)
        {
            try
            {
                if(ShouldSaveMetadata)
                    SaveMetadata(basicEvent);
                Notify(basicEvent, "PROCESSING_STARTED");
                Validate(basicEvent);
                if(ShouldBeFilePreprocessed)
                    Preprocess(basicEvent);
                ProcessEvent(basicEvent);
                Search(basicEvent);
                if (ShouldBeEventStored)
                    Store(basicEvent);
                if(ShouldSaveMetadata)
                    UpdateMetadata(basicEvent);
                Notify(basicEvent, "PROCESSING_FINISHED");
            }
            catch (Exception ex)
            {
                Notify(basicEvent, "PROCESSING_FAILED");
            }
        }
        // Other functionality goes here
}
```

In the preceding examples, we defined an abstract and two concrete pipelines classes that are responsible for processing events in our event hub. The main difference is that they do have public properties on which the **`Process`** functionality depends. Let us review one of the pipelines. For example, we will take **`FileUploadPipeline`**. It has properties that can influence the process. These properties are **`ShouldSaveMetadata`**, **`ShouldBeFilePreProcessed`**, **`ShouldBeEventStored`**, **`TargetSystemUploadUrl`**, **`TargetSystemApiUrl`**. With them, you can control how processing works, and by setting them, you can define different file upload pipelines.

In the next example, we will define a builder that will be able to create various file upload pipelines by using public properties of **FileUploadPipeline** class:

```
public class FilePipelineBuilder<T> where T : FileUploadPipeline, new()
{
        private T pipeline = default;

        public FilePipelineBuilder()
       {
            this.pipeline = new T();
       }
        public FilePipelineBuilder<T> ShouldSaveMetadata(bool shouldSaveMetadata)
        {
            pipeline.ShouldSaveMetadata = shouldSaveMetadata;
            return this;
        }
        public FilePipelineBuilder<T> ShouldBeFilePreprocessed(bool
                                             shouldBeFilePreprocessed)
        {
            pipeline.ShouldBeFilePreprocessed = shouldBeFilePreprocessed;
            return this;
        }
        public FilePipelineBuilder<T> ShouldBeEventStored(bool shouldBeEventStored)
        {
            pipeline.ShouldBeEventStored = shouldBeEventStored;
            return this;
        }
        public FilePipelineBuilder<T> SetTargetSystemApiUrl(string apiUrl)
        {
            pipeline.TargetSystemApiUrl = apiUrl;
            return this;
        }
        public FilePipelineBuilder<T> SetTargetSystemUploadUrl(string targetApiUrl)
        {
            pipeline.TargetSystemUploadUrl = targetApiUrl;
            return this;
        }
```

```
        public T Build()
        {
            return pipeline;
        }
}
```

As you can notice, this class is generic. It will be helpful, for example, when you want to extend the processing procedure and add some new functionality like calling some additional APIs or work. You can simply extend the basic class **FileUploadPipeline** and still use the same builder to create one.

Let us talk about builder. It provides a method that returns the same builder to chain a list of functions you are calling on the builder itself. Moreover, by using these functions, you can configure the pipeline to fulfill your needs.

Let us see an example of the builder that will configure two file upload pipelines with different settings and endpoints:

```
public static class PipelineDirector
{
        private static string targetASystemUploadUrl =
                              "http://file.storage.com/systemA/upload";
        private static string targetASystemApiUrl =
                              "http://systemA.com/api";
        private static string targetBSystemUploadUrl =
                              "http://file.storage.com/systemB/upload";
        private static string targetBSystemApiUrl =
                              "http://systemB.com/api";
        private static string targetCSystemApiUrl =
                              "http://systemC.com/api";
        private static string targetCSystemProcessingApiUrl =
                              "http://systemC.processing.com/api";
        public static AbstractPipeline BuildTypeAPipeline()
        {
            var typeAPipelineBuilder = new
                                FilePipelineBuilder<FileUploadPipeline>();
            return typeAPipelineBuilder.
                ShouldBeFilePreprocessed(false).
                ShouldBeEventStored(true).
                ShouldSaveMetadata(true).
                SetTargetSystemApiUrl(targetASystemUploadUrl).
                SetTargetSystemUploadUrl(targetASystemApiUrl).
```

```
            Build();
    }
    public static AbstractPipeline BuildTypeBPipeline()
    {
        var typeAPipelineBuilder = new
                        FilePipelineBuilder<FileUploadPipeline>();
        return typeAPipelineBuilder.
            ShouldBeFilePreprocessed(false).
            ShouldBeEventStored(true).
            ShouldSaveMetadata(true).
            SetTargetSystemApiUrl(targetBSystemUploadUrl).
            SetTargetSystemUploadUrl(targetBSystemApiUrl).
            Build();
    }
    public static AbstractPipeline BuildTypeCPipeline()
    {
        var typeCPipeline = new IoTPipelineBuilder<IoTPipeline>();
        return typeCPipeline.
            ShouldSaveMetadata(true).
            SetApiUrl(targetCSystemApiUrl).
            SetTargetApiUrl(targetCSystemProcessingApiUrl).
            Build();

    }
}
```

In the preceding example, we look at the utility of our builder. First, **PipelineDirector** is a place where our configuration parameters are kept. So, you will need to change them only once if it will be required. Second, you do not need to instantiate pipelines directly. For this, the **PipelineDirector** exists. It will configure the required pipeline with all the predefined properties and config values.

Let us explore the design of this system, as shown in *Figure 2.7*:

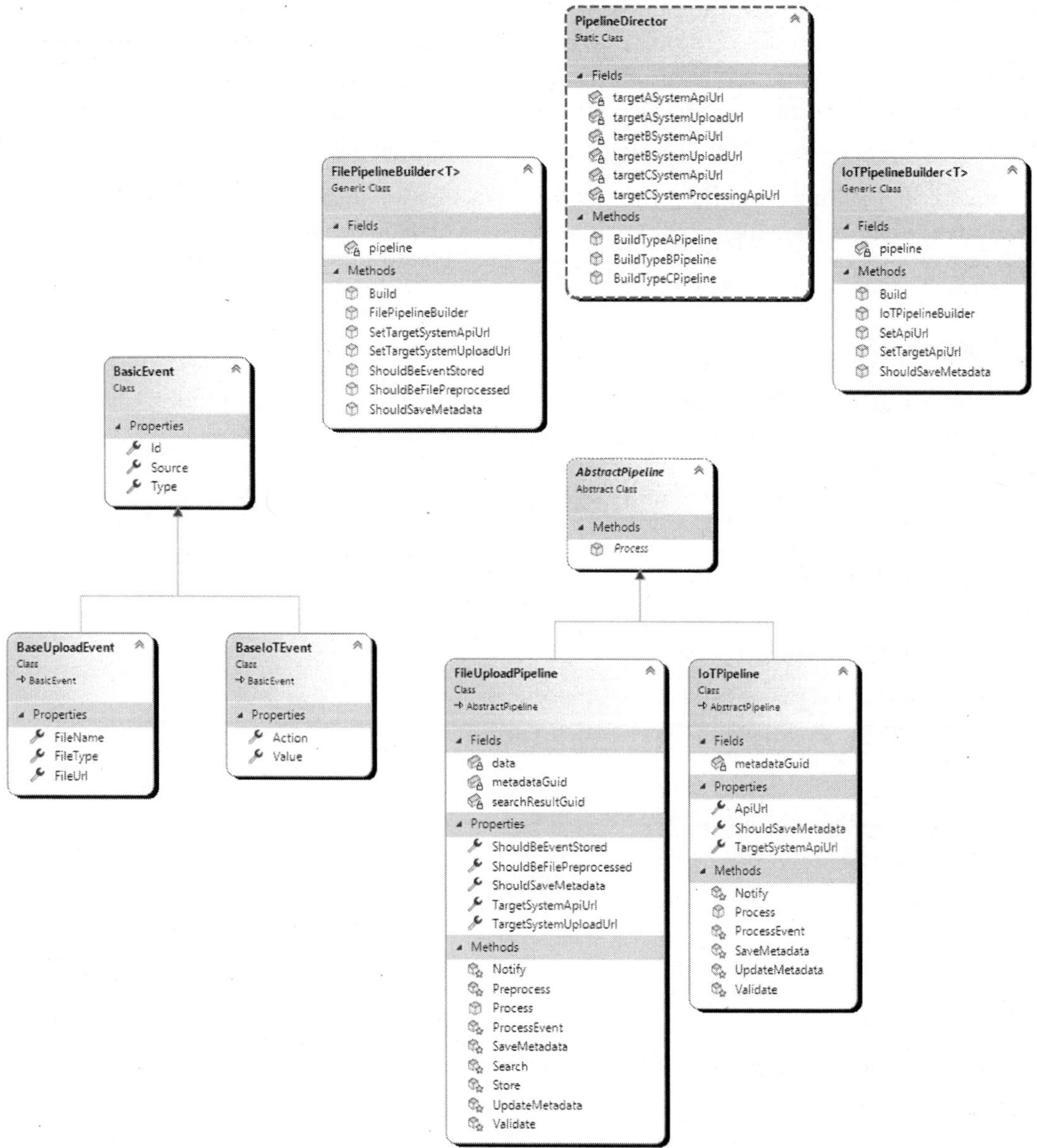

Figure 2.7: Builder design pattern design

On the top of the hierarchy, we have a **`PipelineDirector`** class, which manages pipeline's builders. Builders are responsible for creating concrete pipelines with concrete properties set.

In our case, we have **`FileUploadPipeline`** and **`IoTPipeline`**, which can be configured by various properties they provide. You can notice that **`FileUploadPipeline`** and **`IoTPipeline`** are not abstract classes, and they do not have children.

It is the third reason to use the Builder design pattern. It eliminates redundant derivation of classes. In the preceding chapters, we have used child classes to set the properties that can now be set by using public properties. We do not need to create child classes anymore. We can simply add a new method into the **PipelineDirector**, which will supply us with preconfigured Pipeline instance to use for processing a specific event.

However, it does not eliminate the need of inheritance altogether. In case we need to change the main processing pipeline defined in the **FileUploadPipeline** or **IoTPipeline** classes, we will need to derive one of the classes and make some changes to it.

Code

For now, let us dive into the code. There are some hidden implementation details in the previous section. Therefore, we need to look at each class of the diagram.

We will start with the event object. They are simple and similar to the ones we used in the preceding sections/chapters:

```
public class BasicEvent
{
    public Guid Id { get; set; }
    public string Type { get; set; }
    public string Source { get; set; }
}
public class BaseUploadEvent: BasicEvent
{
    public string FileName { get; set; }
    public string FileUrl { get; set; }
    public string FileType { get; set; }
}
public class BaseIoTEvent: BasicEvent
{
    public string Action { get; set; }
    public string Value { get; set; }
}
```

As you can see, we do not define any **Data** property in each event. They define their properties explicitly. We have a **BasicEvent**, which is used as a base for **BaseUploadEvent** and **BaseIoTEvent**. Each of them has additional properties along with the base class properties.

The next part of the diagram is pipelines:

```
public abstract class AbstractPipeline
{
        public abstract void Process(BasicEvent basicEvent);
}
```

In this case, we define **AbstractPipeline** as the most generic class which has only one function **Process** also called by client code.

Each process pipeline (File or IoT) is different, so they will be defined in appropriate classes.

You can see their interfaces in the following code example:

```
public class FileUploadPipeline : AbstractPipeline
{
        public bool ShouldSaveMetadata { get; set; }
        public bool ShouldBeFilePreprocessed { get; set; }
        public bool ShouldBeEventStored { get; set; }
        public string TargetSystemUploadUrl { get; set; }
        public string TargetSystemApiUrl { get; set; }
        public override void Process(BasicEvent basicEvent)
        {
                if(ShouldSaveMetadata)
                    SaveMetadata(basicEvent);
                Notify(basicEvent, "PROCESSING_STARTED");
                Validate(basicEvent);
                if(ShouldBeFilePreprocessed)
                    Preprocess(basicEvent);
                ProcessEvent(basicEvent);
                Search(basicEvent);
                if (ShouldBeEventStored)
                    Store(basicEvent);
                if(ShouldSaveMetadata)
                    UpdateMetadata(basicEvent);
                Notify(basicEvent, "PROCESSING_FINISHED");
 }
```

```
protected virtual void Preprocess(BasicEvent basicEvent);
        protected virtual void ProcessEvent(BasicEvent basicEvent);
        protected virtual void Search(BasicEvent basicEvent);
        protected virtual void Store(BasicEvent basicEvent);
        protected virtual Guid SaveMetadata(BasicEvent basicEvent);
        protected virtual void UpdateMetadata(BasicEvent basicEvent);
        protected virtual void Notify(BasicEvent badicEvent, string message);
        protected virtual void Validate(BasicEvent basicEvent);
}
```

The full source code can be found on GitHub repository of this book.

We can divide this class into three parts. First, the public properties help us to control the flow of the processing. Second, the public function **Process**, which can be called from the outside code to start processing of the event and is derived from the **AbstractPipeline** class. And third, protected functions which provide functionality for event processing and can be overwritten in the child classes to achieve more precise processing of specific events.

IoTPipeline class looks similar and is demonstrated in the following code example:

```
public class IoTPipeline : AbstractPipeline
{
        public bool ShouldSaveMetadata {get;set;}
        public string ApiUrl { get; set; }
        public string TargetSystemApiUrl { get; set; }
        public override void Process(BasicEvent basicEvent)
        {
                if(ShouldSaveMetadata)
                    SaveMetadata(basicEvent);
                Notify(basicEvent, "PROCESSING_STARTED");
                Validate(basicEvent);
                ProcessEvent(basicEvent);

                if (ShouldSaveMetadata)
                    UpdateMetadata(basicEvent);


                Notify(basicEvent, "PROCESSING_FINISHED");
        }
        protected virtual void ProcessEvent(BasicEvent basicEvent);
```

```
        protected virtual Guid SaveMetadata(BasicEvent basicEvent);
        protected virtual void UpdateMetadata(BasicEvent basicEvent);
        protected virtual void Notify(BasicEvent badicEvent, string message);
        protected virtual void Validate(BasicEvent basicEvent);
}
```

For now, we have defined our events and pipeline classes. Further, let us define our builder, responsible for creating various pipelines.

On the top of the hierarchy, we have a **PipelineDirector** class, which contains all the information needed to provide our pipelines with configuration data and defines methods that return preconfigured pipelines for event processing:

```
public static class PipelineDirector
{
        private static string targetASystemUploadUrl =
                                "http://file.storage.com/systemA/upload";
        private static string targetASystemApiUrl =
                                "http://systemA.com/api";
        private static string targetBSystemUploadUrl =
                                "http://file.storage.com/systemB/upload";
        private static string targetBSystemApiUrl =
                                "http://systemB.com/api";
        private static string targetCSystemApiUrl =
                                "http://systemC.com/api";
        private static string targetCSystemProcessingApiUrl =
                                "http://systemC.processing.com/api";
        public static AbstractPipeline BuildTypeAPipeline()
        {
            var typeAPipelineBuilder = new
                                FilePipelineBuilder<FileUploadPipeline>();
            return typeAPipelineBuilder.
                ShouldBeFilePreprocessed(false).
                ShouldBeEventStored(true).
                ShouldSaveMetadata(true).
                SetTargetSystemApiUrl(targetASystemUploadUrl).
                SetTargetSystemUploadUrl(targetASystemApiUrl).
                Build();
        }
        public static AbstractPipeline BuildTypeBPipeline()
```

```
        {
            var typeAPipelineBuilder = new
                            FilePipelineBuilder<FileUploadPipeline>();
            return typeAPipelineBuilder.
                ShouldBeFilePreprocessed(false).
                ShouldBeEventStored(true).
                ShouldSaveMetadata(true).
                SetTargetSystemApiUrl(targetBSystemUploadUrl).
                SetTargetSystemUploadUrl(targetBSystemApiUrl).
                Build();
        }
        public static AbstractPipeline BuildTypeCPipeline()
        {
            var typeCPipeline = new IoTPipelineBuilder<IoTPipeline>();
            return typeCPipeline.
                ShouldSaveMetadata(true).
                SetApiUrl(targetCSystemApiUrl).
                SetTargetApiUrl(targetCSystemProcessingApiUrl).
                Build();
        }
}
```

In our case, it contains URLs of APIs and three methods to create two types of pipelines. The end of the diagram is dedicated to pipeline builders.

We have defined two of them: **IoTPipelineBuilder** and **FileUploadPipelineBuilder**.

Let us examine these further:

```
public class IoTPipelineBuilder<T> where T: IoTPipeline, new()
{
        private T pipeline = default;
        public IoTPipelineBuilder()
        {
            this.pipeline = new T();
        }
        public IoTPipelineBuilder<T> ShouldSaveMetadata(bool shouldSaveMetadata)
        {
            pipeline.ShouldSaveMetadata = shouldSaveMetadata;
```

```
            return this;
        }
        public IoTPipelineBuilder<T> SetApiUrl(string apiUrl)
        {
            pipeline.ApiUrl = apiUrl;
            return this;
        }
        public IoTPipelineBuilder<T> SetTargetApiUrl(string targetApiUrl)
        {
            pipeline.TargetSystemApiUrl = targetApiUrl;
            return this;
        }
        public T Build()
        {
            return this.pipeline;
        }
}
```

As you can see, they are straightforward. The main feature of the Builder design pattern is that it provides the possibility to hide some underlying initialization features. Also, the **PipelineDirector** class makes a chain of configuration method calls. **FileUploadPipepelineBuilder** will not be provided because it looks the same as **IoTPipelineBuilder**.

In this section, we reviewed the Builder design pattern. We have seen that it has great capabilities to split class definition from class configuration and decouple the creation of an instance from its usage. Also, we could eliminate redundant child classes because earlier, they were created only for making some adjustments to pipeline flow configuration. Now, it can be done using public properties set through the builder.

We can use these new pipelines without the builder but then in each place where you going to use it, you will need to get config values and configure these pipelines with required properties. It is complex and error prone. In our example, we have only used simple types like strings and bool values, but in the real-life system you will have to configure such pipelines with many support classes, services and so on.

In our next section, we will merge **AbstractFactory** and **Builder** approaches to see how it helps us to build a processing event hub.

Synergy of the patterns

For now, we are ready to merge all the three patterns. Let us see how it looks in the design. Refer to the following *Figure 2.8*:

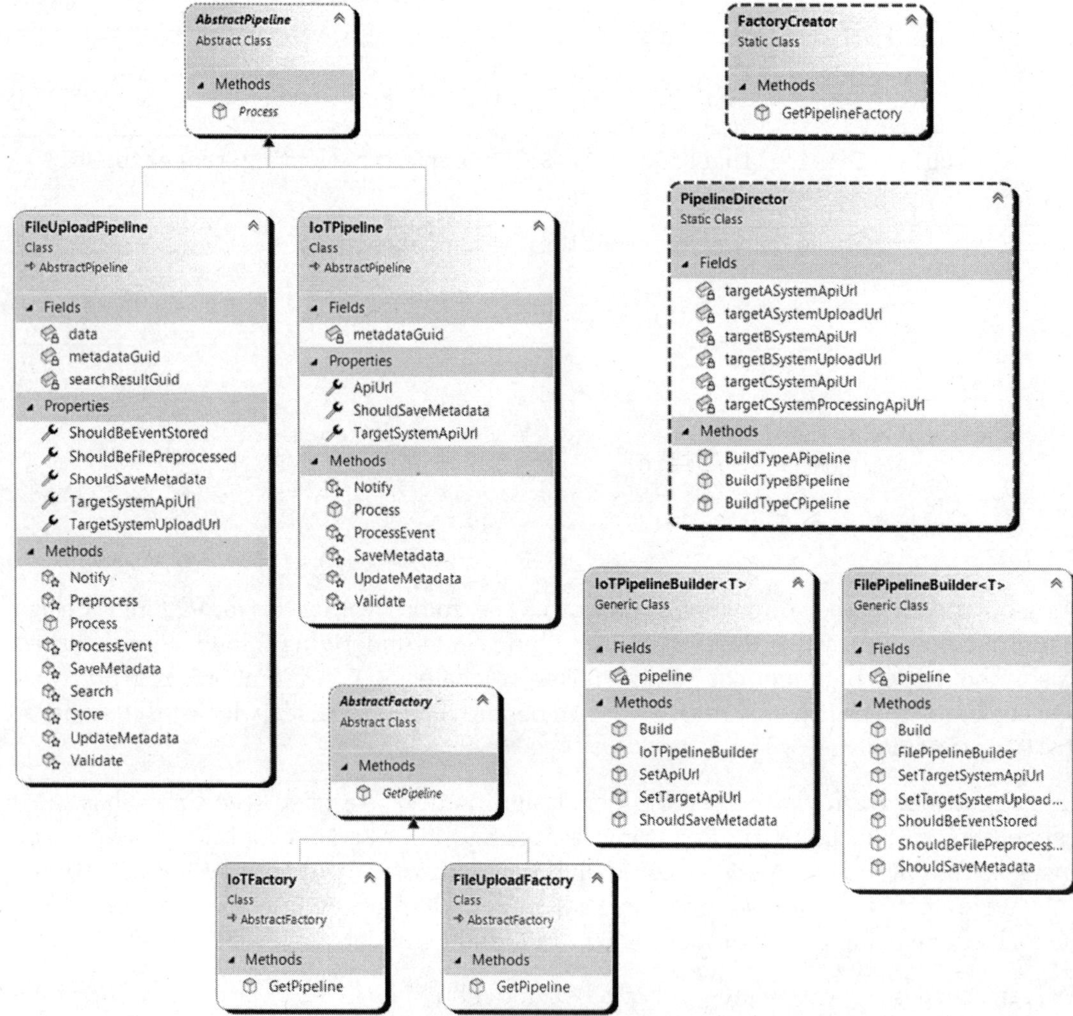

Figure 2.8: The core of processing engine

In the bottom of the diagram, we have **`AbstractFactory`** with two child classes: **`IoTFactory`** and **`FileUploadFactory`**. They are responsible for producing concrete pipelines based on information from event. Internally, they use **`PipelineDirector`** to produce the requested pipeline for an event. **`PipelineDirector`** is in turn responsible for keeping configuration parameters for pipelines and contains three methods which provide possibility to create a specific pipeline. When these three methods are called, **`IoTPipelineBuilder<T>`** or **`FilePipelineBuilder<T>`** is created with specific pipeline, returned by builders.

Let us look from the client code perspective. When system receives an event, it calls **FactoryCreator** to create a factory. Depending on the **Source** property of the event, **IoTFactory** or **FileUploadFactory** is created. Both have a method **GetPipeline** that uses **PipelineDirector** internally to get a pipeline.

If we try to make a more schematic view, it will look like this:

FactoryCreator | **Factory** (IoT or FileUpload) | **PipelineDirector** | **PipelineBuilder** (IoT or FileUpload) | **Pipeline** (IoT or FileUpload).

In the end, you receive a preconfigured pipeline on which you can call **ProcessEvent** method and pass your incoming event to be processed.

Code

In this section, we need to look only at factory class.

Instead of using the old approach demonstrated in the following code.

```
public class FileUploadFactory: AbstractFactory
{
        public override AbstractPipeline GetPipeline(BasicEvent basicEvent)
        {
            return basicEvent.Type switch
            {
                "TypeA" => new TypeAPipeline(),
                "TypeB" => new TypeBPipeline(),
                _ => throw new NotImplementedException()
            };
        }
}
```

We are using the **PipelineDirector** to make our pipelines. Take a look at the code:

```
public class FileUploadFactory: AbstractFactory
{
        public override AbstractPipeline GetPipeline(BasicEvent basicEvent)
        {
            return basicEvent.Type switch
            {
                "TypeA" => PipelineDirector.BuildTypeAPipeline(),
                "TypeB" => PipelineDirector.BuildTypeBPipeline(),
```

```
            _ => throw new NotImplementedException()
        };
    }
}
```

That is all we need to do to integrate our **PipelineDirector** class into our codebase and produce ready-to-use pipelines using its methods.

From a client code perspective, it looks like this:

```
var event1 = new BaseUploadEvent
{
            Source = "FILE",
            Type = "TypeA",
            FileName = "TypeAFilename.jpg",
            FileType = ".jpg",
            FileUrl = «http://typeA.file.url»,
            Id = Guid.NewGuid()
        };
        var event2 = new BaseUploadEvent
        {
            Source = "FILE",
            Type = "TypeB",
            FileName = "TypeBFilename.jpg",
            FileType = ".jpg",
            FileUrl = "http://typeB.file.url",
            Id = Guid.NewGuid()
        };
        var event3 = new BaseIoTEvent
        {
            Source = "IOT",
            Type = "TypeC",
            Action = "TEMP_UPDATE",
            Value = 92.2.ToString(),
            Id = Guid.NewGuid()
        };
        List<BasicEvent> eventList = new List<BasicEvent> { event1,
                                                   event2, event3 };
```

```
            eventList.ForEach(eventObj =>
            {
                FactoryCreator.GetPipelineFactory(eventObj).
                                GetPipeline(eventObj).Process(eventObj);
});
```

As you can see, you can chain the calls to get the result of pipeline processing. In the event handler, you do not need to spend a line of code to determine which pipeline should handle this event. In this case, the configuration of the processing pipeline is happening automatically.

In result of executing this code, you will see the following *Figure 2.9*:

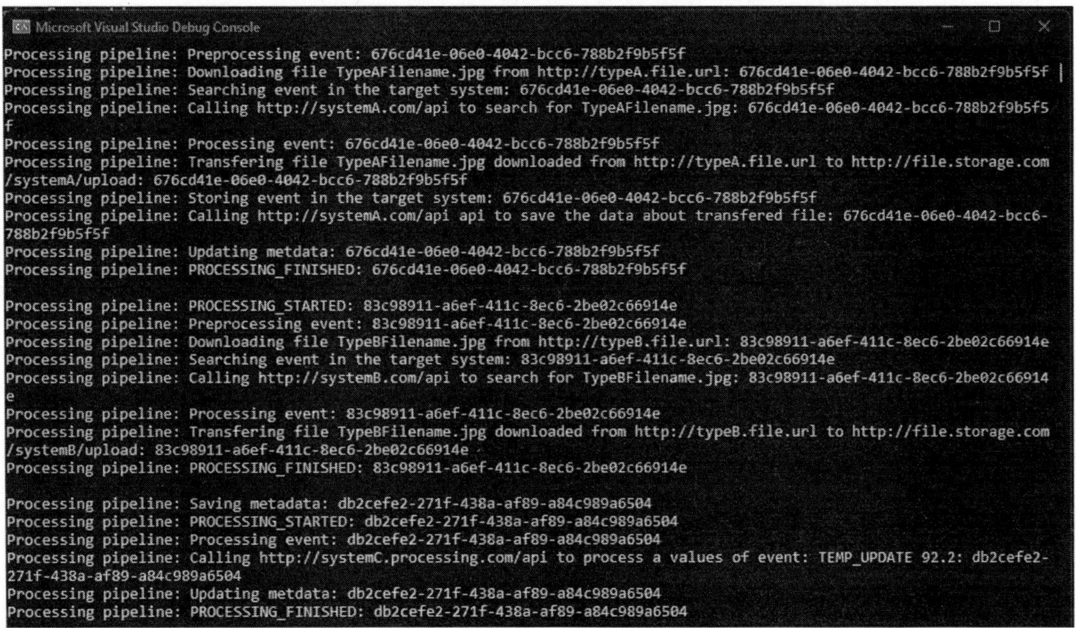

Figure 2.9: *Summary of 3 patterns build together*

Conclusion

Factory, Abstract Factory, and Builder design patterns help you to separate the configuration, instantiation, and utility from each other. It is important because each of these steps can be changed in the future. If you have all these steps in one place and a couple or more such places, you will need to change them all. At this moment, we have a foundation to build a service that will handle all nuances of event handling in a simpler way. It will allow us to make changes more effectively than *spaghetti-code*.

We can easily add a new class of events and a separate pipeline without changing the main processing client code or existing pipeline to add some additional methods. Also, we can separate some types of events to be processed by different pipelines. Some changes will require more work, but it is still manageable because we have a separation. When we have a separation, we can split the required job into smaller tasks, make them more concrete, and better estimate the time needed to make the changes.

In the next chapter, we will continue to explore Creational design patterns. Our next target is to review singleton and prototype design patterns. They will help us to build a cloneable pipeline and manage connection strings through the Configuration class.

Join our book's Discord space

Join the book's Discord Workspace for Latest updates, Offers, Tech happenings around the world, New Release and Sessions with the Authors:

https://discord.bpbonline.com

CHAPTER 3

Creational Design Patterns: Singleton and Prototype

Introduction

This chapter will introduce you to singleton and prototype design patterns. These are some of the simplest and most useful patterns. Singleton provides the possibility to create only one instance of a class. It is useful when you want to load some data on initialization and then just use this data during an application lifetime.

The second design pattern is prototype. It provides a mechanism to copy an existing object's main properties without calling heavy logic to create it from scratch.

Structure

The chapter covers the following topics:

- Singleton
- Design
    - Designing the configuration provider
    - Code
- Prototype
    - Designing a cloneable pipeline
    - Code

- Synergy of the patterns
  - o Adjusting the processing engine
  - o Code

Objectives

At the end of this chapter, you will be able to describe singleton and prototype design patterns and apply them to real-world problems.

We will design and code a support class that will help us to manage configuration and API tokens to make our lives easier and much faster during events processing.

Singleton

Singleton design pattern is a creational design pattern that restricts a class to have no more than one instance of a class, providing a single point of access to this instance.

It provides the possibility to optimize memory consumption and performance simultaneously: less instances on the heap | less memory consumption | less load of resources | and less performance footprint.

Designing the configuration provider

Let us start with the basic definition of singleton design pattern. In *Chapter 2, Fundamental Programming Structures*, we started working with factories. In this chapter, we will continue this way and optimize **`PipelineDirector`**.

Design

Let us start with the technical aspects. In **`PipelineDirector`**, as you remember, we had all our API addresses hardcoded. It is not the right way to keep configuration data. So, we will start by defining our requirements for the **`Configuration`** class:

- **`Configuration`** must reside in a separate class.
- The class should be initialized on startup.
- The class should be initialized only once during lifetime.
- Only one instance of the class should be used.

With these requirements in mind, let us design one. Refer to the following *Figure 3.1*:

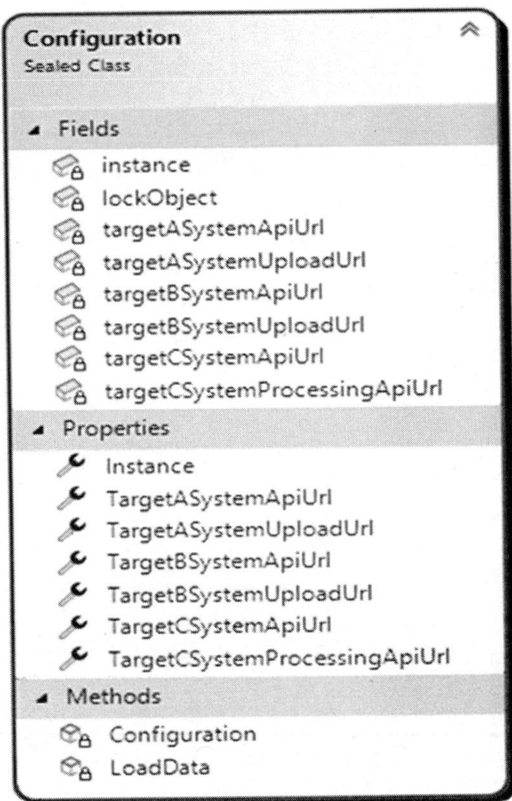

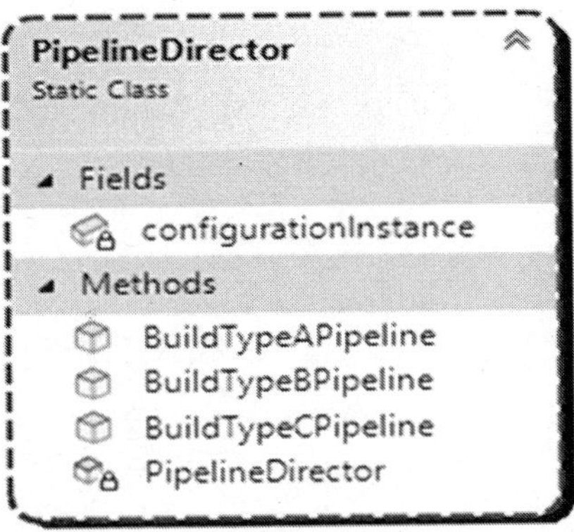

***Figure 3.1:** Configuration class diagram*

As you can see in the figure, we have added a new class **`Configuration`**. It has a bunch of private variables in which configuration values are kept with the same public properties. They should be read only to allow read access without modification possibility. Also, it has the method **`LoadData`**, which loads the config into the memory. In our case, it contains only variable setters, but in a real system, it can be file loading and parsing or database connection with loading data from some tables.

In the **`PipelineDirector`** class, we have added a variable named **`configurationInstance`**. We are using it to initialize config and access config data during the initialization of requested pipeline classes.

Code

Take a look at the code of **`Configuration`** class:

```
public sealed class Configuration
{
        private static Configuration instance = null;
```

```
        private Configuration() { }
        private void LoadData()
        {
            this.TargetASystemUploadUrl =
                    "http://file.storage.com/systemA/upload";
            // Define other private properties
        }
        public static Configuration Instance
        {
            get
            {
                    if (instance == null)
                    {
                        instance = new Configuration();
                        instance.LoadData();
                    }
                    return instance;
            }
        }
        public string TargetASystemUploadUrl
        {
            get; private set;
        }
        public String TargetASystemApiUrl
        {
            get; private set;
        }
        public string TargetBSystemApiUrl
        {
            get; private set;
        }
       // Other Properties
}
```

In this code example, you can notice a few things. The **Configuration** class is sealed, so one can derive from it. Constructor is private, and no one can create an instance of this class. For accessing an instance of the **Configuration** class, a developer can use the

`Instance` property. It checks if the instance is already initialized and if not, it creates a new one and loads config data. Otherwise, it returns the current instance.

Next, we will look at the **`PipelineDirector`**'s code, which now uses the **`Configuration`** class to supply pipelines with the required properties:

```
public static class PipelineDirector
{
        private static Configuration configurationInstance;
        static PipelineDirector()
        {
            configurationInstance = Configuration.Instance;
        }
        public static AbstractPipeline BuildTypeAPipeline()
        {
            var typeAPipelineBuilder = new
                                FilePipelineBuilder<FileUploadPipeline>();
            return typeAPipelineBuilder.
                ShouldBeFilePreprocessed(true).
                ShouldBeEventStored(true).
                ShouldSaveMetadata(true).
                SetTargetSystemApiUrl(configurationInstance.
                                    TargetASystemApiUrl).
                SetTargetSystemUploadUrl(configurationInstance.
                                    TargetASystemUploadUrl).
                Build();
        }
        public static AbstractPipeline BuildTypeBPipeline()
        {
            var typeAPipelineBuilder =
                    new FilePipelineBuilder<FileUploadPipeline>();
            return typeAPipelineBuilder
              .ShouldBeFilePreprocessed(true)
              .ShouldBeEventStored(false).ShouldSaveMetadata(false)
              .SetTargetSystemApiUrl(configurationInstance.
              TargetBSystemApiUrl)
              .SetTargetSystemUploadUrl(configurationInstance.
              TargetBSystemUploadUrl)
              .Build();
        }
```

```
        public static AbstractPipeline BuildTypeCPipeline()
        {
            var typeCPipeline = new IoTPipelineBuilder<IoTPipeline>();
             return typeCPipeline.ShouldSaveMetadata(true).
             SetApiUrl(configurationInstance.TargetCSystemApiUrl).
             SetTargetApiUrl(configurationInstance.
             TargetCSystemProcessingApiUrl).Build();
        }
}
```

We have added a private variable **configurationInstance**, which is initialized in the static constructor of the **PipelineDirector** class. It means that when a developer calls any function of **PipelineDirector**'s class to be executed, the **configurationInstance** will already be initialized.

From the preceding code example, we can see that the **PipelineDirector** class became cleaner. Also, all functionality connected to dynamic properties of pipelines (URLs are dynamic by their nature) moved to a different class. It means that we do not need to think about the details of the configuration while we are using it. It can be loaded from a file or database, but in **PipelineDirector**, we only use a high-level interface provided by the **Configuration** class instance.

Also, it is worth mentioning that configuration data is loaded only once during the lifetime of an application. Imagine that for each pipeline instance (for each event), you would need to load configuration data, and it would take some 150ms. In this case, the processing time of event is 10ms, and configuration loading takes 150ms. You need to process 1 million events. 1,000,000 * 10 * 150 / 1000 / 60 / 60 equals 410 hours. Without configuration loading for each event, it will take 2.7 hours + 150ms for initial configuration loading.

Singleton design pattern introduces the possibility of providing a single access point to some resources. In our example, it was configuration. In another case, it can be a managed resource, like a database connection, system resource, or something similar.

Sometimes, it can greatly improve performance (in our example, it worked as a cache). In others, it helps to manage concurrent access to a resource.

Before you try to transform any class into a singleton, ask yourself the following questions:

- Should it manage concurrent access to a shared resource?
- Will access be requested from separate parts of the system?
- Will you benefit from performance, access control, or both by introducing singleton?

If your answer is *yes* to at least two of these questions, then it is meaningful to consider reviewing the possibility of introducing the Singleton design pattern in your system.

Prototype

Prototype is a creational design pattern that allows you to copy an existing object without making your code dependent on its internal structure.

It provides you the possibility to create a new object without knowing anything about its internals. Also, it allows you to optimize the performance if internal objects of the class require a heavy loading operation to create them.

Designing a cloneable pipeline

Imagine that our API requires us to request a token before executing any operation on target systems A, B, or C. For simplicity of design, let us define that the token is valid for a lifetime. Token requests can take up to 200ms. Again, 1,000,000 events multiplied by 200ms will be a huge number of hours required to process many objects.

The solution is to introduce a cloneable pipeline that will copy token properties. Our example will be artificial; see *Figure 3.2*:

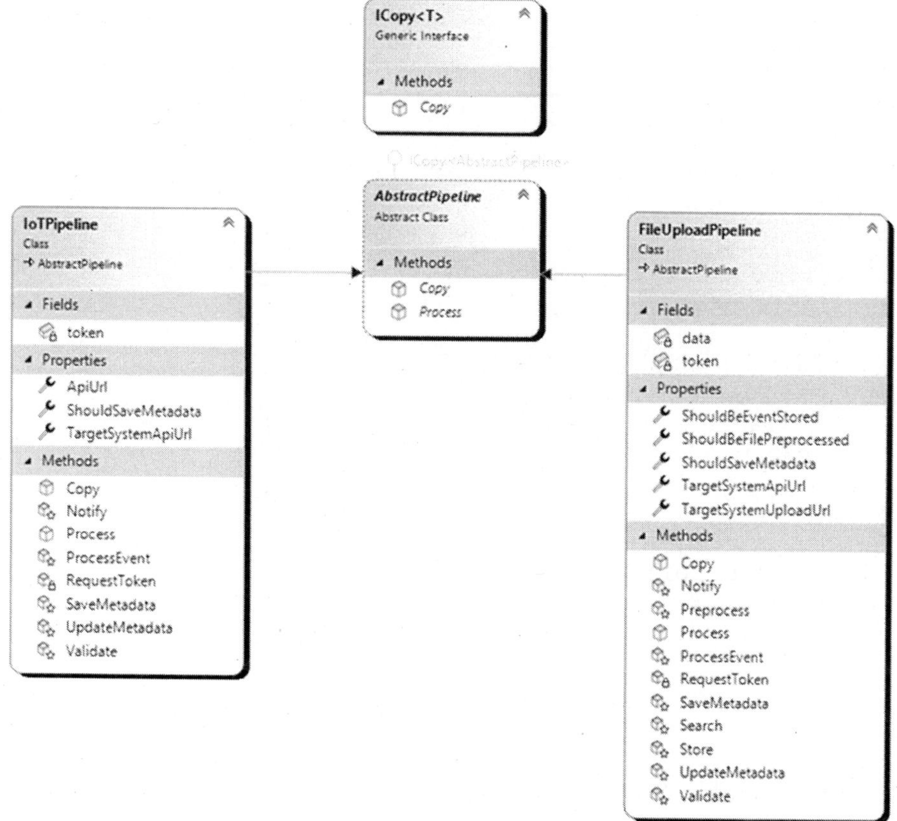

Figure 3.2: *Prototype design pattern diagram*

In this figure, you can see that we have defined a new interface **ICopy<T>**, and **AbstractPipeline** now derives it with a generic parameter of itself. For this case, we have added a **Copy** method for each pipeline, including **AbstractPipeline**.

Let us see what it looks like in the code.

Code

Firstly, we will define our **Copy<T>** interface:

```
public interface ICopy<T>
{
        public T Copy();
}
```

It contains only one method **Copy** and is parameterized with type parameter **T**, which has no constraints.

Then, we should derive our **AbstractPipeline** class from it:

```
public abstract class AbstractPipeline: ICopy<AbstractPipeline>
{
        public abstract AbstractPipeline Copy();
        public abstract void Process(BasicEvent basicEvent);
}
```

At this level, we define that our **ICopy<T>** interface will be implemented with **AbstractPipeline** as a type parameter.

Then, we define the **Copy** method and an additional variable token in our concrete pipelines. Take a look at the following code:

```
public class FileUploadPipeline : AbstractPipeline
{
      private string token;
    public override void Process(BasicEvent basicEvent)
        {
                RequestToken();
           // Other Processing stuff
        }
         public override AbstractPipeline Copy()
         {
             FileUploadPipeline result = new FileUploadPipeline();
```

```
            result.ShouldBeEventStored = this.ShouldBeEventStored;
           result.ShouldBeFilePreprocessed = this.ShouldBeFilePreprocessed;
            result.ShouldSaveMetadata = this.ShouldSaveMetadata;
            result.TargetSystemApiUrl = this.TargetSystemApiUrl;
            result.TargetSystemUploadUrl = this.TargetSystemApiUrl;
            result.token = this.token;
            return result;
        }
        private async void RequestToken()
        {
            if (!string.IsNullOrWhiteSpace(token))
                return;

            await Task.Delay(200);
            this.token = $"Token: {Guid.NewGuid()}";
        }
    // All other stuff
}
```

The same code will be used by the **IoTPipeline** class.

Let us see how the **PipelineDirector** class should adapt to these changes:

```
public static class PipelineDirector
{
        private static Configuration configurationInstance;
        private static FileUploadPipeline typeAPipeline;
        private static FileUploadPipeline typeBPipeline;
        private static IoTPipeline typeCPipeline;

        static PipelineDirector()
        {
             configurationInstance = Configuration.Instance;
             var typeAPipelineBuilder =
                 new FilePipelineBuilder<FileUploadPipeline>();
           typeAPipeline = typeAPipelineBuilder.
               ShouldBeFilePreprocessed(true).
               ShouldBeEventStored(true).
               ShouldSaveMetadata(true).
```

```
            SetTargetSystemApiUrl(configurationInstance.TargetASystemApiUrl).
      SetTargetSystemUploadUrl(configurationInstance.TargetASystemUploadUrl).
                Build();
            // Initialize other pipelines in the same manner
        }
        public static AbstractPipeline BuildTypeAPipeline()
        {
            typeAPipeline = typeAPipeline.Copy();
            return typeAPipeline;
        }
        public static AbstractPipeline BuildTypeBPipeline()
        {
            typeBPipeline = typeBPipeline.Copy();
            return typeBPipeline;
        }
        public static AbstractPipeline BuildTypeCPipeline()
        {
            typeCPipeline = typeCPipeline.Copy();
            return typeCPipeline;
        }
}
```

We have moved the initialization of pipelines into a static constructor. It means that it will be called before any static member execution. In our case, it will initialize pipelines, which can later be copied into appropriate methods.

`Copy()` method will be called before pipeline execution. In the pipeline execution method, we will call the **`RequestToken`** method in which the token variable will be set. When the next event comes into our processing engine, **`PipelineDirector`** will copy an instance of pipeline with an existing token.

Prototype design pattern is useful when you have some part of an object that requires too many resources to be instantiated. In our artificial example, a token request could take up to 200ms. When a system built is going to process large events in a short time, requesting token for each event can take a lot of time and can hurt overall system performance. In our case, we are simply copying existing data from the pipeline that we already have.

There is one more example that you can take from the gaming industry. When you are loading an image for a graphical object, you need to display 1000 of them in parallel. You can use the **`.Copy`** method to copy reference to img byte array and set new coordinates for each object. It will help you to reduce memory usage and time needed to display a concrete object.

In .NET, there is an interface called **`ICloneable`** that is used across .NET Core for the same purpose.

Synergy of the patterns

In this section, we will review how the described design patterns can be used together to help developers maintain a codebase, support, and create an easy-to-use class hierarchy.

Adjusting the processing engine

In this section, we will unite the patterns together. We will have a **Builder**, **Factory**, **AbstractFactory**, singleton, and prototype in *Figure 3.3*:

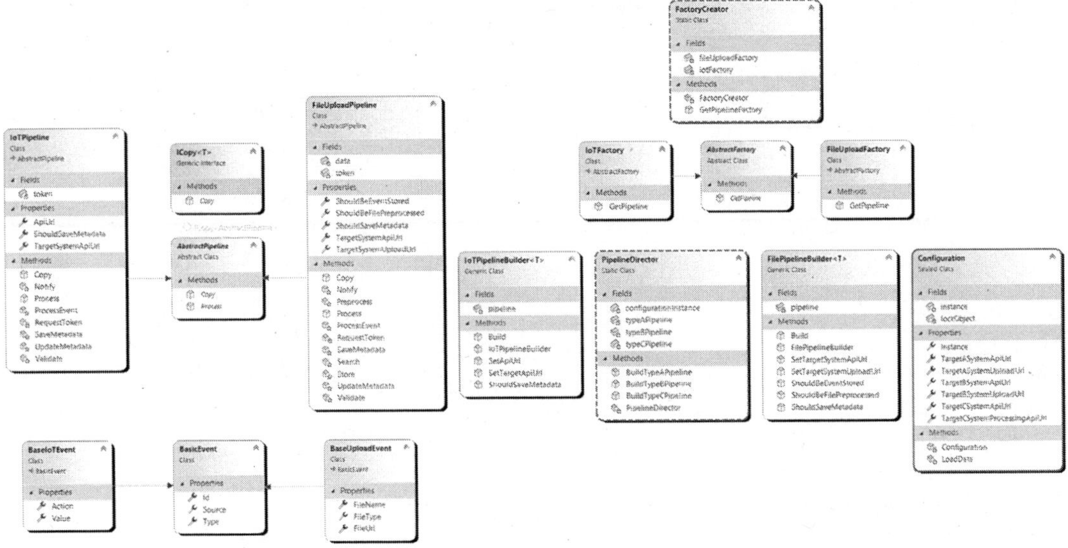

Figure 3.3: *AbstractFactory, Factory, Builder, singleton, and prototype diagram*

You have already seen the separate parts of this figure before.

We have separated it into parts as it is too large to display all classes in one diagram. Refer to the following *Figure 3.3(a)*:

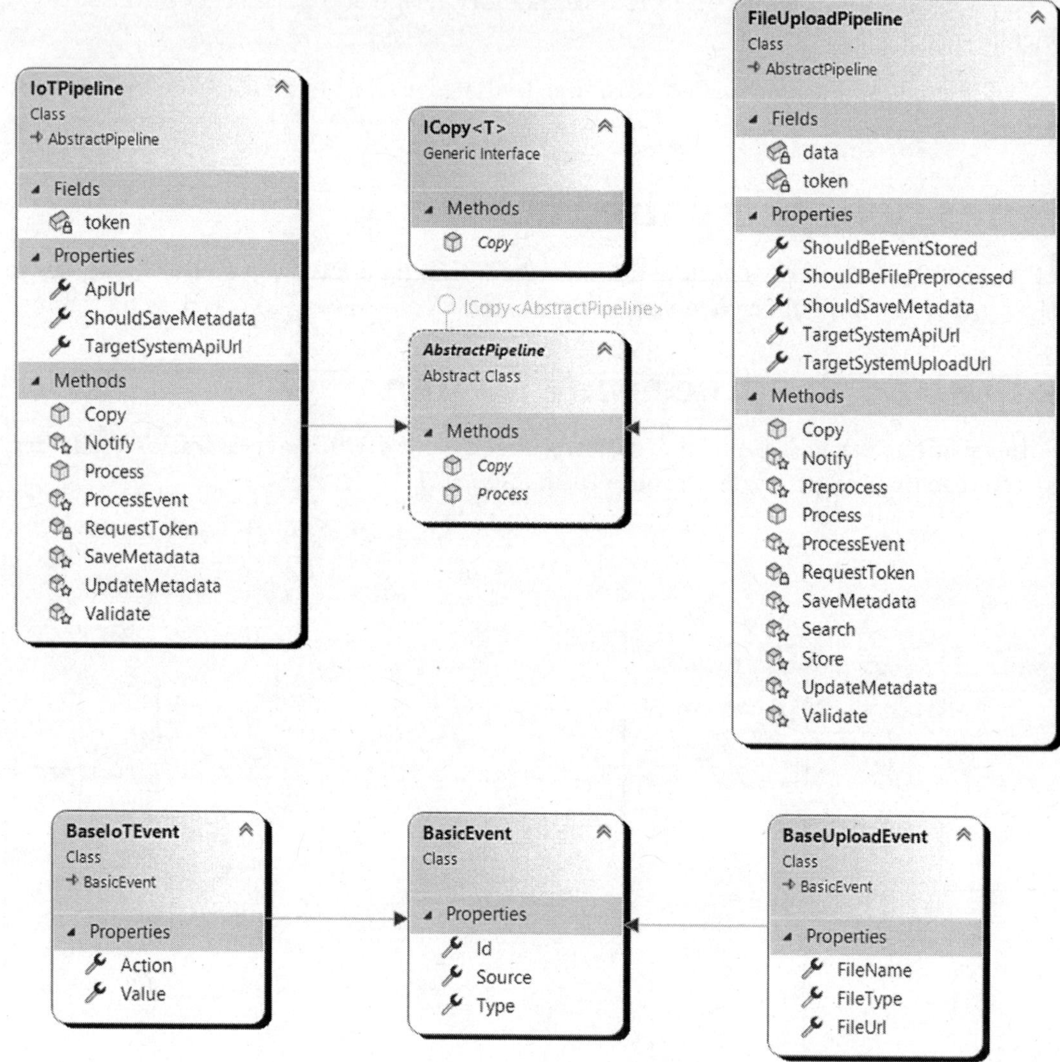

Figure 3.3(a): *Synergy of patterns. Prototype diagram*

In this figure, you can look at the pipeline part, which includes **`AbstractPipeline`** and derived classes like **`IoT`** and **`FileUpload`** pipelines.

In *Figure 3.3(b)*, you can look at the **`Configuration`** and **`PipelineDirector`** classes, which use configuration as a private variable to get the required configuration properties to build concrete pipelines:

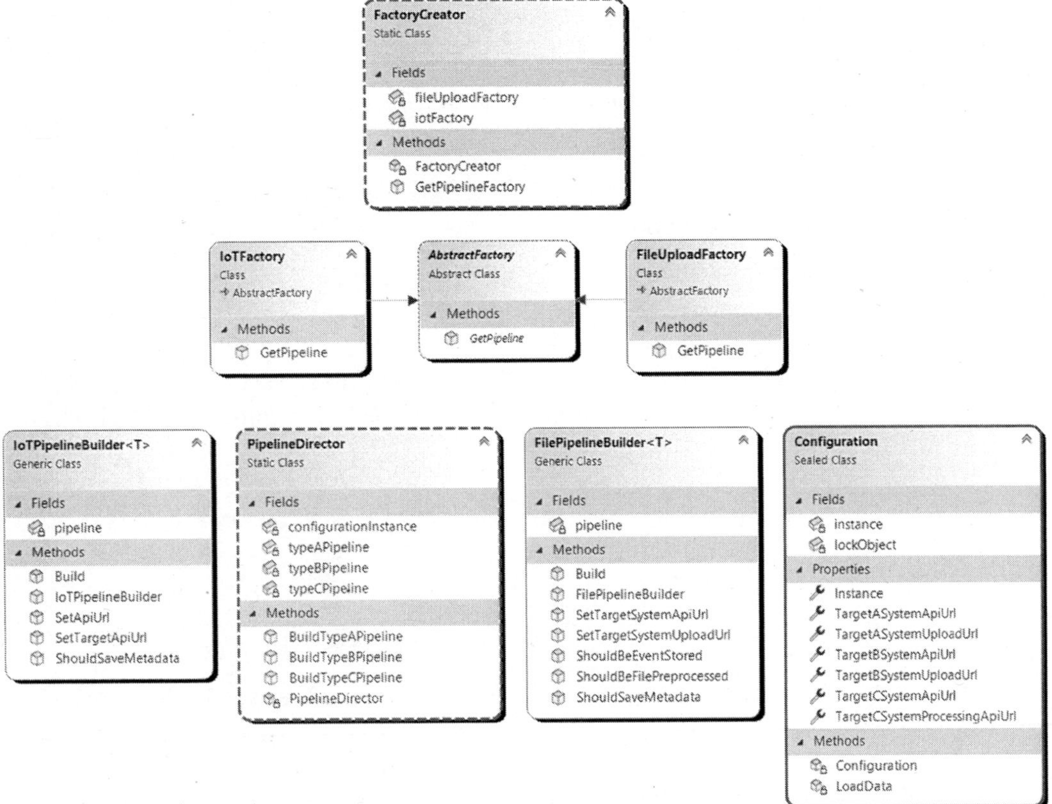

Figure 3.3(b): *Synergy of pattens. Singleton diagram*

Also, it contains the Factory part, which includes **`FactoryCreator`**, **`AbstractFactory`** and its derived classes, and concrete **`Pipeline`** builder classes.

Code

In the preceding section of this chapter, you have already seen all parts of the code that were added. Here, we can check how our addition to the existing design influenced the time needed to process the six events.

Take a look at this code. It is the simplest code to experiment with:

```
public static void Main()
{
            Stopwatch watch = new Stopwatch();
            watch.Start();

            var event1 = new BaseUploadEvent
```

```
            {
                Source = "FILE",
                Type = "TypeA",
                FileName = "TypeAFilename.jpg",
                FileType = ".jpg",
                FileUrl = "http://typeA.file.url",
                Id = Guid.NewGuid()
            };
            // Definition of additional 5 events

            List<BasicEvent> eventList = new List<BasicEvent> { event1,
                              event2, event3, event4, event5, event6 };
            eventList.ForEach(eventObj =>
                    FactoryCreator
                    .GetPipelineFactory(eventObj)
                    .GetPipeline(eventObj)
                    .Process(eventObj));

            watch.Stop();
            Console.WriteLine($"MS ellapsed: {watch.ElapsedMilliseconds}");
}
```

We will check how long will it take if we remove token copying:

```
public override FileUploadPipeline Copy()
{
            FileUploadPipeline result = new FileUploadPipeline();
            result.ShouldBeEventStored = this.ShouldBeEventStored;
            result.ShouldBeFilePreprocessed = this.ShouldBeFilePreprocessed;
            result.ShouldSaveMetadata = this.ShouldSaveMetadata;
            result.TargetSystemApiUrl = this.TargetSystemApiUrl;
            result.TargetSystemUploadUrl = this.TargetSystemApiUrl;
            result.token = this.token;
            return result;
        }
```

For this, we will need to remove the line: **`result.token = this.token;`** in both pipelines.

As an example, take a look at **`FileUploadPipeline`**:

```
public override FileUploadPipeline Copy()
{
        FileUploadPipeline result = new FileUploadPipeline();
        result.ShouldBeEventStored = this.ShouldBeEventStored;
        result.ShouldBeFilePreprocessed = this.ShouldBeFilePreprocessed;
        result.ShouldSaveMetadata = this.ShouldSaveMetadata;
        result.TargetSystemApiUrl = this.TargetSystemApiUrl;
        result.TargetSystemUploadUrl = this.TargetSystemApiUrl;
        return result;
}
```

As you can notice, we removed the line **`result.token = this.token;`** and now, for all new instances of this pipeline, we should request the token again. Refer to the following *Figure 3.4*:

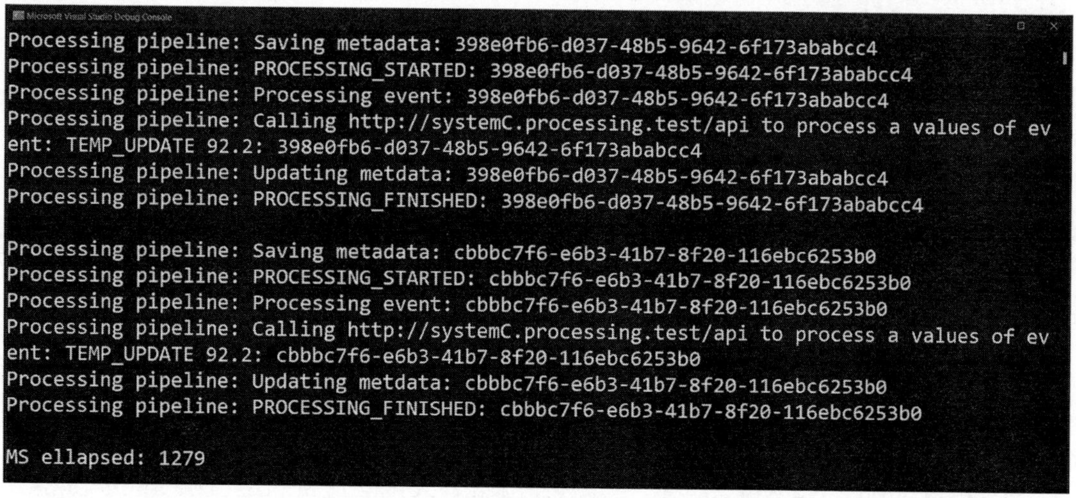

```
Microsoft Visual Studio Debug Console
Processing pipeline: Saving metadata: 398e0fb6-d037-48b5-9642-6f173ababcc4
Processing pipeline: PROCESSING_STARTED: 398e0fb6-d037-48b5-9642-6f173ababcc4
Processing pipeline: Processing event: 398e0fb6-d037-48b5-9642-6f173ababcc4
Processing pipeline: Calling http://systemC.processing.test/api to process a values of ev
ent: TEMP_UPDATE 92.2: 398e0fb6-d037-48b5-9642-6f173ababcc4
Processing pipeline: Updating metdata: 398e0fb6-d037-48b5-9642-6f173ababcc4
Processing pipeline: PROCESSING_FINISHED: 398e0fb6-d037-48b5-9642-6f173ababcc4

Processing pipeline: Saving metadata: cbbbc7f6-e6b3-41b7-8f20-116ebc6253b0
Processing pipeline: PROCESSING_STARTED: cbbbc7f6-e6b3-41b7-8f20-116ebc6253b0
Processing pipeline: Processing event: cbbbc7f6-e6b3-41b7-8f20-116ebc6253b0
Processing pipeline: Calling http://systemC.processing.test/api to process a values of ev
ent: TEMP_UPDATE 92.2: cbbbc7f6-e6b3-41b7-8f20-116ebc6253b0
Processing pipeline: Updating metdata: cbbbc7f6-e6b3-41b7-8f20-116ebc6253b0
Processing pipeline: PROCESSING_FINISHED: cbbbc7f6-e6b3-41b7-8f20-116ebc6253b0

MS ellapsed: 1279
```

Figure 3.4: *Execution result without token copying*

In the end, it took **`1279 ms`** to process the six events.

Let us execute our optimized code with the prototype design pattern and try again.

In the following *Figure 3.5*, you can look at the result of execution of our optimized code:

```
Processing pipeline: Updating metdata: 2b7ac6ac-e519-4c2d-b4cc-449b53042c35
Processing pipeline: PROCESSING_FINISHED: 2b7ac6ac-e519-4c2d-b4cc-449b53042c35

Processing pipeline: Saving metadata: 3481e7e9-4529-41dc-af83-c8e31b5087d6
Processing pipeline: PROCESSING_STARTED: 3481e7e9-4529-41dc-af83-c8e31b5087d6
Processing pipeline: Processing event: 3481e7e9-4529-41dc-af83-c8e31b5087d6
Processing pipeline: Calling http://systemC.processing.test/api to process a values of ev
ent: TEMP_UPDATE 92.2: 3481e7e9-4529-41dc-af83-c8e31b5087d6
Processing pipeline: Updating metdata: 3481e7e9-4529-41dc-af83-c8e31b5087d6
Processing pipeline: PROCESSING_FINISHED: 3481e7e9-4529-41dc-af83-c8e31b5087d6

Processing pipeline: Saving metadata: 0e3001fa-1be0-4697-8a6a-b80501d9c311
Processing pipeline: PROCESSING_STARTED: 0e3001fa-1be0-4697-8a6a-b80501d9c311
Processing pipeline: Processing event: 0e3001fa-1be0-4697-8a6a-b80501d9c311
Processing pipeline: Calling http://systemC.processing.test/api to process a values of ev
ent: TEMP_UPDATE 92.2: 0e3001fa-1be0-4697-8a6a-b80501d9c311
Processing pipeline: Updating metdata: 0e3001fa-1be0-4697-8a6a-b80501d9c311
Processing pipeline: PROCESSING_FINISHED: 0e3001fa-1be0-4697-8a6a-b80501d9c311

MS ellapsed: 664
```

***Figure 3.5**: Execution result with token copying*

The system has spent **644ms** to execute this code. It is two times faster than the code that is run without optimization. With more events to be processed, this difference will become larger.

Conclusion

Singleton and prototype design patterns provide a nice way to optimize access to resources, memory consumption, and loading time. Do not look at them as primitive patterns. They are not very complex to understand and implement, but sometimes, adopting these patterns can simplify your code and make it more understandable.

Implementing these patterns provides you with the possibility to manage access to resources, reduce execution time on time-consuming operations, and make your code as clean as possible.

In the next chapter, we will start to review structural design patterns. The intention is to help developers optimize the structure of types and their connections with each other.

Chapter 4
Structural Design Patterns: Adapter, Composite, and Flyweight

Introduction

This chapter explores object composition using Adapter, Composite, and Flyweight design patterns.

These three patterns provide the cornerstones of structural decomposition: interface to the outside world, encapsulation of a group of objects, and sharing a common state between a group of objects.

Structure

The chapter covers the following topics:

- Adapter
  - Design the interface to outside world
  - Code
- Composite
  - Design bulk processing pipeline
  - Code

- Flyweight
  - Sharing a common state
  - Code
- Synergy of the patterns
  - Adjusting the processing engine
  - Code

Objectives

At the end of this chapter, you will be able to describe Adapter, Composite, and Flyweight design patterns and apply them to real-world problems.

Let us dive in!

Adapter

Adapter design pattern is a structural design pattern that provides one interface to different types. For example, we can use different endpoints which use different protocols.

Design interface to the outside world

We should notify a couple of systems about incoming events. For example, one system uses `http` protocol, and the second uses `gRpc`. With this in mind, we will start designing our class hierarchy to support such a scenario.

In `PipelineDirector`, as you remember, we had set all our API addresses from the configuration instance and then passed them into pipelines directly. The problem is that the pipeline should decide what to do with these API addresses independently. With the help of Adapter design pattern, we will move API clients initialization outside of pipeline's code. Let us define the requirements for our class hierarchy:

- `Pipeline` should accept initialized unified communication client instead of API address.
- `PipelineDirector` should be able to initialize communication clients.
- Communication clients should be initialized only once during their lifetime.
- Communication clients should have only one method to be executed.
- Types of request and response should be specified as type parameters on abstraction type.

With these requirements in mind, let us design one! Refer to the following *Figure 4.1*:

***Figure 4.1:** Adapter design pattern diagram*

As you can see, the high ground was taken by **`ICommunicationClient<TRequest, TResponse>`** interface. It has only one method, which is named **`ExecuteRequest`**. It accepts one input parameter, **`TRequest`**, and returns **`TResponse`**, defined by type parameters in the interface definition. Then, we defined **`FileDownload`** and **`FileUpload`** clients for file handling and **`SystemAApiClient`** to deal with APIs provided by target systems. In our case, let us imagine that third-party systems upload files only to one storage, so we do not need to create additional file-downloading clients. Also, we have only one storage for uploaded files that are saved and registered in our system, so we do not need different uploading clients. **`SystemA`** and **`SystemC`** API clients are different because they use different protocols to communicate with their target systems.

At the same time, the **`PipelineDirector`** class no longer contains API addresses as private variables. From this moment, it keeps instances of various **`ICommunicationClient`** classes.

Code

First, we will define the **ICommunicationClient<TRequest, TResponse>** interface:

```
public interface ICommunicationClient<TRequest, TResponse>
{
        Task<TResponse> ExecuteRequest(TRequest request);
}
```

As you can see, there are two type parameters in the interface definition and one method **ExecuteRequest**.

Then we will look at communication clients that we have created to derive this interface:

```
public class SystemAApiClient : ICommunicationClient<string, string>
{
        private string baseUrl = string.Empty;
        public SystemAApiClient(string baseUrl)
        {
            this.baseUrl = baseUrl;
        }
        public async Task<string> ExecuteRequest(string data)
        {
            Console.WriteLine($"Sending message to {baseUrl}. Message: {data}");
            return await Task.FromResult(string.Empty);
        }
}
public class FileUploadClient : ICommunicationClient<UploadFileInfo, int>
{
        private string baseUrl = string.Empty;
        public FileUploadClient(string baseUrl)
        {
            this.baseUrl = baseUrl;
        }
        public async Task<int> ExecuteRequest(UploadFileInfo data)
        {
            string jsonString = JsonSerializer.Serialize(data);
            Console.WriteLine($"Uploading file to {this.baseUrl}. File:
                                                                {jsonString}");
            return await Task.FromResult(0);
        }
}
```

At the same time, **FileUploadClient** requires **UploadFileInfo** to be passed as input parameters:

```
public class UploadFileInfo
{
        public string FileName { get; set; }
        public byte[] Content { get; set; }
}
```

As mentioned, we have only one storage for upload and download, so all pipelines can use the same **FileUploadClient** instance to upload their files. If the path of a file is different for some pipeline, we can create a new instance with an appropriate address passed as a parameter into the constructor and use this instance instead.

FileUploadInfo contains only basic information like **FileName** and **Content** as a byte array.

The next class for our review is **FileDownloadClient**:

```
public class FileDownloadClient : ICommunicationClient<string, byte[]>
{
        public async Task<byte[]> ExecuteRequest(string fileUrl)
        {
            Console.WriteLine($"Downloading file from  {fileUrl}.");
            return await Task.FromResult(new byte[0]);
        }
}
```

This class does not contain any constructors, accepts file URL as an input parameter, and should return an array of bytes.

The last one is **SystemCApiClient**:

```
public class SystemCApiClient : ICommunicationClient<IoTData, string>
{
        private string baseUrl = string.Empty;
        public SystemCApiClient(string baseUrl)
        {
            this.baseUrl = baseUrl;
        }
        public async Task<string> ExecuteRequest(IoTData data)
        {
            string jsonString = JsonSerializer.Serialize(data);
```

```
            Console.WriteLine($"Sending message to {this.baseUrl}.
                                                    Message: {jsonString}");
            return await Task.FromResult("Success!");
        }
}
public class IoTData
{
        public string Source { get; set; }
        public string Action { get; set; }
        public string Value { get; set; }
}
```

It accepts **IoTData** as a **TRequest** type parameter, converts data to JSON, and sends it using **baseUrl** as an endpoint. It has a return type defined as string so that JSON could be passed back, or an error message tells you that an internal API server error has occurred so that we can finish or fail the processing.

The last class that will manage all changes together is **PipelineDirector**:

```
public static class PipelineDirector
{
        private static Configuration configurationInstance = Configuration.Instance;
        private static FileUploadPipeline typeAPipeline;
        private static FileUploadPipeline typeBPipeline;
        private static IoTPipeline typeCPipeline;

        private static SystemAApiClient systemASearchClient =
       new SystemAApiClient(configurationInstance.TargetASystemSearchApiUrl);
        private static SystemAApiClient systemAStoreClient =
       new SystemAApiClient(configurationInstance.TargetASystemStoreApiUrl);
        private static FileUploadClient fileUploadAClient =
       new FileUploadClient(configurationInstance.TargetASystemUploadUrl);
        private static FileUploadClient fileUploadBClient =
       new FileUploadClient(configurationInstance.TargetBSystemUploadUrl);
        private static FileDownloadClient fileDownloadClient =
          new FileDownloadClient();
        private static SystemCApiClient systemCApiClient =
   new SystemCApiClient(configurationInstance.TargetCSystemProcessingApiUrl);
        static PipelineDirector()
        {
```

```
    var typeAPipelineBuilder = new FilePipelineBuilder<FileUploadPipeline>();
        typeAPipeline = typeAPipelineBuilder.
            ShouldBeFilePreprocessed(true).
            ShouldBeEventStored(true).
            ShouldSaveMetadata(true).
            SetTargetSystemUploadClient(fileUploadAClient).
            SetTargetSystemDownloadClient(fileDownloadClient).
            SetTargetSystemSearchApiClient(systemASearchClient).
            SetTargetSystemStoreApiClient(systemAStoreClient).
            Build();
    var typeBPipelineBuilder = new FilePipelineBuilder<FileUploadPipeline>();
        typeBPipeline = typeBPipelineBuilder.
            ShouldBeFilePreprocessed(true).
            ShouldBeEventStored(false).
            ShouldSaveMetadata(false).
            SetTargetSystemUploadClient(fileUploadBClient).
            SetTargetSystemDownloadClient(fileDownloadClient).
            SetTargetSystemSearchApiClient(systemASearchClient).
            Build();
        var typeCPipelineBuilder = new IoTPipelineBuilder<IoTPipeline>();
        typeCPipeline = typeCPipelineBuilder.
            ShouldSaveMetadata(true).
            SetTargetApiClient(systemCApiClient).
            Build();
    }

    // Methods to build concrete pipelines
}
```

As you can notice, we have changed it in the private variables definition section. Now, it does not keep any string variables. It only has initialized instances of the **ICommunicationClient** derived classes.

Adapter design pattern provides you with the possibility to unify different approaches under one interface. At some point in time, the interface/protocol of the target system can be changed, and you simply need to switch an implementation in **PipelineDirector** to a new one.

Composite

Composite is a creational design pattern that allows you to compose objects into tree structure and use this structure through a common interface.

Design bulk processing pipeline

Imagine that in our solution, we can have an event composed of two different types of events. The event can be from the IoT device hub, which will send a report if some threshold is reached. In this case, we will receive an event with all the properties from **`BasicEvent`**, **`UploadFileEvent`**, and **`IoTEvent`**. For such a case, we can design a new composite pipeline containing two pipelines, **`IoT`** and **`FileUpload`**, and execute them one by one. Refer to the following *Figure 4.2*:

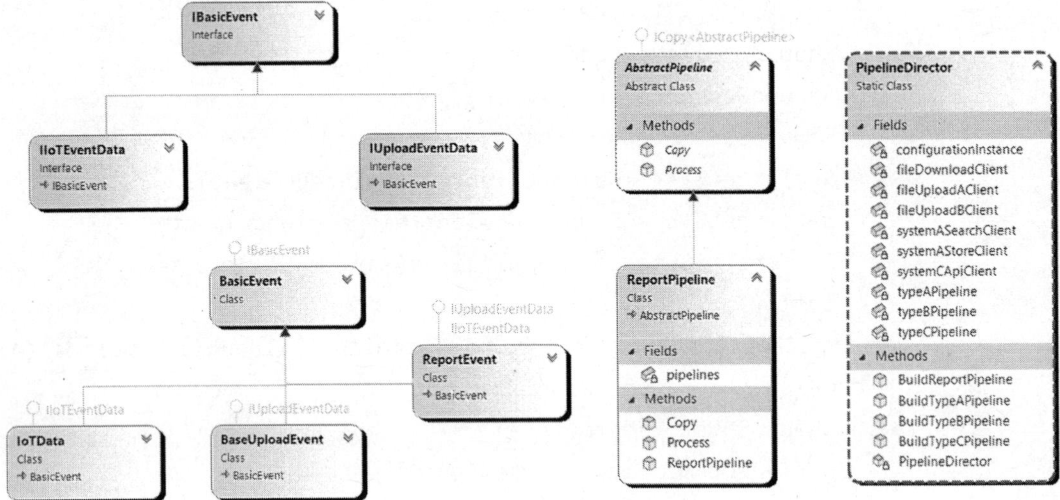

***Figure 4.2:** Composite design pattern diagram*

You can see that we have defined new interfaces: **`IBasicEvent`**, **`IIotEventData`**, and **`IUploadEventData`**. They are created to ease our re-usage of existing pipelines with different types of events. We have added a new event named **`ReportEvent`** to be passed as the input parameter to our new pipeline **`ReportPipeline`**. It has private variables of type List, which contains all the pipelines that should be executed for the concrete event. And lastly, we have extended the **`PipelineDirector`** class with the method **`BuildReportPipeline`**.

Let us see how it looks in the code.

Code

First, we will define our **`new`** interfaces:

```
public interface IBasicEvent
{
        Guid Id { get; set; }
        string Type { get; set; }
        string Source { get; set; }
}
public interface IUploadEventData: IBasicEvent
{
        string FileName { get; set; }
        string FileUrl { get; set; }
        string FileType { get; set; }
}
public interface IIoTEventData: IBasicEvent
{
        string Action { get; set; }
        string Value { get; set; }
}
```

They contain all the data we have already defined in the existing events, so they are needed only for inheritance.

The next step is to define the events derived from them:

```
public class BasicEvent: IBasicEvent
{
        public Guid Id { get; set; }
        public string Type { get; set; }
        public string Source { get; set; }
}
public class IoTData: BasicEvent, IIoTEventData
{
        public string Action { get; set; }
        public string Value { get; set; }
}
public class BaseUploadEvent: BasicEvent, IUploadEventData
{
        public string FileName { get; set; }
        public string FileUrl { get; set; }
        public string FileType { get; set; }
    }
```

These events are the same that we have used before in other chapters. The only difference is that they derive from interfaces.

And now, the last event is as follows:

```
public class ReportEvent : BasicEvent, IUploadEventData, IIoTEventData
{
        public string FileName { get ; set ; }
        public string FileUrl { get ; set ; }
        public string FileType { get; set; }
        public string Action { get; set; }
        public string Value { get; set; }
}
```

The last event object is **ReportEvent**. It implements all three interfaces to be passed to any of the three pipelines we already have.

The next class to be reviewed is **ReportPipeline**:

```
public class ReportPipeline : AbstractPipeline
{
        private List<AbstractPipeline> pipelines;
        public ReportPipeline(List<AbstractPipeline> pipelines)
        {
            this.pipelines = pipelines;
        }
        public override AbstractPipeline Copy()
        {
              ReportPipeline pipeline = new ReportPipeline(this.pipelines.
                                                Select(x=> x.Copy()).ToList());
            return pipeline;
        }
        public override void Process(IBasicEvent basicEvent)
        {
            this.pipelines.ForEach(x => x.Process(basicEvent));
        }
}
```

It is a simple class. It has pipelines private variables of type List, which contains pipelines that should be executed to process passed event to method **Process**. In this method, we execute each pipeline over the event sequentially.

PipelineDirector is responsible for building an instance of **ReportPipeline**:

```
public static class PipelineDirector
{
        // Private variables definition
        static PipelineDirector()
        {
            // pipelines initialization
        }
        // Pipelines build methods

        public static AbstractPipeline BuildReportPipeline()
        {
            return new ReportPipeline(new List<AbstractPipeline>
                          { BuildTypeBPipeline(), BuildTypeCPipeline() });
        }
}
```

In **PipelineDirector**, we have added a new method, **BuildReportPipeline**, built from existing pipelines. You can use it to instantiate a **ReportPipeline** instance for **ReportEvent** processing.

We need to create a **Factory** for **ReportPipeline** and extend **FactoryCreator** to add the extension for this new factory:

```
public class ReportFactory : AbstractFactory
{
        public override AbstractPipeline GetPipeline(BasicEvent basicEvent)
        {
            return basicEvent.Type switch
            {
                "TypeR" => PipelineDirector.BuildReportPipeline(),
                _ => throw new NotImplementedException()
            };
        }
}
public static class FactoryCreator
{
        private static AbstractFactory iotFactory;
        private static AbstractFactory fileUploadFactory;
        private static AbstractFactory reportFactory;
```

```
        static FactoryCreator()
        {
            iotFactory = new IoTFactory();
            fileUploadFactory = new FileUploadFactory();
            reportFactory = new ReportFactory();
}
public static AbstractFactory GetPipelineFactory(BasicEvent basicEvent)
{
            return basicEvent.Source switch
            {
                "IOT" => iotFactory,
                "FILE" => fileUploadFactory,
                "REPORT" => reportFactory,
              _ => throw new NotImplementedException("Cannot create a factory
                                                   for non known source"),
            };
        }
}
```

New **Factory** supports only events with type **"TypeR"**, and we have added support for **REPORT** source in the **FactoryCreator**.

Let us see how this pipeline looks in the code:

```
var event1 = new ReportEvent
{
        Source = "REPORT",
        Type = "TypeR",
        FileName = "TypeBFilename.jpg",
        FileType = ".jpg",
        FileUrl = "http://typeA.file.url",
        Id = Guid.NewGuid() ,
        Action = "TEMP_UPDATE",
        Value = 92.2.ToString()
};
FactoryCreator.GetPipelineFactory(event1).GetPipeline(event1).Process(event1);
```

We are creating a simple **ReportEvent** and requesting a pipeline to process it.

The result is shown in *Figure 4.3*:

```
Microsoft Visual Studio Debug Console
Processing pipeline: PROCESSING_STARTED: 76643241-e80c-4bbb-b885-dd8c12ca683a
Processing pipeline: Preprocessing event: 76643241-e80c-4bbb-b885-dd8c12ca683a
Downloading file from  http://typeA.file.url.
Processing pipeline: Searching event in the target system: 76643241-e80c-4bbb-b885-dd8c12ca683a
Sending message to http://systemA.com/api/search. Message: TypeBFilename.jpg
Processing pipeline: Processing event: 76643241-e80c-4bbb-b885-dd8c12ca683a
Uploading file to http://file.storage.com/systemB/upload. File: {"FileName":"TypeBFilename.jpg","Content":""}
Processing pipeline: PROCESSING_FINISHED: 76643241-e80c-4bbb-b885-dd8c12ca683a

Processing pipeline: Saving metadata: 76643241-e80c-4bbb-b885-dd8c12ca683a
Processing pipeline: PROCESSING_STARTED: 76643241-e80c-4bbb-b885-dd8c12ca683a
Processing pipeline: Processing event: 76643241-e80c-4bbb-b885-dd8c12ca683a
Sending message to http://systemC.processing.com/api. Message: {"Source":"REPORT","Action":"TEMP_UPDATE","Value":"92.2"}Processing pipeline:
 Updating metdata: 76643241-e80c-4bbb-b885-dd8c12ca683a
Processing pipeline: PROCESSING_FINISHED: 76643241-e80c-4bbb-b885-dd8c12ca683a
```

***Figure 4.3:** Composite design pattern implementation execution result*

Composite design pattern is useful when you call a function on a list of objects that implements a unified interface. We have used this design pattern over our pipelines to provide the possibility to process one event by a new composite pipeline. In addition to the introduction of the new **`ReportPipeline`** class, we were forced to derive our events classes from interfaces to be able to implement this. You may notice that we have not provided any implementation besides executing two child pipelines. However, it is possible to add the same functionality for other pipelines.

Flyweight

Flyweight design pattern's aim is to move outside of the class state that could be shared among instances.

Sharing a common state

We can examine the token variable currently scored in the pipelines. The time has come to move it outside of the pipelines to their own store and provide token per request to Communication clients. Refer to the following *Figure 4.4*:

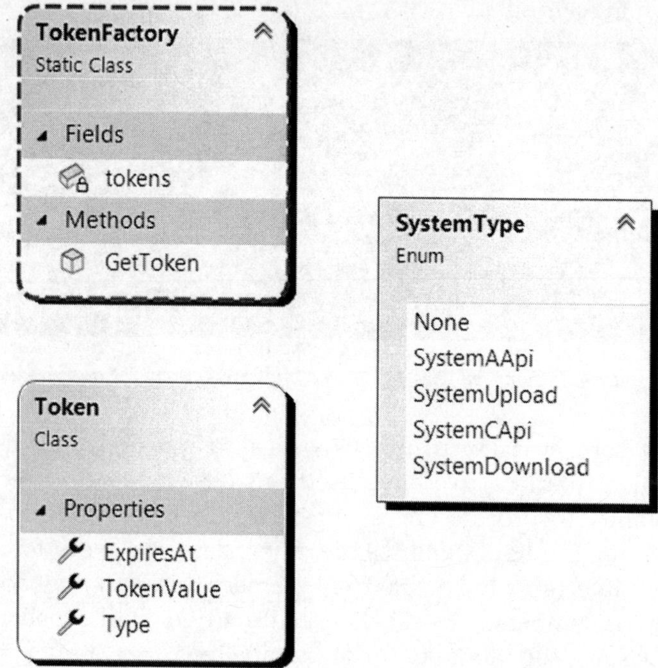

***Figure 4.4:** Flyweight design pattern diagram*

Here, you can see the three entities we will use in our Flyweight design pattern implementation. **TokenFactory** is responsible for requesting, storing, and providing tokens to classes per request. **Token** is an entity in which token information is stored. **SystemType** is an enumeration that allows us to identify the system for which **Token** should be provided.

Code

Let us start with **TokenFactory**:

```
public static class TokenFactory
{
        private static Dictionary<SystemType,Token> tokens =
                                       new Dictionary<SystemType,Token>();
        public static Token GetToken(SystemType system)
        {
            if(tokens.ContainsKey(system) && tokens[system].ExpiresAt >
                                       DateTime.Now.AddMinutes(1))
            {
                return tokens[system];
```

```
            }
            // Imitating token request
            Thread.Sleep(200);
            tokens[system] = new Token
            {
                ExpiresAt = DateTime.Now.AddHours(2),
                TokenValue = Guid.NewGuid().ToString(),
                Type = system
            };
            return tokens[system];
        }
}
public class Token
{
        public SystemType Type { get; init; }
        public DateTime ExpiresAt { get; init; }
        public string TokenValue { get; init; }
}
public enum SystemType
{
        None  = 0,
        SystemAApi = 1,
        SystemUpload = 2,
        SystemCApi = 3,
        SystemDownload = 4
}
```

TokenFactory contains two members: private variable tokens of type **Dictionary** for storing and accessing tokens and method **GetToken**, responsible for tokens management.

Let us see how we are using **TokenFactory** in the code.

We need to refactor **PipelineDirector** and remove pipelines private variables from it:

```
public static class PipelineDirector
{
       private static Configuration config = Configuration.Instance;
       private static SystemAApiClient systemASearchClient = new (config.
```

```
ASystemSearchApi);
            private static SystemAApiClient systemAStoreClient =
                                        new (config.ASystemStoreApi);
            private static FileUploadClient fileUploadAClient =
                                        new (config.ASystemUploadUrl);
            private static FileUploadClient fileUploadBClient =
                                        new (config.BSystemUploadUrl);
            private static FileDownloadClient fileDownloadClient = new ();
            private static SystemCApiClient systemCApiClient =
                                        new (config.CSystemApi);
            public static AbstractPipeline BuildTypeAPipeline()
{
      var typeAPipelineBuilder = new FilePipelineBuilder<FileUploadPipeline>();
      return typeAPipelineBuilder
      .ShouldBeFilePreprocessed(true)
      .ShouldBeEventStored(true)
      .ShouldSaveMetadata(true)
      .SetUploadClient(fileUploadAClient)
      .SetDownloadClient(fileDownloadClient)
      .SetSearchApiClient(systemASearchClient)
      .SetStoreApiClient(systemAStoreClient).Build();
}
public static AbstractPipeline BuildTypeBPipeline()
{
      var typeBPipelineBuilder = new FilePipelineBuilder<FileUploadPipeline>();
            return typeBPipelineBuilder.
            ShouldBeFilePreprocessed(true).ShouldBeEventStored(false).
      ShouldSaveMetadata(false).SetUploadClient(fileUploadBClient).
      SetDownloadClient(fileDownloadClient)
      .SetSearchApiClient(systemASearchClient).Build();
}
public static AbstractPipeline BuildTypeCPipeline()
{
      var typeCPipelineBuilder = new IoTPipelineBuilder<IoTPipeline>();
      return typeCPipelineBuilder.ShouldSaveMetadata(true).
      SetTargetApiClient(systemCApiClient).Build();
}
```

```
public static AbstractPipeline BuildReportPipeline()
{
      return new ReportPipeline(new List<AbstractPipeline>
      { BuildTypeBPipeline(), BuildTypeCPipeline() });
      }
}
```

As you can see, **PipelineDirector** has become clearer. Now, we are creating an instance of pipeline by request. We do not need to keep their private variables anymore, and **PipelineDirector** does not know anything about tokens.

At the current moment, **token** is directly requested from **TokenFactory** by concrete **ICommunicationClient** implementation:

```
public class SystemAApiClient : ICommunicationClient<string, string>
{
        private string baseUrl = string.Empty;
        public SystemAApiClient(string baseUrl)
        {
            this.baseUrl = baseUrl;
        }
        public async Task<string> ExecuteRequest(string data)
        {
            var token = TokenFactory.GetToken(SystemType.SystemAApi);
            Console.WriteLine($"Token received {token}");

         Console.WriteLine($"Sending message to {this.baseUrl}. Message: {data}");
            return await Task.FromResult(string.Empty);
        }
}
```

On each request, we request a token from **TokenFactory**. If there is no token for a specific system or it is expired, the **TokenFactory** requests it for us. Otherwise, it returns the existing token instance from the **Dictionary**.

As we do not have to keep the token variable inside the pipeline instance anymore, we have removed all variables and methods connected to the token from pipelines classes.

We have changed each implementation of pipelines. We removed the implementation of the **ICopy** interface because it is no longer necessary, given that we have implemented **TokenFactory**. There is no reason to keep it because we copied the entire pipelines for the token variable. For example, we can look at **TypeCPipeline**:

```
public class IoTPipeline : AbstractPipeline
{
        public bool ShouldSaveMetadata {get;set;}
        public ICommunicationClient<IoTData, string> SystemCApiClient { get; set; }

        public override void Process(IBasicEvent basicEvent)
        {
            var data = basicEvent as IIoTEventData;
            if (this.ShouldSaveMetadata) this.SaveMetadata(data);
            this.Notify(data, "PROCESSING_STARTED");
            this.Validate(data);
            this.ProcessEvent(data);
            if (this.ShouldSaveMetadata) this.UpdateMetadata(data);
            this.Notify(data, "PROCESSING_FINISHED");
}
protected void ProcessEvent(IIoTEventData basicEvent)
{
            var iotEvent = basicEvent as IIoTEventData;
            Notify(basicEvent, "Processing event");
            var data = new IoTData(iotEvent.Source, iotEvent.Action,
                                                    iotEvent.Value);
            SystemCApiClient.ExecuteRequest(data);
        }

        protected virtual Guid SaveMetadata(IIoTEventData basicEvent)
        {
            this.Notify(basicEvent, "Saving metadata");
            return Guid.NewGuid();
        }
        protected virtual void UpdateMetadata(IIoTEventData basicEvent)
        {
            this.Notify(basicEvent, "Updating metdata");
        }
        protected virtual void Validate(IIoTEventData basicEvent)
        {
            // Validation stuff
        }
}
```

It has become cleaner and more focused on its main goal, event processing.

What have we achieved by introducing Flyweight design pattern for token management?

- Clean code for all parties
- Shared responsibility
- Focused functionality
- Performance

From this moment, all token management functionality is encapsulated in **`concrete`** class, so no other classes need to know about the details of token obtainment. Communication clients do not need to know much about tokens themselves. They are using **`TokenFactory`** as the source of tokens for their needs. Only **`TokenFactory`** is responsible for managing tokens and knows how to get and keep them. Neither **`PipelineDirector`** nor pipelines, nor communication clients, should implement additional functionality to manage tokens. Each class is responsible for its own goals and uses others to execute functionality that it requires. Because of this, each class has become more focused on the functionality that it provides to the outside world. Such classes are easier to modify and support. We still get the same performance benefits as with the Prototype design pattern but in a cleaner way!

Synergy of the patterns

In this chapter, we have introduced Adapter, Composite, and Flyweight design patterns.

They allowed us to decouple pipelines and communication clients, add composite pipelines and decouple token storage from pipelines and communication clients.

Adjusting the processing engine

Let us look at the final design in *Figure 4.5*:

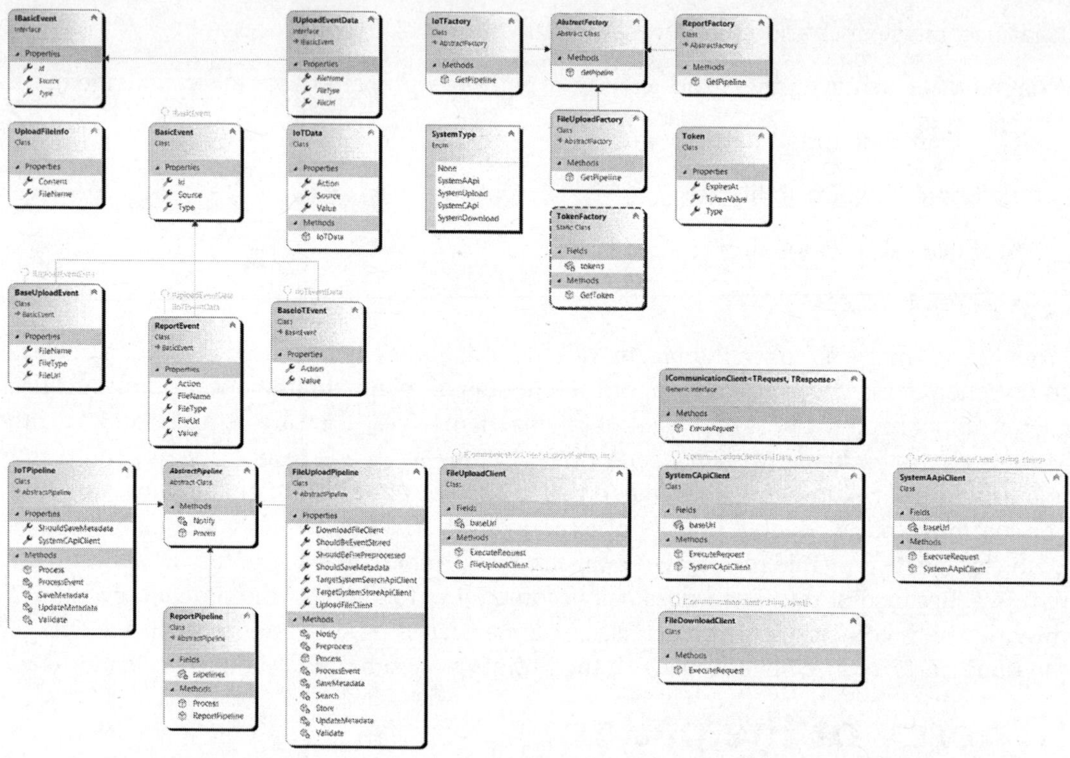

Figure 4.5: Synergy of patterns. Adapter, Composite, Flyweight, and Factories design patterns diagram

In *Figure 4.5(a)*, you can see the Pipelines part in which we have added the **`ReportPipeline`**. It allows us to process one event with multiple pipelines:

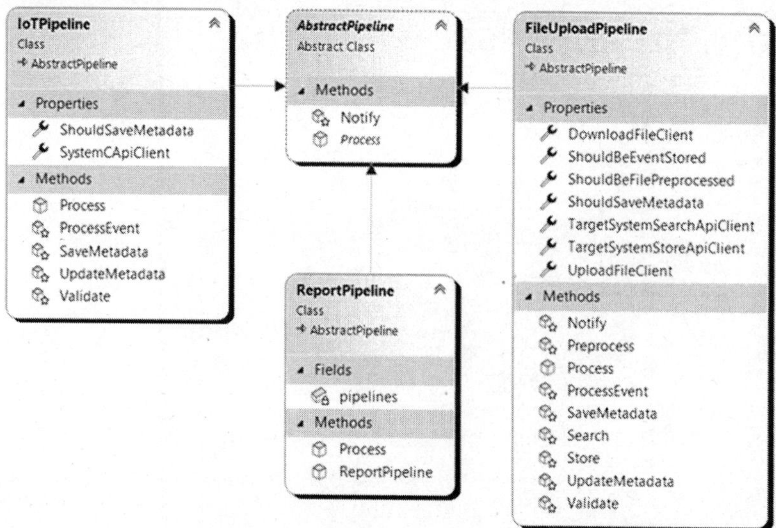

Figure 4.5(a): Synergy of patterns. Pipelines diagram

In *Figure 4.5(b)*, we have placed new interfaces for events classes:

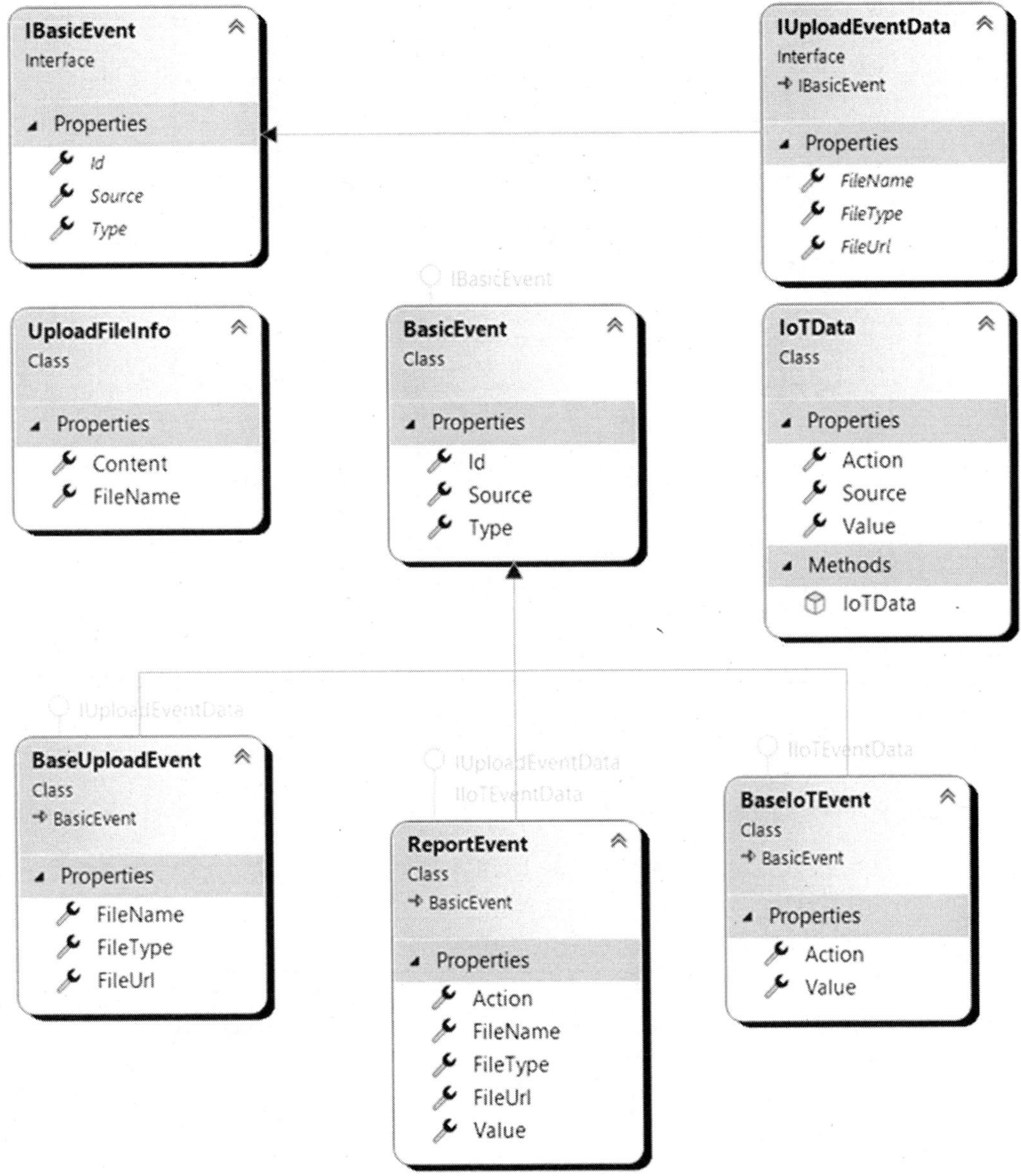

***Figure 4.5(b):** Synergy of patterns. Events types diagram.*

It was required because **`ReportPipeline`** accepts composite event which consists of data for **`BasicEvent`**, **`IoTEvent`**, and **`BaseUploadEvent`**. In C#, multiple inheritance is prohibited for classes, but if we are using interfaces, we can derive entity from multiple interface. At the top center, you can look at **`ReportEvent`**, derived from **`IUploadEventData`** and **`IIoTEventData`** interfaces at the same as from **`BasicEvent`** class.

In *Figure 4.5(c)*, we have placed the **`Factories`** classes:

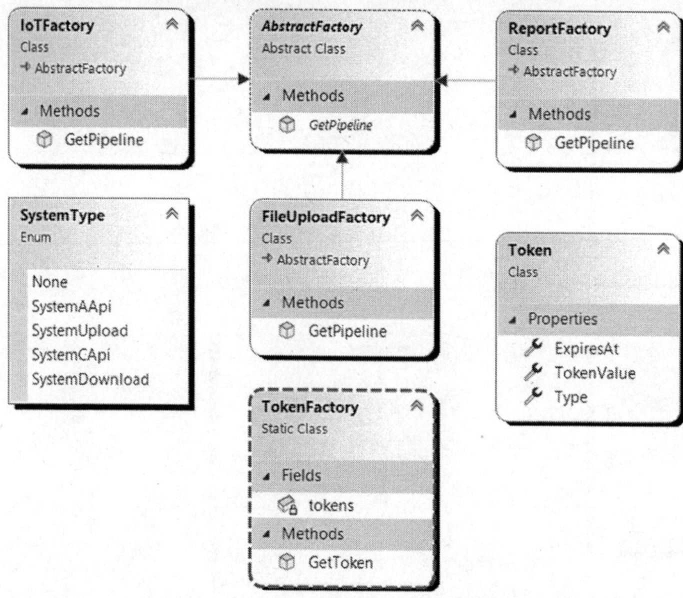

Figure 4.5(c): *Synergy of patterns. Factories types diagram.*

As you can see, we have added a new class **`ReportFactory`**, which produces **`ReportPipeline`** for processing the **`ReportEvent`** instance, and **`TokenFactory`** with **`Token`** class, responsible for token management for our communication clients.

The last part is shown in *Figure 4.5(d)*:

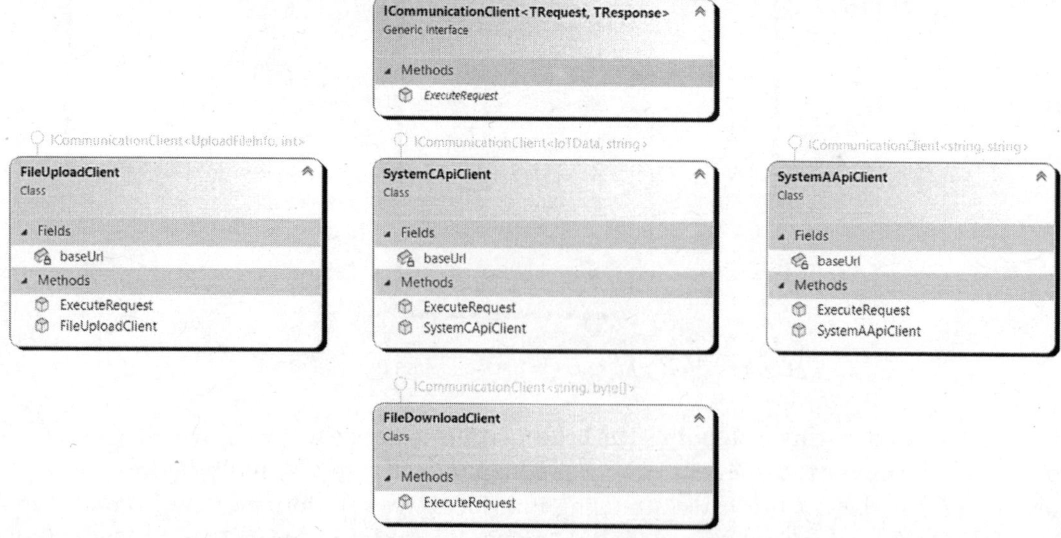

Figure 4.5(d): *Synergy of patterns. Communication clients diagram.*

It contains **ICommunicationClient<TRequest, TResponse>** definition, and **CommunicationClient** classes derived from the above-mentioned interface.

Code

As we have changed our design pattern that was used to work with **Token**, let us repeat the Prototype design pattern test again:

```
Stopwatch watch = new Stopwatch();
watch.Start();
var event1 = new BaseUploadEvent
{
      Source = "FILE",
      Type = "TypeA",
      FileName = "TypeAFilename.jpg",
      FileType = ".jpg",
      FileUrl = "http://typeA.file.url",
      Id = Guid.NewGuid()
};

// Others events definition

var reportEvent = new ReportEvent
{
      Source = "REPORT",
      Type = "TypeR",
      FileName = "TypeBFilename.jpg",
      FileType = ".jpg",
      FileUrl = "http://typeA.file.url",
      Id = Guid.NewGuid(),
      Action = "TEMP_UPDATE",
      Value = 92.2.ToString()
};
List<BasicEvent> eventList = new List<BasicEvent> { event1, event2, event3,
event4, event5, event6, reportEvent };
eventList.ForEach(eventObj =>
{
FactoryCreator.GetPipelineFactory(eventObj).GetPipeline(eventObj).
Process(eventObj);
```

```
        Console.WriteLine();
});
watch.Stop();
Console.WriteLine($"MS ellapsed: {watch.ElapsedMilliseconds}");
```

In the result of code execution, we will receive the following, as shown in *Figure 4.6*:

```
Microsoft Visual Studio Debug Console
Processing pipeline: Saving metadata: 455aa087-5434-4248-a0de-4b5111cf5315
Processing pipeline: PROCESSING_STARTED: 455aa087-5434-4248-a0de-4b5111cf5315
Processing pipeline: Processing event: 455aa087-5434-4248-a0de-4b5111cf5315
Token received afb48ca9-abbd-416b-ba91-afe0a7600eb7
Sending message to http://systemC.processing.com/api. Message: {"Source":"IOT","Action":"TEMP_UPDATE","Value":"92.2"}
Processing pipeline: Updating metdata: 455aa087-5434-4248-a0de-4b5111cf5315
Processing pipeline: PROCESSING_FINISHED: 455aa087-5434-4248-a0de-4b5111cf5315

Processing pipeline: PROCESSING_STARTED: 538a7ff3-6d15-4cf8-b006-9df5f1356436
Processing pipeline: Preprocessing event: 538a7ff3-6d15-4cf8-b006-9df5f1356436
Token received 128edfef-9c5b-42b6-9a91-31a3efd3bea8
Downloading file from  http://typeA.file.url.
Processing pipeline: Searching event in the target system: 538a7ff3-6d15-4cf8-b006-9df5f1356436
Token received 6e8cf674-d274-4348-b271-16dbb9fc9bbb
Sending message to http://systemA.com/api/search. Message: TypeBFilename.jpg
Processing pipeline: Processing event: 538a7ff3-6d15-4cf8-b006-9df5f1356436
Token received 0cf31e49-898d-4eba-8c4b-31b7035d3176
Uploading file to http://file.storage.com/systemB/upload. File: {"FileName":"TypeBFilename.jpg","Content":""}
Processing pipeline: PROCESSING_FINISHED: 538a7ff3-6d15-4cf8-b006-9df5f1356436

Processing pipeline: Saving metadata: 538a7ff3-6d15-4cf8-b006-9df5f1356436
Processing pipeline: PROCESSING_STARTED: 538a7ff3-6d15-4cf8-b006-9df5f1356436
Processing pipeline: Processing event: 538a7ff3-6d15-4cf8-b006-9df5f1356436
Token received afb48ca9-abbd-416b-ba91-afe0a7600eb7
Sending message to http://systemC.processing.com/api. Message: {"Source":"REPORT","Action":"TEMP_UPDATE","Value":"92.2"}
Processing pipeline: Updating metdata: 538a7ff3-6d15-4cf8-b006-9df5f1356436
Processing pipeline: PROCESSING_FINISHED: 538a7ff3-6d15-4cf8-b006-9df5f1356436

MS ellapsed: 893
```

***Figure 4.6:** Synergy of composite design patterns test*

In *Figure 4.6*, we can see two things: the **`ReportEvent`** instance with id **`538a7ff3-6d15-4cf8-b006-9df5f1356436`** is processed by two different pipelines, and our new code with Flyweight design pattern is also fast as it took only **`~900 ms`** to be executed. The difference between Flyweight design pattern and Prototype design pattern implementations in **`200ms`** could be explained by additional output for tokens, one additional event, and two additional pipelines executions.

Conclusion

These simple but effective structural design patterns provided us with a way to decouple and simplify our structural design without affecting performance.

Adapter pattern works well when you need to isolate different implementations of one functionality. In our case, it was multiple communication channels functionality under one unified interface that can be called independently from the internal structure of this functionality.

Composite pattern allows us to hide differences between single and bulk processing of some objects. In our case, we have used it to define a composite pipeline that consists of multiple stages. However, for the outside world, it has the same interface as the usual single-stage pipeline.

Flyweight design pattern was used to manage tokens for our communication clients. In this situation, it works better than the Prototype design pattern we used in the preceding chapter because it provides a better decomposition of structure and separation of responsibility.

In the next chapter, we will continue to review structural design patterns. We will focus on Proxy, Façade, Bridge, and Decorator design patterns.

Join our book's Discord space

Join the book's Discord Workspace for Latest updates, Offers, Tech happenings around the world, New Release and Sessions with the Authors:

https://discord.bpbonline.com

CHAPTER 5
Structural Design Patterns: Object Composition

Introduction

This chapter uses Proxy, Facade, Bridge, and Decorator design patterns to explore object composition.

These four patterns provide a similar approach, but the implementation is different. Each will be applied to the same task to highlight their differences and similarities.

Structure

The chapter covers the following topics:

- Proxy
    - o Design the interface to outside world
    - o Code
- Facade
    - o Code

- Bridge
  - o Ease of changes
  - o Code
- Decorator
  - o Making functionality modular
  - o Code
- Synergy of the patterns
  - o Adjusting the processing pipeline
  - o Code

Objectives

At the end of this chapter, you will be able to describe Proxy, Facade, Bridge, and Decorator design patterns, apply them to real-world problems, and describe their differences and similarities.

Proxy

Let us start with the basic definition of Proxy design pattern. Proxy design pattern is a structural design pattern that provides the possibility to perform actions before and after function execution in the wrapping object. In many cases, you may not want to include additional functionality into your carefully designed and coded class, but you should. Logging or exception handling adds a lot of noise to the main functionality and, at times, disturbs people from understanding the main purpose of the class.

In this case, we can use Proxy to handle all of this in a hidden and transparent way.

Design the interface to outside world

In our case, we want to clean up our pipelines, add the possibility to log each step of concrete pipeline execution and handle exceptions at the same time.

Firstly, we need a new pipeline which will work as a Proxy. It will provide the following functions:

- Exception handling
- Logging
- Communication with dashboard to save logs.

Secondly, we need to add delegate and event objects to pipelines to delegate logging of executed steps. Also, new communication client and Builder will be added. New communication client will be responsible for interacting with a hypothetical dashboard and Builder will be used to build a new pipeline type.

In the end, our class hierarchy should look like the following, as shown in *Figure 5.1*:

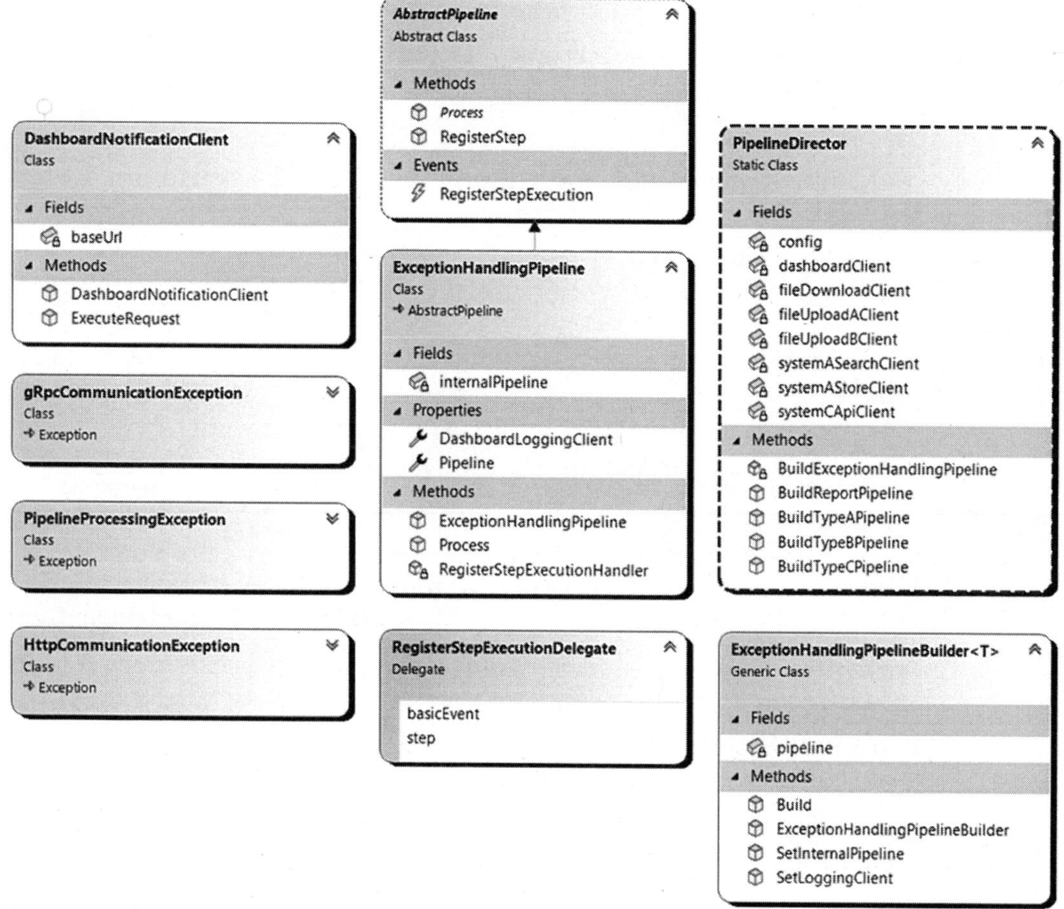

Figure 5.1: *Proxy design pattern diagram*

In *Figure 5.1*, you can see **`ExceptionHandlingPipeline`** in the center. Our new pipeline will handle communication, logging, and exception handling. On the left, you can see the new **`DashboardCommunicationClient`** and three exception classes, which we will use to notify that something has gone wrong. On the right, we have added **`ExceptionHandlingPipelineBuilder`**, which will be responsible for creating a new Proxy pipeline. In **`PipelineDirector`**, we have added a new method called **`BuildExceptionHandlingPipeline`** to be used to create each of the pipelines.

Code

In this section, our main focus is on **ExceptionHandlingPipeline**. Let us see how it looks from the code perspective:

```
public class ExceptionHandlingPipeline : AbstractPipeline
{
        private AbstractPipeline internalPipeline;
        public ICommunicationClient<string, string> LoggingClient { get; set; }
        public ExceptionHandlingPipeline()
        {
            RegisterStepExecution += RegisterStepExecutionHandler;
        }
        public AbstractPipeline Pipeline
        {
            set
            {
                if(internalPipeline != null)
                    internalPipeline.RegisterStepExecution -=
                                                RegisterStepExecutionHandler;
                internalPipeline = value;
                internalPipeline.RegisterStepExecution +=
                                                RegisterStepExecutionHandler;
            }
        }
        private void RegisterStepExecutionHandler(IBasicEvent basicEvent,
                                                   string step)
        {
            var message = $"Executing step: {step} for event: {basicEvent.
                           Id}-{basicEvent.Source}-{basicEvent.Type}";
            DashboardLoggingClient.ExecuteRequest(message);
        }
        public override void Process(IBasicEvent basicEvent)
        {
            try
            {
                RegisterStep(basicEvent, "PROCESSING_STARTED");
                internalPipeline.Process(basicEvent);
```

```
                RegisterStep(basicEvent, "PROCESSING_FINISHED");
            }
            catch (gRpcCommunicationException)
            {
                RegisterStep(basicEvent, "PROCESSING_FAILED");
                Console.WriteLine("gRpc communication error received");
            }
            catch (HttpCommunicationException)
            {
                RegisterStep(basicEvent, "PROCESSING_FAILED");
                Console.WriteLine("Http communication error received");
            }
            catch (FileCommunicationException)
            {
                RegisterStep(basicEvent, "PROCESSING_FAILED");
                Console.WriteLine("File communication error received");
            }
            catch (PipelineProcessingException)
            {
                RegisterStep(basicEvent, "PROCESSING_FAILED");
                Console.WriteLine("Pipeline business error received");
            }
        }
}
```

From an interface perspective, it is identical to the other pipelines. It is derived from the **AbstractPipeline** class and has the same default methods. However, the following differences can be noticed from the beginning:

- It has an **internalPipeline** private variable of type **AbstractPipeline** type.
- It has a public property **Pipeline** of type **AbstractPipeline**. This property subscribes to an event called **RegisterStepExecution**. It will notify the parent pipeline about step execution processing in the child pipeline.
- It has a **RegisterStepExecutionHandler** function, which is responsible for communication with the dashboard (in our case, console).

The **Process** method forwards a request to **internalPipeline** and provides exception handling capabilities.

The next class that we will review is **AbstractPipeline**:

```
public delegate void RegisterStepExecutionDelegate(IBasicEvent basicEvent,
string step);
public abstract class AbstractPipeline
{
        public event RegisterStepExecutionDelegate RegisterStepExecution;
        public abstract void Process(IBasicEvent basicEvent);
        public virtual void RegisterStep(IBasicEvent basicEvent, string step)
        {
            if (RegisterStepExecution != null)
                RegisterStepExecution(basicEvent, step);
        }
}
```

As you can see, we have modified it a little. You can notice that we have added **RegisterStepExecutionDelegate.** It is used in the definition of **RegisterStepExecution event**, which we have added to the **AbstractPipeline** class.

RegisterStep function executes the **RegisterStepExecution** event of anyone who has subscribed to it. It is called from the **IoTPipeline** and **FileUploadPipeline** during execution.

Then, we have added a **Builder** class to our new pipeline:

```
public class ExceptionHandlingPipelineBuilder<T> where T
                                        : ExceptionHandlingPipeline, new()
{
        public ExceptionHandlingPipelineBuilder()
        {
            pipeline = new T();
        }
        public ExceptionHandlingPipelineBuilder<T> SetLoggingClient
        (ICommunicationClient<string, string> dashboardLoggingClient)
        {
            pipeline.DashboardLoggingClient = dashboardLoggingClient;
            return this;
        }
        public ExceptionHandlingPipelineBuilder<T>
         SetInternalPipeline(AbstractPipeline internalPipeline)
        {
```

```
            pipeline.Pipeline = internalPipeline;
            return this;
        }
        public ExceptionHandlingPipeline Build() => pipeline;
}
```

Two functions allow us to set the **LoggingClient** and **internalPipeline**: **SetLoggingClient** and **SetInternalPipeline** methods. They are used to configure this instance of pipeline in **PipelineDirector**:

```
public static class PipelineDirector
{
       private static DashboardNotificationClient dashboardClient =
       new(config.DashboardLoggingUrl);
       // Private variables
        public static AbstractPipeline BuildTypeAPipeline();
        public static AbstractPipeline BuildTypeBPipeline();
        public static AbstractPipeline BuildTypeCPipeline()
        {
           var typeCPipelineBuilder = new IoTPipelineBuilder<IoTPipeline>();
            return BuildExceptionHandlingPipeline(typeCPipelineBuilder.
                ShouldSaveMetadata(true).
                SetTargetApiClient(systemCApiClient).
                Build());
        }
        private static AbstractPipeline
          BuildExceptionHandlingPipeline(AbstractPipeline internalPipeline)
        {
            var exceptionPipelineBuilder =
          new ExceptionHandlingPipelineBuilder<ExceptionHandlingPipeline>();
            return exceptionPipelineBuilder.
                SetLoggingClient(dashboardClient).
                SetInternalPipeline(internalPipeline).
                Build();
        }
}
```

We have cut out the part that did not change and left only that is necessary for understanding.

So, here we have added a private method named **BuildExceptionHandlingPipeline**, which accepts **AbstractPipeline** instance as a parameter and sets it through the Builder property. Also, logging client is set from the private variable. In the **BuildTypeCPipeline** method, you can notice that we wrap builder code with the **BuildExceptionHandling-Pipeline** method. As a result, when **TypeCTypeline** is configured with the appropriate Builder, it will be passed directly to the previously mentioned method and wrapped by **ExceptionHandlingPipeline**.

Let us check how the **IoTPipeline** looks after refactoring:

```
public class IoTPipeline : AbstractPipeline
{
        public bool ShouldSaveMetadata {get;set;}
        public ICommunicationClient<IoTData, string> SystemCApiClient
                                                            { get; set; }
        protected void ProcessEvent(IIoTEventData basicEvent)
        {
            RegisterStep(basicEvent, "EVENT_PROCESSING");
            var data = new IoTData(basicEvent.Source,
                                basicEvent.Action, basicEvent.Value);
            SystemCApiClient.ExecuteRequest(data);
        }
        public override void Process(IBasicEvent basicEvent)
        {
            var data = basicEvent as IIoTEventData;
            SaveMetadata(data);
            Validate(data);
            ProcessEvent(data);
            UpdateMetadata(data);
        }
        protected virtual Guid SaveMetadata(IIoTEventData basicEvent)
        {
            if (!ShouldSaveMetadata)
                return Guid.Empty;
            RegisterStep(basicEvent, "SAVE_METADATA");
            return Guid.NewGuid();
        }
        protected virtual void UpdateMetadata(IIoTEventData basicEvent)
        {
```

```
            if (!ShouldSaveMetadata)
                return;
            RegisterStep(basicEvent, "UPDATE_METADATA");
        }
        protected virtual void Validate(IIoTEventData basicEvent)
        {
            if (basicEvent.Action == null)
                throw new PipelineProcessingException(
                                "Action of the event cannot be null");
            if (basicEvent.Value == null)
                throw new PipelineProcessingException(
                                "Value of the event cannot be null");
        }
}
```

As you can notice, some of the code was wiped out. For example, the method **Notify** was previously used for logging steps. We are currently using the **RegisterStep** method derived from **AbstractPipeline**, which executes the event to which **ExceptionHandlingPipeline** is subscribed. So, all the logging data goes directly to our Dashboard through **DashboardCommunicationClient**.

In the method **Validate**, we have added new exception throws. It is of type **PipelineProcessingException**, handled by **ExceptionHandlingPipeline** by an appropriate catch block.

Our basic exceptions are very simple. We derive their implementation from the base **Exception** class provided by the .NET Core infrastructure:

```
public class FileCommunicationException: Exception
{
}
public class gRpcCommunicationException: Exception
{
}
public class HttpCommunicationException: Exception
{
}
public class PipelineProcessingException: Exception
{
        public PipelineProcessingException(string message): base(message)
        {
        }
}
```

In **PipelineProcessingException**, we have added a constructor to describe the error in detail. It calls for a base constructor of the **Exception** class to provide a message to be saved and propagated to the catch block.

The last support class is **DashboardCommunicationClient**:

```
public class DashboardNotificationClient : ICommunicationClient<string, string>
{
        private string baseUrl;
        public DashboardNotificationClient(string baseUrl)
        {
            this.baseUrl = baseUrl;
        }
        public string ExecuteRequest(string request)
        {
            Console.WriteLine(request);
            return string.Empty;
        }
}
```

It only provides one method: **ExecuteRequest** (like other communication clients) and its purpose is to send a message (in our case, console).

We can test this code on our existing example that we have used to test the **ReportPipeline** event. Refer to the following *Figure 5.2*:

```
Microsoft Visual Studio Debug Console
DASHBOARD_CLIENT: Executing step: PROCESSING_STARTED for event: 04945fa2-6105-477c-86b2-d8fcd4166178-IOT-TypeC
DASHBOARD_CLIENT: Executing step: SAVE_METADATA for event: 04945fa2-6105-477c-86b2-d8fcd4166178-IOT-TypeC
DASHBOARD_CLIENT: Executing step: EVENT_PROCESSING for event: 04945fa2-6105-477c-86b2-d8fcd4166178-IOT-TypeC
SYSTEM_C_API_CLIENT: Sending message to http://systemC.processing.com/api. Message: {"Source":"IOT","Action":"TEMP_UPDATE","Value":"92.2"}
DASHBOARD_CLIENT: Executing step: UPDATE_METADATA for event: 04945fa2-6105-477c-86b2-d8fcd4166178-IOT-TypeC
DASHBOARD_CLIENT: Executing step: PROCESSING_FINISHED for event: 04945fa2-6105-477c-86b2-d8fcd4166178-IOT-TypeC

DASHBOARD_CLIENT: Executing step: PROCESSING_STARTED for event: 9c5feb2d-b9da-4335-9b68-c4f352dd4528-IOT-TypeC
DASHBOARD_CLIENT: Executing step: SAVE_METADATA for event: 9c5feb2d-b9da-4335-9b68-c4f352dd4528-IOT-TypeC
DASHBOARD_CLIENT: Executing step: EVENT_PROCESSING for event: 9c5feb2d-b9da-4335-9b68-c4f352dd4528-IOT-TypeC
SYSTEM_C_API_CLIENT: Sending message to http://systemC.processing.com/api. Message: {"Source":"IOT","Action":"TEMP_UPDATE","Value":"92.2"}
DASHBOARD_CLIENT: Executing step: UPDATE_METADATA for event: 9c5feb2d-b9da-4335-9b68-c4f352dd4528-IOT-TypeC
DASHBOARD_CLIENT: Executing step: PROCESSING_FINISHED for event: 9c5feb2d-b9da-4335-9b68-c4f352dd4528-IOT-TypeC

DASHBOARD_CLIENT: Executing step: PROCESSING_STARTED for event: 8d7a555c-43db-4e83-ab71-a129561d6d82-REPORT-TypeR
DASHBOARD_CLIENT: Executing step: EVENT_PREPROCESSING for event: 8d7a555c-43db-4e83-ab71-a129561d6d82-REPORT-TypeR
DOWNLOAD_CLIENT: Downloading file from  http://typeA.file.url.
DASHBOARD_CLIENT: Executing step: EVENT_SEARCH for event: 8d7a555c-43db-4e83-ab71-a129561d6d82-REPORT-TypeR
SYSTEM_A_API_CLIENT: Sending message to http://systemA.com/api/search. Message: TypeBFilename.jpg
DASHBOARD_CLIENT: Executing step: EVENT_PROCESSING for event: 8d7a555c-43db-4e83-ab71-a129561d6d82-REPORT-TypeR
FILE_UPLOAD_CLIENT: Uploading file to http://file.storage.com/systemB/upload. File: {"FileName":"TypeBFilename.jpg","Content":""}
DASHBOARD_CLIENT: Executing step: PROCESSING_FINISHED for event: 8d7a555c-43db-4e83-ab71-a129561d6d82-REPORT-TypeR
DASHBOARD_CLIENT: Executing step: PROCESSING_STARTED for event: 8d7a555c-43db-4e83-ab71-a129561d6d82-REPORT-TypeR
DASHBOARD_CLIENT: Executing step: SAVE_METADATA for event: 8d7a555c-43db-4e83-ab71-a129561d6d82-REPORT-TypeR
DASHBOARD_CLIENT: Executing step: EVENT_PROCESSING for event: 8d7a555c-43db-4e83-ab71-a129561d6d82-REPORT-TypeR
SYSTEM_C_API_CLIENT: Sending message to http://systemC.processing.com/api. Message: {"Source":"REPORT","Action":"TEMP_UPDATE","Value":"92.2"}
DASHBOARD_CLIENT: Executing step: UPDATE_METADATA for event: 8d7a555c-43db-4e83-ab71-a129561d6d82-REPORT-TypeR
DASHBOARD_CLIENT: Executing step: PROCESSING_FINISHED for event: 8d7a555c-43db-4e83-ab71-a129561d6d82-REPORT-TypeR
```

***Figure 5.2:** Proxy execution result*

As you can see, the existing testing code works well, and all the steps of our pipelines are logged cleanly.

Proxy design pattern provides the possibility to extend the existing class with additional functionality without including it in the base class. There is a little overhead in the line of code of creation of any instance of the class for which the Proxy class should be created. However, if this line is contained in a single point of creation like **`PipelineDirector`** class, it looks good enough. Later, we will see how this can be simplified with the help of .NET AOP.

The second concern is that it looks very similar to the Composite design pattern, which it is. The main difference, however, is that it proxies only one instance of pipeline and provides additional functionality for pre- and post-processing. In our example, we passed **`ReportPipeline`**, created using the Composite design pattern to **`ExceptionHandlingPipeline`** as **`internalPipeline`**, so the two patterns can be used together without any problem.

Facade

Facade is a structural design pattern that allows you to provide a simplified interface to any library / framework.

In our case, we can virtually incorporate Builders and Pipelines classes into one virtual library. At the current moment, **`PipelineDirector`** is responsible for the following:

- Communication clients creation and configuration
- Builder selection
- Builder configuration
- ExceptionHandling middleware configuration
- Composite pipeline creation

Let us create a facade class named **`PipelineCreationFacade`** and move 2, 4, and 5 points into it. Refer to the following *Figure 5.3*:

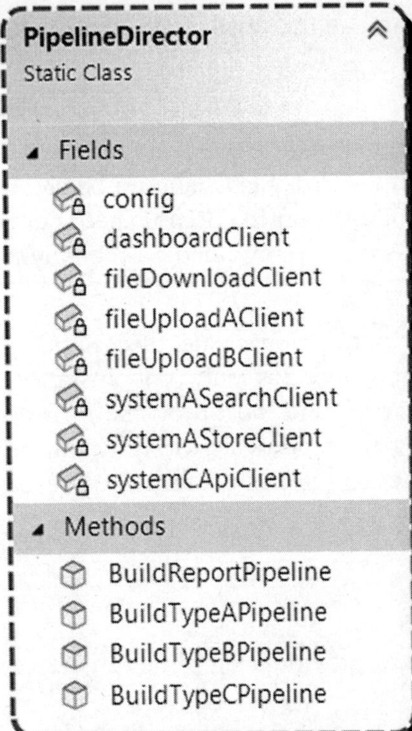

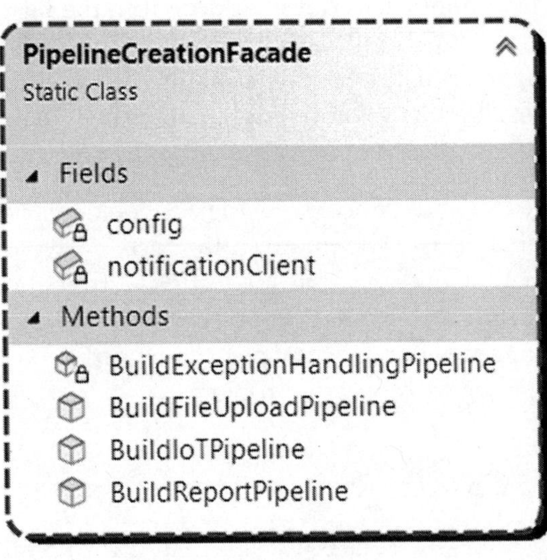

Figure 5.3: Facade design pattern diagram

In this case, we will split responsibility and clean up the **`PipelineDirector`** class.

`PipelineCreationFacade` will keep secret details about ExceptionHandling, middleware pipeline creation and configuration, and **`ReportPipeline`** creation. For **`PipelineDirector`**, all pipelines are **`AbstractPipeline`** instances that should be configured by a specific set of parameters to be passed as method input parameters.

Code

Let us look at the refactored **`PipelineDirector`** class:

```
public static class PipelineDirector
{
        private static Configuration config = Configuration.Instance;
        private static SystemAApiClient systemASearchClient = new (config.
                                              ASystemSearchApi);
        private static SystemAApiClient systemAStoreClient = new (config.
                                              ASystemStoreApi);
```

```
        private static FileUploadClient fileUploadAClient = new (config.
                                                    ASystemUploadUrl);
        private static FileUploadClient fileUploadBClient = new (config.
                                                    BSystemUploadUrl);
        private static FileDownloadClient fileDownloadClient = new ();
        private static SystemCApiClient systemCApiClient = new (config.
                                                    CSystemApi);
        private static DashboardNotificationClient dashboardClient =
                                     new(config.DashboardLoggingUrl);

        public static AbstractPipeline BuildTypeAPipeline()
        {
            return PipelineCreationFacade.BuildFileUploadPipeline(true,
                                                           true, true,
                fileUploadAClient, fileDownloadClient, systemASearchClient,
                                                    systemAStoreClient);
        }
        public static AbstractPipeline BuildTypeBPipeline()
        {
            return PipelineCreationFacade.BuildFileUploadPipeline(true,
                                                      false, false,
              fileUploadBClient, fileDownloadClient, systemASearchClient, null);
        }
        public static AbstractPipeline BuildTypeCPipeline()
        {
           return PipelineCreationFacade.BuildIoTPipeline(true, systemCApiClient);
        }

        public static AbstractPipeline BuildReportPipeline()
        {
            return new ReportPipeline(new List<AbstractPipeline> {
                       BuildTypeBPipeline(), BuildTypeCPipeline() });
        }
}
```

It looks a lot cleaner and simpler than in the preceding chapter. We kept communication clients and their instantiation and methods to create pipelines of concrete type. Other functionality was moved to **PipelineCreationFacade**. You can notice it in the following code example:

```
public static class PipelineCreationFacade
{
    private static Configuration config = Configuration.Instance;
    private static DashboardNotificationClient notificationClient =
            new DashboardNotificationClient(config.DashboardLoggingUrl);

    public static AbstractPipeline BuildFileUploadPipeline(
    bool shouldBeFileProcessed, bool shouldEventBeStored,
    bool shouldSaveMetadataICommunicationClient<UploadFileInfo, int>
    fileUploadClient, ICommunicationClient<string, byte[]> fileDownloadClient,
    ICommunicationClient<string, string> searchApiClient,
    ICommunicationClient<string, string> storeApiClient)
{
    var typeAPipelineBuilder =
                new FilePipelineBuilder<FileUploadPipeline>();
            return BuildExceptionHandlingPipeline(typeAPipelineBuilder.
                ShouldBeFilePreprocessed(shouldBeFileProcessed).
                ShouldBeEventStored(shouldEventBeStored).
                ShouldSaveMetadata(shouldSaveMetadata).
                SetUploadClient(fileUploadClient).
                SetDownloadClient(fileDownloadClient).
                SetSearchApiClient(searchApiClient).
                SetStoreApiClient(storeApiClient).
                Build());
}
public static AbstractPipeline BuildIoTPipeline(bool shouldSaveMetadata,
ICommunicationClient<IoTData, string> apiClient)
{
            var typeCPipelineBuilder =
                    new IoTPipelineBuilder<IoTPipeline>();
            return BuildExceptionHandlingPipeline(typeCPipelineBuilder.
                ShouldSaveMetadata(shouldSaveMetadata).
                SetTargetApiClient(apiClient).
                Build());
}
public static AbstractPipeline BuildReportPipeline(
    bool shouldBeFileProcessed, bool shouldEventBeStored, bool
```

```
shouldSaveMetadata,
            ICommunicationClient<UploadFileInfo, int> fileUploadClient,
            ICommunicationClient<string, byte[]> fileDownloadClient,
            ICommunicationClient<string, string> searchApiClient,
            ICommunicationClient<string, string> storeApiClient,
            bool shouldSaveIoTMetadata, ICommunicationClient<IoTData,
            string> apiClient)
      {
            return new ReportPipeline(new List<AbstractPipeline>
      {
               BuildFileUploadPipeline(
                  shouldBeFileProcessed, shouldEventBeStored,
                  shouldSaveMetadata, fileUploadClient,
                  fileDownloadClient, searchApiClient, storeApiClient),
                  BuildIoTPipeline(shouldSaveIoTMetadata, apiClient)
      });
}
private static AbstractPipeline BuildExceptionHandlingPipeline(
                                          AbstractPipeline internalPipeline)
{
      var exceptionPipelineBuilder =
      new ExceptionHandlingPipelineBuilder<ExceptionHandlingPipeline>();
      return exceptionPipelineBuilder.
         SetLoggingClient(notificationClient).
         SetInternalPipeline(internalPipeline).
         Build();
      }
}
```

PipelineCreationFacade class provides public methods to build **IoTPipeline**, **FileUploadPipeline**, and **ReportPipeline**. All requested pipelines are wrapped in by **ExceptionHandlingPipeline**. All configuration is passed through input parameters. It does not know how to configure any specific pipeline, for example, **TypeAPipeline**. This information is kept by the **PipelineDirector**.

Facade design pattern is useful when you need to simplify the usage of a library / framework or hide the composition of classes. Facade pattern implementation will provide a simplified interface that you can use in your code without knowing all the details covered under the hood. It also provides a good opportunity to split responsibility between classes and clean them to be more focused on the functionality they provide.

Bridge

The mission of Bridge design pattern is to provide a unified interface for different classes that provide similar functionality. In our case, we can implement such interfaces for pipeline step processing logging.

Ease of changes

In the preceding chapter, we made **ExceptionHandlingPipeline**, responsible for steps and fails logging. In that version, all output was directed to the **DashboardClient**. What if we want to save output to a file? To solve this problem, we will create a new class: **Logger** and **ILoggingDestination interface**. They will provide us with unified interfaces for different logger classes. Refer to the following *Figure 5.4*:

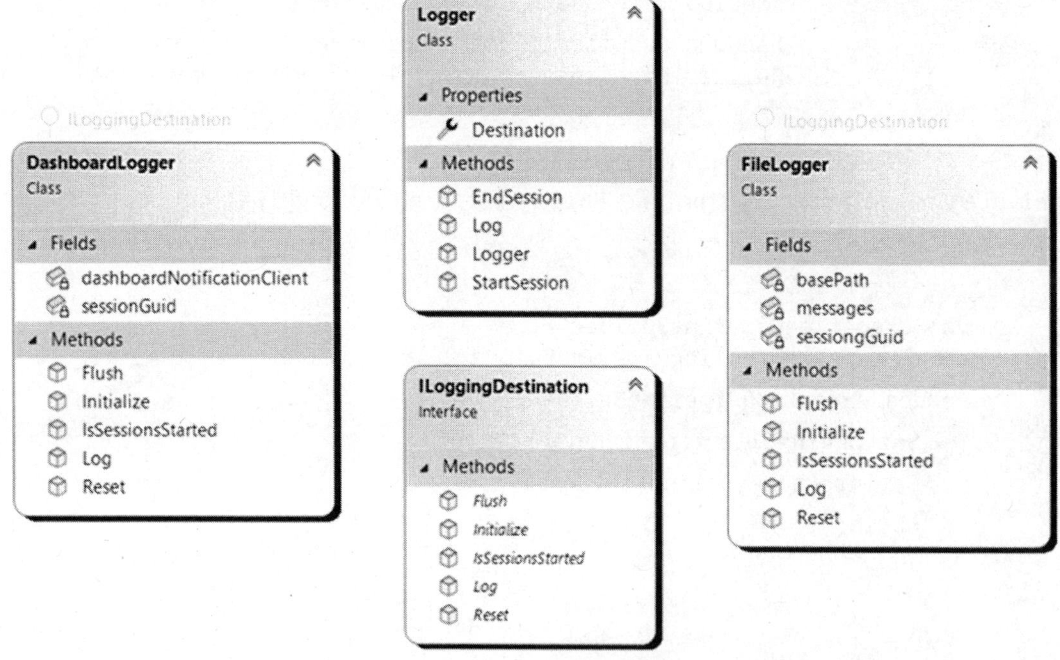

***Figure 5.4:** Bridge design pattern diagram*

In this figure, you can see four entities that we will use in our Bridge design pattern implementation. Logger class is our bridge to **ILoggingDestination** usage in our application. It has three methods: **StartSession**, **EndSession**, and **Log**. Internally, all these methods are calling the **ILoggingDestination** interface members. Next, we have the **ILoggingDestination** interface, which defines the standard contract for a logger. It should support five methods that are listed in the figure. The last two are concrete implementations of the **ILoggingDestination** interface: **DashboardLogger** and **FileLogger**. The first one uses an already-used **DashboardCommunicationClient** class, and the second writes all logs into files.

Code

Let us start with the **Logger** class:

```
public class Logger
{
        public ILoggingDestination Destination { get; set; }
        public Logger(ILoggingDestination destination)
        {
            Destination = destination;
        }

        public void StartSession(Guid logGuid)
        {
            Destination.Initialize(logGuid);
        }
        public void EndSession()
        {
            Destination.Flush();
            Destination.Reset();
        }
        public void Log(string message)
        {
            if (!Destination.IsSessionsStarted())
                throw new InvalidOperationException("Logging sessions is
                                                    not initialized");

            Destination.Log(message);
        }
}
```

This class accepts **ILoggingDestination** interface implementation as a constructor parameter and uses the provided object in its methods:

```
public interface ILoggingDestination
{
        void Initialize(Guid sessionsGuid);
        void Flush();
        void Reset();
        void Log(string message);
        bool IsSessionsStarted();
}
```

ILoggingDestination interface is simple and contains methods for sessions starting/ending, logging, and status checking:

```
public class DashboardLogger : ILoggingDestination
{
        private DashboardNotificationClient dashboardNotificationClient =
                                      new DashboardNotificationClient(string.Empty);
        private Guid sessionGuid = Guid.Empty;
        public void Flush()
        {
            // do nothing
        }
        public void Initialize(Guid sessionsGuid)
        {
            sessionGuid = sessionsGuid;
        }
        public bool IsSessionsStarted()
        {
            return sessionGuid != Guid.Empty;
        }
        public void Log(string message)
        {
            dashboardNotificationClient.ExecuteRequest(message);
        }
        public void Reset()
        {
            sessionGuid = Guid.Empty;
        }
}
```

```
public class FileLogger : ILoggingDestination
{
        private string basePath =
                "C:\\Users\\Timur\\source\\repos\\Book_Pipelines\\Logs";
        private List<string> messages = new List<string>();
        private Guid sessiongGuid = Guid.Empty;

        public void Flush()
        {
          File.AppendAllLines($"{basePath}\\{sessiongGuid}.txt", messages);
            messages.Clear();
        }

        public void Initialize(Guid sessionsGuid)
        {
            sessiongGuid = sessionsGuid;
        }

        public bool IsSessionsStarted()
        {
            return sessiongGuid != Guid.Empty;
        }

        public void Log(string message)
        {
            messages.Add(message);
        }

        public void Reset()
        {
            messages.Clear();
            sessiongGuid = Guid.Empty;
        }
}
```

Loggers are simple, however, there are some differences in implementation. They use different destinations to save logs. There are some differences in terms of method implementation. For example, **FileLogger** can implement the **Flush** method easily (which gives some performance benefits), while it does not make any sense for **DashboardLogger** since logs are created one by one anyway.

The result of execution can be seen in *Figure 5.5*:

```
Microsoft Visual Studio Debug Console
DOWNLOAD_CLIENT: Downloading file from  http://typeA.file.url.
SYSTEM_A_API_CLIENT: Sending message to http://systemA.com/api/search. Message: TypeAFilename.jpg
FILE_UPLOAD_CLIENT: Uploading file to http://file.storage.com/systemA/upload. File: {"FileName":"TypeAFilename.jpg","Content":""}
SYSTEM_A_API_CLIENT: Sending message to http://systemA.com/api/store. Message: TypeAFilename.jpg

DOWNLOAD_CLIENT: Downloading file from  http://typeB.file.url.
SYSTEM_A_API_CLIENT: Sending message to http://systemA.com/api/search. Message: TypeBFilename.jpg
FILE_UPLOAD_CLIENT: Uploading file to http://file.storage.com/systemB/upload. File: {"FileName":"TypeBFilename.jpg","Content":""}

DOWNLOAD_CLIENT: Downloading file from  http://typeB.file.url.
SYSTEM_A_API_CLIENT: Sending message to http://systemA.com/api/search. Message: TypeB2Filename.jpg
FILE_UPLOAD_CLIENT: Uploading file to http://file.storage.com/systemB/upload. File: {"FileName":"TypeB2Filename.jpg","Content":""}

SYSTEM_C_API_CLIENT: Sending message to http://systemC.processing.com/api. Message: {"Source":"IOT","Action":"TEMP_UPDATE","Value":"92.2"}

SYSTEM_C_API_CLIENT: Sending message to http://systemC.processing.com/api. Message: {"Source":"IOT","Action":"TEMP_UPDATE","Value":"92.2"}

SYSTEM_C_API_CLIENT: Sending message to http://systemC.processing.com/api. Message: {"Source":"IOT","Action":"TEMP_UPDATE","Value":"92.2"}

DOWNLOAD_CLIENT: Downloading file from  http://typeA.file.url.
SYSTEM_A_API_CLIENT: Sending message to http://systemA.com/api/search. Message: TypeBFilename.jpg
FILE_UPLOAD_CLIENT: Uploading file to http://file.storage.com/systemB/upload. File: {"FileName":"TypeBFilename.jpg","Content":""}
SYSTEM_C_API_CLIENT: Sending message to http://systemC.processing.com/api. Message: {"Source":"REPORT","Action":"TEMP_UPDATE","Value":"92.2"}

MS ellapsed: 879
```

Figure 5.5: *Bridge design pattern execution result*

In this example, we have used **`FileLogger`** class as the main logger for pipeline steps registration. Our console output now contains only some messages from support classes like API clients.

In the file system, you can see that the application has generated a bunch of files. Refer to the following *Figure 5.6*:

Timur › source › repos › Book_Pipelines › Logs

Name	Date modified	Type	Size
9d74052d-42cd-477d-8b1e-f37ad3041951.txt	3/29/2023 9:55 PM	Text Document	1 KB
22ac3f3c-d286-4ad6-8310-ce97ff7d75ee.txt	3/29/2023 9:55 PM	Text Document	1 KB
76a480b2-fbca-4786-b4d8-f33f5b8c051f.txt	3/29/2023 9:55 PM	Text Document	1 KB
467b2bba-21da-4697-a368-2a223c5fab59.txt	3/29/2023 9:55 PM	Text Document	1 KB
779daa6b-cbc8-4d01-a033-8c845165c4cf.txt	3/29/2023 9:55 PM	Text Document	1 KB
071168c7-fdfc-4e1d-80d7-23af1dd35db8.txt	3/29/2023 9:55 PM	Text Document	1 KB
a0355b7b-e5b3-4ea1-b72e-3373dd1136e7.txt	3/29/2023 9:55 PM	Text Document	1 KB
cd624d23-27ed-426c-bfdc-f37f4a683bae.txt	3/29/2023 9:55 PM	Text Document	1 KB
d999f857-b3e4-40a4-b96e-32a13bd6c328.txt	3/29/2023 9:55 PM	Text Document	1 KB

Figure 5.6: *Bridge design pattern execution logs*

Each pipeline generates its own file with information about its execution.

In our case, we are documenting the executed steps, which you can see in *Figure 5.7*:

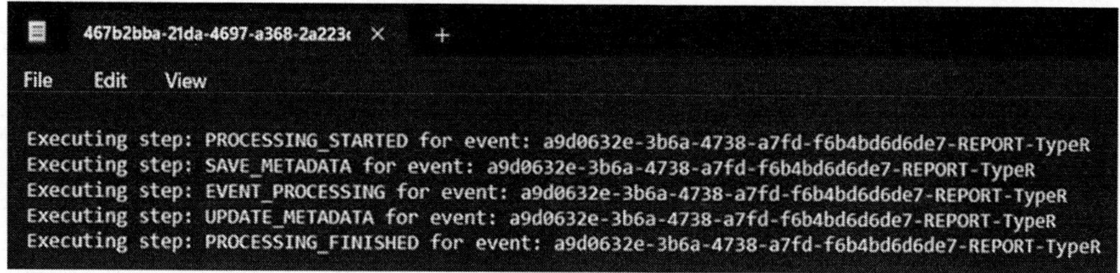

Figure 5.7: Bridge design pattern log example

We can list improvements to our code that we have achieved because of Bridge design pattern:

- Separate logger class can log information to different destinations
- Unified interface for different logging destinations
- Easy switch between logging destinations
- Possibility to improve performance

We have isolated pipelines logging from pipelines execution code, which is crucial in some situations. This information can be displayed on the UI to allow users to track the pipelines execution process.

Each logging source has a unified interface to interact with any destinations. We can switch between logging destinations easily as **`Logger`** class works as a Bridge with a unified interface. You will need to change the storage of logs by implementing a new class, which is derived from the **`IloggingDestination`** interface, and pass it to **`Logger`** class constructor. Some of the loggers can improve performance by utilizing the **Flush** method to write kept logs all at once.

Decorator

Decorator is a structural design pattern that provides the possibility to attach additional functionality to an object.

We can imagine decorators as layers of onion. Each layer provides its own functionality, and in the result of execution of all these layers, we will receive the final objects. It is like a conveyer at each step, we are modifying existing objects to make a final product.

Making functionality modular

In our case, we can modify our logging system to be layered. For this, we need to create **`LoggingDestinationDecorator`** class and derive actual decorators from it. We will add two additional decorators: **`DateLoggingDecorator`** and **`NewLineLoggingDecorators`**. Refer to the following *Figure 5.8*:

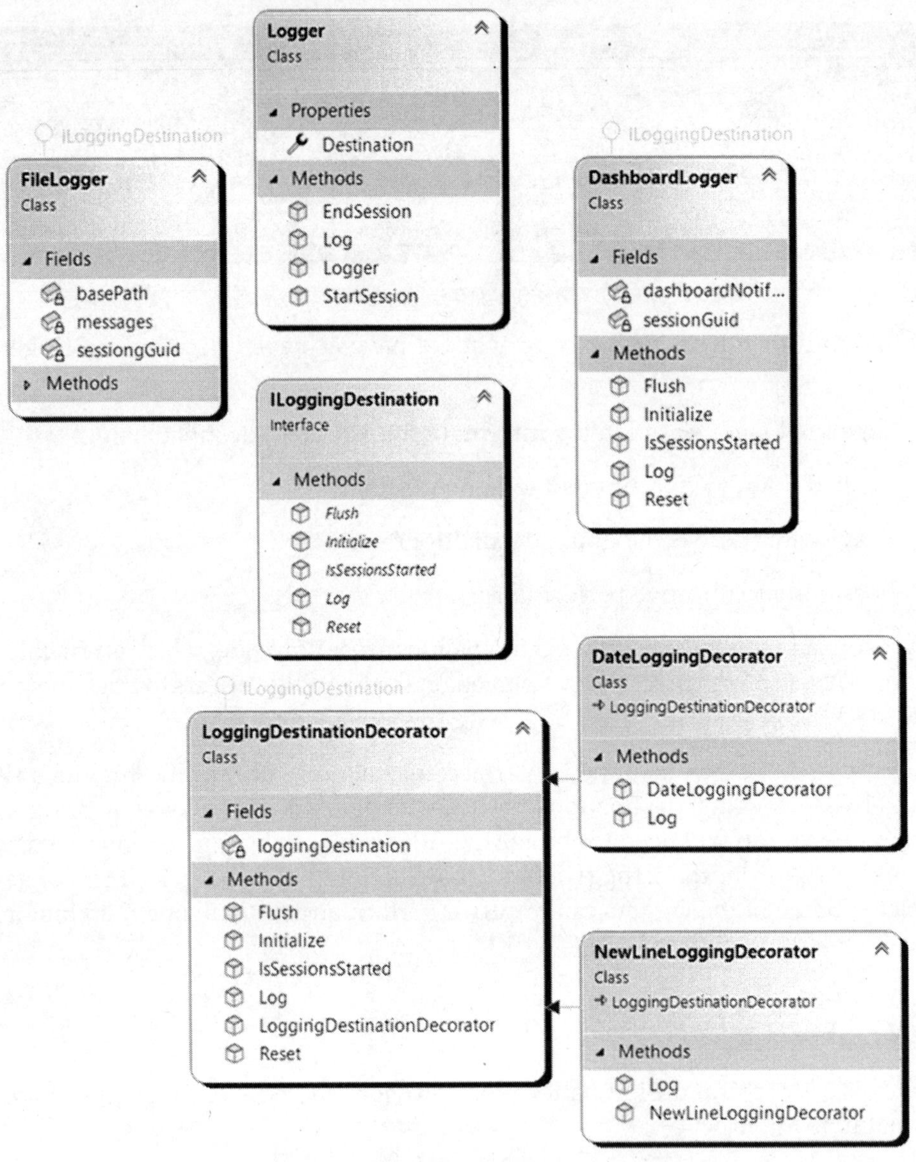

Figure 5.8: Decorator design pattern diagram

At the top of *Figure 5.8*, you can see already-used entities like **`Logger`** and **`ILoggerDestination`**. At the bottom, there is a new class that is included in our logging system: **`LoggingDestinationDecorator`**, which implements the **`ILoggingDestination`**. Two concrete classes derive from it: **`DateLoggingDecarotar`** and **`NewLineLoggingDecorator`**. The first adds date in the beginning of the message logged, and second adds a new line after each message.

Let us see how it looks in the code:

Code

We will start with **`LoggingDestinationDecorator`**. It is like a wrapper that works as a Proxy for an underlying object. However, there is a small difference with the Proxy object; some methods are marked as virtual so that we can override or extend existing functionality.

`LoggingDestinationDecorator` is our main point of logging system extension:

```
public class LoggingDestinationDecorator : ILoggingDestination
{
        private ILoggingDestination loggingDestination;

        public LoggingDestinationDecorator(ILoggingDestination loggingDestination)
        {
            this.loggingDestination = loggingDestination;
        }

        public void Flush()
        {
            loggingDestination.Flush();
        }

        public void Initialize(Guid sessionsGuid)
        {
            loggingDestination.Initialize(sessionsGuid);
        }

        public bool IsSessionsStarted()
        {
            return loggingDestination.IsSessionsStarted();
        }

        public virtual void Log(string message)
        {
            loggingDestination.Log(message);
        }

        public void Reset()
        {
            loggingDestination.Reset();
        }
}
```

Then, we are introducing two new Decorators:

```
public class NewLineLoggingDecorator : LoggingDestinationDecorator
{
        public NewLineLoggingDecorator(ILoggingDestination
                        loggingDestination) : base(loggingDestination)
        {
        }

        public override void Log(string message)
        {
            string dateTimeMessage = $"{message}{Environment.NewLine}";
            base.Log(dateTimeMessage);
        }
}
public class DateLoggingDecorator: LoggingDestinationDecorator
{
        public DateLoggingDecorator(ILoggingDestination loggingDestination)
                                                    : base(loggingDestination)
        {
        }
        public override void Log(string message)
        {
            string dateTimeMessage = $"{DateTime.UtcNow.
                                      ToShortDateString()}: {message}";
            base.Log(dateTimeMessage);
        }
}
```

Each of them overrides the **Log** method to add additional information to the message.

In the end, we can make an onion of wrappers around concrete **LoggingDestination** object:

```
var fileLogger = new FileLogger();
return new NewLineLoggingDecorator(
new DateLoggingDecorator(
         new LoggingDestinationDecorator(fileLogger)));
```

The result of code execution is shown in *Figure 5.9*:

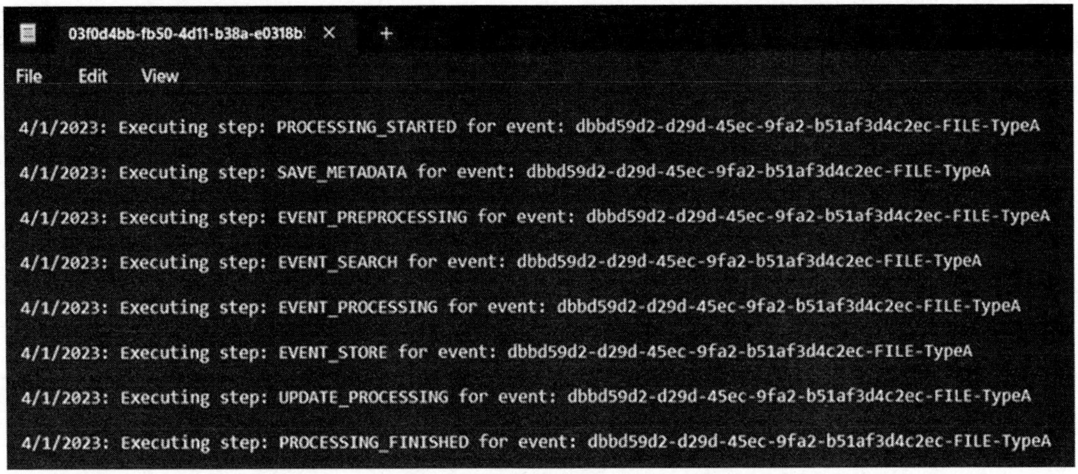

```
03f0d4bb-fb50-4d11-b38a-e0318b  ×  +
File   Edit   View

4/1/2023: Executing step: PROCESSING_STARTED for event: dbbd59d2-d29d-45ec-9fa2-b51af3d4c2ec-FILE-TypeA
4/1/2023: Executing step: SAVE_METADATA for event: dbbd59d2-d29d-45ec-9fa2-b51af3d4c2ec-FILE-TypeA
4/1/2023: Executing step: EVENT_PREPROCESSING for event: dbbd59d2-d29d-45ec-9fa2-b51af3d4c2ec-FILE-TypeA
4/1/2023: Executing step: EVENT_SEARCH for event: dbbd59d2-d29d-45ec-9fa2-b51af3d4c2ec-FILE-TypeA
4/1/2023: Executing step: EVENT_PROCESSING for event: dbbd59d2-d29d-45ec-9fa2-b51af3d4c2ec-FILE-TypeA
4/1/2023: Executing step: EVENT_STORE for event: dbbd59d2-d29d-45ec-9fa2-b51af3d4c2ec-FILE-TypeA
4/1/2023: Executing step: UPDATE_PROCESSING for event: dbbd59d2-d29d-45ec-9fa2-b51af3d4c2ec-FILE-TypeA
4/1/2023: Executing step: PROCESSING_FINISHED for event: dbbd59d2-d29d-45ec-9fa2-b51af3d4c2ec-FILE-TypeA
```

Figure 5.9: *Decorator design pattern execution result log*

As you can see at the beginning of each **Executing step** log, the date has been added, and each log is separated by a new line.

Decorator design pattern provides a good opportunity to decouple the logic of an object creation/usage and makes your codebase more modular. After applying it, you achieve the decoupling of concrete functionality from your codebase by separating classes/functionality that should not be exposed to outside code. At the same time, you can combine these classes without any additional code changes. A good example of such modularity is when you are writing a messaging application where it is possible to send large amounts of encrypted texts. The execution flow could be the following:

- User inputs a text
- System applies compression
- System applies encryption
- Message is sent to another user

Compression and encryption can be created as Decorators, so they will be easy to switch if you need to change compression or encryption algorithms. At the same time, for some chats, it is possible that you do not want to use encryption. In this case, you can simply remove the redundant Decorator.

Synergy of the patterns

In this chapter, we have introduced Proxy, Facade, Bridge, and Decorator design patterns. They allowed us to decouple exception handling and step execution process logging into a general pipeline, clean up **`PipelineDirector`**, move part of functionality to outside class, move loggers to separate classes, provide access to different logging capabilities by using a unified interface, and add the possibility to enhance existing loggers without touching the internals.

Adjusting the processing pipeline

Let us look at the final design in *Figure 5.10*:

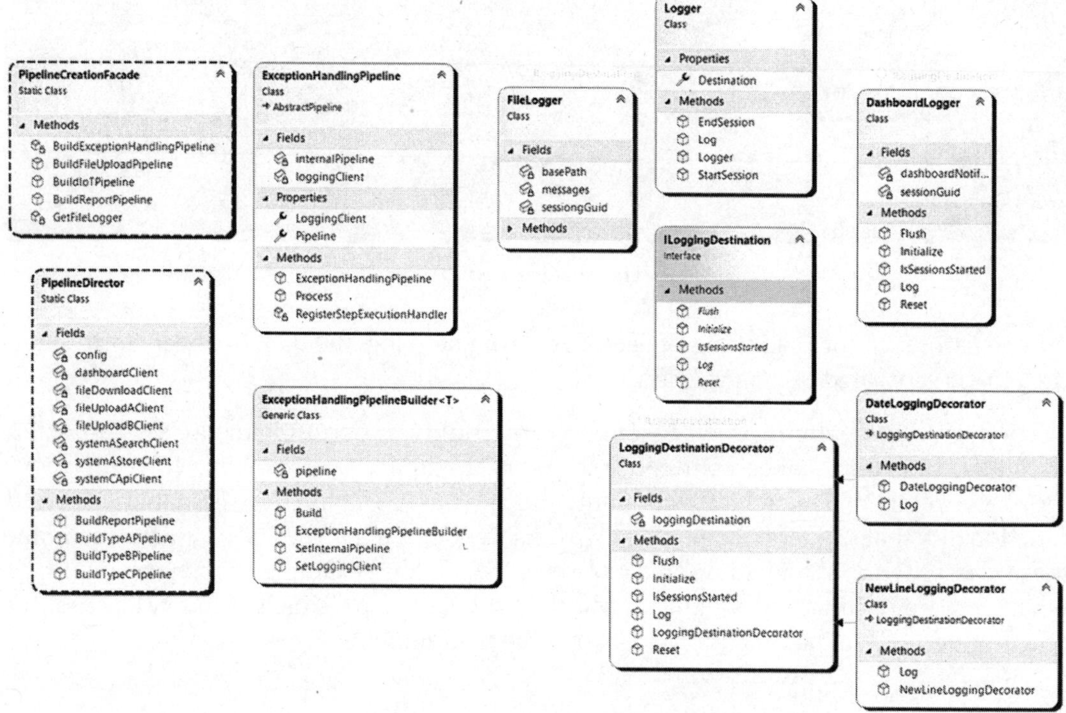

***Figure 5.10:** Synergy of patterns: Adapter, Composite, Flyweight, and Factories design patterns diagram*

The left side of the image is given away for Facade and Proxy design patterns. They are responsible for separating **`PipelineCreationFacade`** from **`PipelineDirector`** and making **`ExceptionHandlingPipeline`**. On the right side, we can find Bridge and Decorator design patterns responsible for making logging systems and applying Decorators for them independently.

Code

We have added a lot of code that could influence the performance of the pipelines. For example, logging and one proxy pipeline. Let us test it with the same example as in the preceding chapters to see if there is any difference:

```
Stopwatch watch = new Stopwatch();
watch.Start();

var event1 = new BaseUploadEvent(Guid.NewGuid(), "TypeA", "FILE",
                    "TypeAFilename.jpg", "http://typeA.file.url", ".jpg");

var event2 = new BaseUploadEvent(Guid.NewGuid(), "TypeB", "FILE",
                    "TypeBFilename.jpg", "http://typeB.file.url", ".jpg");

var event3 = new BaseUploadEvent(Guid.NewGuid(), "TypeB", "FILE",
                   "TypeB2Filename.jpg", "http://typeB.file.url", ".jpg");

var event4 = new BaseIoTEvent(Guid.NewGuid(), "TypeC", "IOT",
                                              "TEMP_UPDATE", "92.2");
var event5 = new BaseIoTEvent(Guid.NewGuid(), "TypeC", "IOT",
                                              "TEMP_UPDATE", "92.2");
var event6 = new BaseIoTEvent(Guid.NewGuid(), "TypeC", "IOT",
                                              "TEMP_UPDATE", "92.2");
var reportEvent = new ReportEvent(Guid.NewGuid(), "TypeR", "REPORT",
                       "TypeRFilename.jpg", "http://typeR.file.url",
                       ".jpg", "TEMP_UPDATE", "93.2");

List<BasicEvent> eventList = new List<BasicEvent>
{
          event1, event2, event3, event4, event5, event6, reportEvent };
eventList.ForEach(eventObj =>
{
          FactoryCreator.GetPipelineFactory(eventObj)
                        .GetPipeline(eventObj).Process(eventObj);
         Console.WriteLine();
});

watch.Stop();
Console.WriteLine($"MS ellapsed: {watch.ElapsedMilliseconds}");
```

We have cleaned the code and moved all initialization to constructors, so for now, we can observe all seven events being used for testing.

In the result of code execution, we will receive the following *Figure 5.11*:

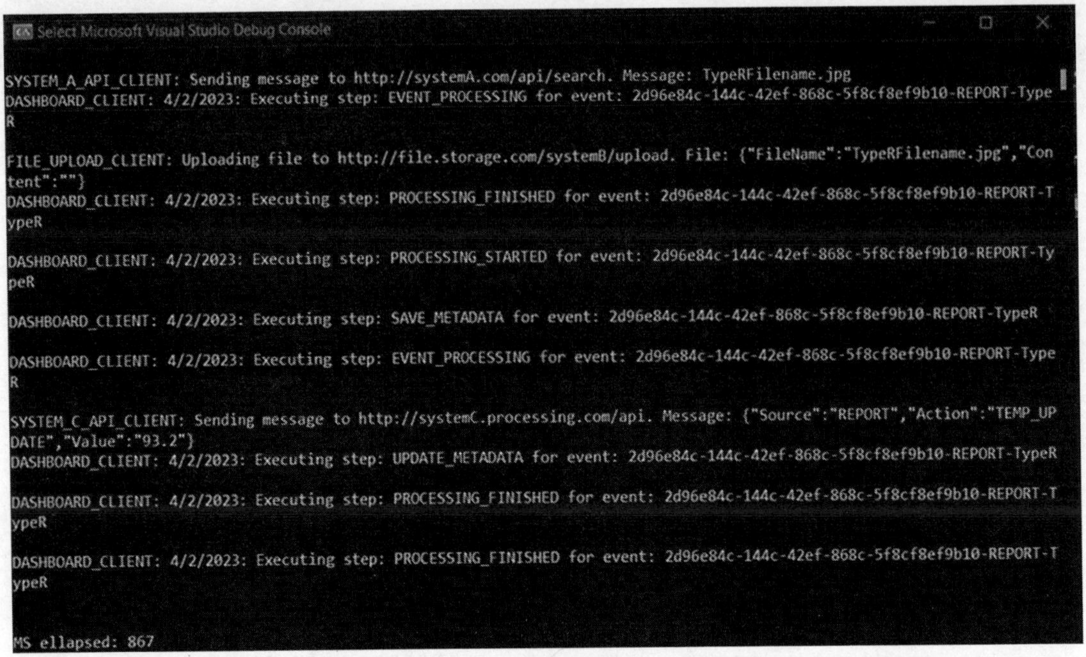

```
Select Microsoft Visual Studio Debug Console

SYSTEM_A_API_CLIENT: Sending message to http://systemA.com/api/search. Message: TypeRFilename.jpg
DASHBOARD_CLIENT: 4/2/2023: Executing step: EVENT_PROCESSING for event: 2d96e84c-144c-42ef-868c-5f8cf8ef9b10-REPORT-Type
R

FILE_UPLOAD_CLIENT: Uploading file to http://file.storage.com/systemB/upload. File: {"FileName":"TypeRFilename.jpg","Con
tent":""}
DASHBOARD_CLIENT: 4/2/2023: Executing step: PROCESSING_FINISHED for event: 2d96e84c-144c-42ef-868c-5f8cf8ef9b10-REPORT-T
ypeR

DASHBOARD_CLIENT: 4/2/2023: Executing step: PROCESSING_STARTED for event: 2d96e84c-144c-42ef-868c-5f8cf8ef9b10-REPORT-Ty
peR

DASHBOARD_CLIENT: 4/2/2023: Executing step: SAVE_METADATA for event: 2d96e84c-144c-42ef-868c-5f8cf8ef9b10-REPORT-TypeR

DASHBOARD_CLIENT: 4/2/2023: Executing step: EVENT_PROCESSING for event: 2d96e84c-144c-42ef-868c-5f8cf8ef9b10-REPORT-Type
R

SYSTEM_C_API_CLIENT: Sending message to http://systemC.processing.com/api. Message: {"Source":"REPORT","Action":"TEMP_UP
DATE","Value":"93.2"}
DASHBOARD_CLIENT: 4/2/2023: Executing step: UPDATE_METADATA for event: 2d96e84c-144c-42ef-868c-5f8cf8ef9b10-REPORT-TypeR

DASHBOARD_CLIENT: 4/2/2023: Executing step: PROCESSING_FINISHED for event: 2d96e84c-144c-42ef-868c-5f8cf8ef9b10-REPORT-T
ypeR

DASHBOARD_CLIENT: 4/2/2023: Executing step: PROCESSING_FINISHED for event: 2d96e84c-144c-42ef-868c-5f8cf8ef9b10-REPORT-T
ypeR


MS ellapsed: 867
```

Figure 5.11: *Synergy of pattens, Execution result*

With all our additions, it still takes **`~900ms`** to process the same events. We have achieved good results by adding modularity and decoupling the classes while keeping our performance on the same level.

Conclusion

The patterns we have reviewed are not simple, but they provide a good foundation for good OOP design of your class hierarchy. Most structural design patterns are similar in some parts, but the difference is in their usage. For example, we can notice that Proxy and Decorator are similar in idea, however, some nuances uncover the difference.

Proxy design pattern provides us with the capability to extend existing functionality with pre-and post-processing of the function execution. This can include logging, exception handling, object transformation, etc.

Facade pattern allows us to aggregate a wide range of class usage under one simple interface. It is helpful when you want to incorporate some framework/library into one interface or have a lot of classes for supporting some part of your application and keeping business logic under one interface.

In our case, the Bridge design pattern was used to manage pipeline logging capabilities. It provides the capability to use different classes for one purpose under a unified interface. It is helpful when you have multiple ways to solve one problem and want to switch between these ways without modifying the internals of your application.

Decorator design pattern provides us with the capability to extend the base object with additional information. The base object goes through a line of decorators, and each adds additional information, thus extending it. And the most important part is that it can be done modularly with decoupling in mind.

In the next chapter, we will explore behavioral design patterns. These patterns help with customization of behavior depending on a context. We will start with the template method, strategy, and chain of responsibility design patterns.

Join our book's Discord space

Join the book's Discord Workspace for Latest updates, Offers, Tech happenings around the world, New Release and Sessions with the Authors:

https://discord.bpbonline.com

CHAPTER 6
Object Behavioral Design Patterns

Introduction

This chapter explores object behavioral design using the template method, strategy, and chain of responsibility design patterns.

These three patterns are cornerstones for modifying the behavior of objects.

Structure

The chapter covers the following topics:

- Template method
  - Simplify pipelines creation and design
  - Code
- Strategy
  - Functionality split
  - Code

- Chain of responsibility
  - o Modularizing the pipeline
  - o Code
- Synergy of the patterns

Objectives

At the end of this chapter, you will be able to describe the template method, strategy, and chain of responsibility design patterns and apply them to real-world problems.

Let us dive in!

Template method

The idea of Template method design pattern is to make an ideal process and then simply change some parts of it for a specific case. We have already seen it in *Chapter 1, Main OOP Standpoints,* where we discussed abstract class definition.

First, we need an abstract class that will define a flow of execution. Then, we should identify our specific cases and create classes for each of the identified cases, derive them from the defined abstract class, and modify/implement the required functionality.

In our case, we want to clean up our pipelines to make them more standardized.

Simplify pipelines creation and design

We will need an abstract pipeline to work as the definition of the base processing flow.

Then, we need to refactor our existing pipelines to adapt to changes (and all other classes like builders, PipelineDirector, etc).

Refer to the following *Figure 6.1*:

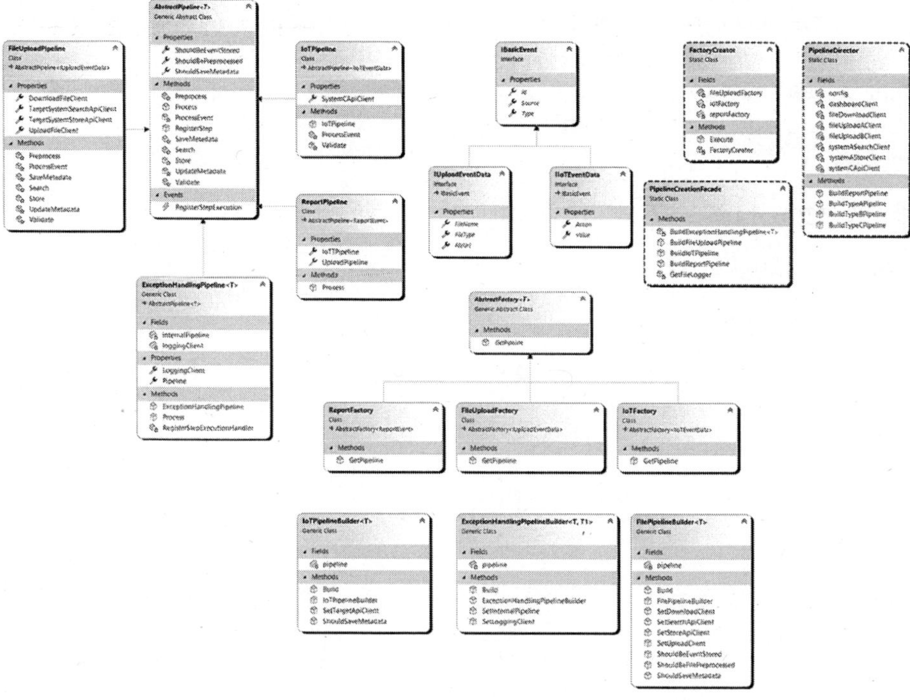

Figure 6.1: Template method design pattern diagram

Let us first look at **AbstractPipeline** and its derived classes in the following *Figure 6.2*:

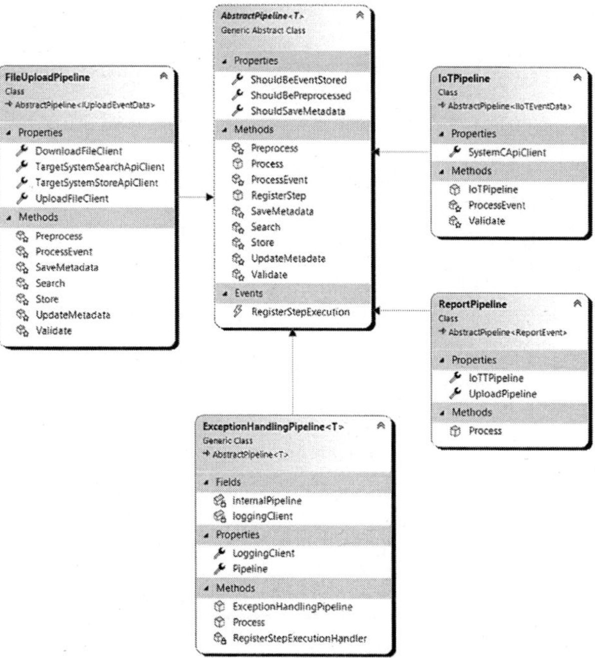

Figure 6.2: Abstract pipeline diagram

Now, the **AbstractPipeline** class has more members than before. Its main method, **Process**, defines a basic flow of event processing. All other methods are abstract and should be overridden in derived classes. **FileUploadPipeline** and **IoTPipeline** are pipelines that provide the main functionality of processing. They override derived methods and provide their own functionality. They fill the process flow with meaningful functionality.

ReportPipeline combines them to process composite **ReportEvent** objects.

ExceptionHandlingPipeline is refactored and now accepts generic type parameter.

Let us go further, see the following *Figure 6.3*:

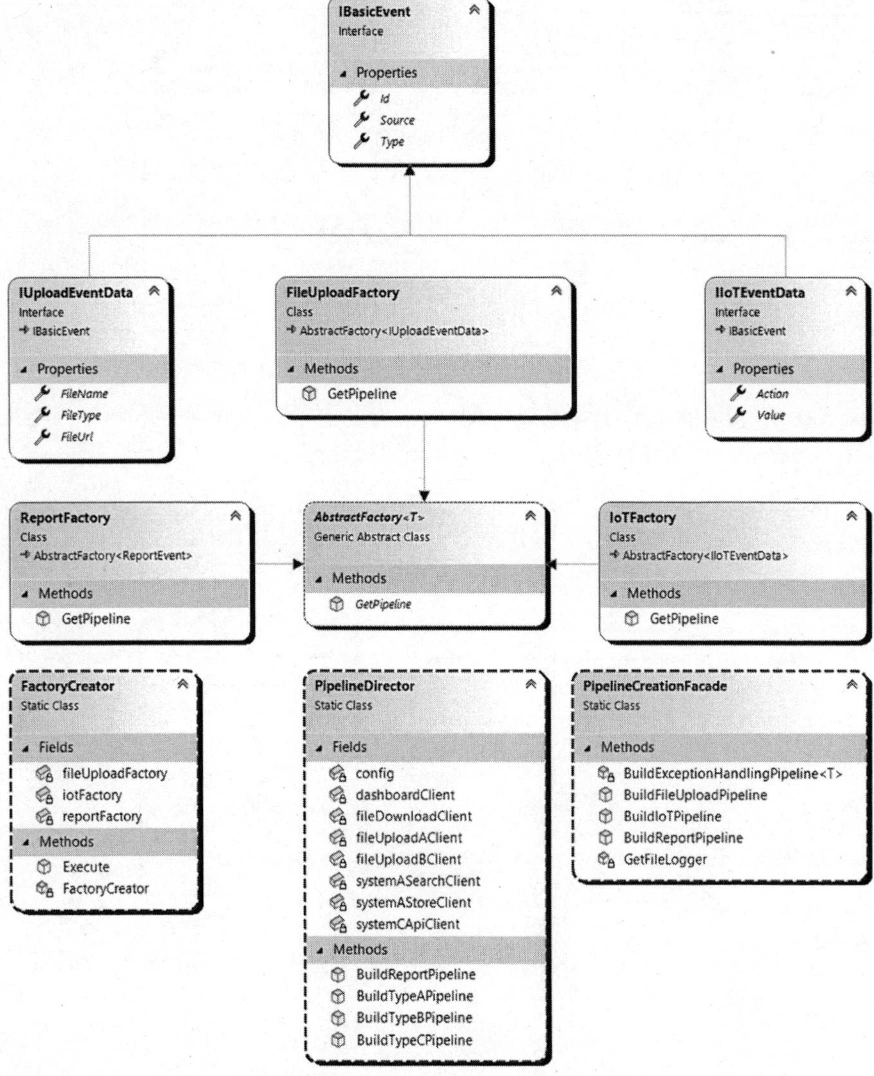

Figure 6.3: Factories diagram

FactoryCreator has changed a little. For now, it contains the **Execute** method instead of **GetPipelineFactory**. It is easier for us to execute pipeline inside the **FactoryCreator** instead of returning it because of generics type parameters (it is not easy to cast them). All other classes contain the same methods. However, **AbstractFactory** has also received a type parameter. All generic details will be reviewed in the *Code* section. Refer to the following *Figure 6.4*:

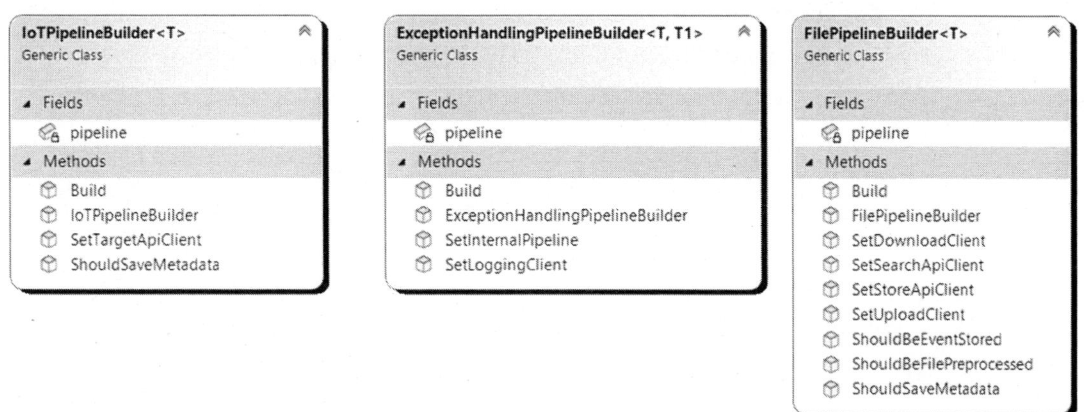

***Figure 6.4:** Pipelines diagram*

The last section is about builders. We added generic type parameters to all of them to make them more adaptive to different events.

Code

Let us start with the AbstractPipeline class:

```
public delegate void RegisterStepExecutionDelegate(IBasicEvent basicEvent,
                                                      string step);
public abstract class AbstractPipeline<T> where T : IBasicEvent
{
        public event RegisterStepExecutionDelegate RegisterStepExecution;
        public bool ShouldSaveMetadata { get; set; }
        public bool ShouldBePreprocessed { get; set; }
        public bool ShouldBeEventStored { get; set; }
        public virtual void RegisterStep(T basicEvent, string step)
        {
                if (this.RegisterStepExecution != null)
                this.RegisterStepExecution(basicEvent, step);
        }
```

```
        public virtual void Process(T basicEvent)
        {
            if (this.ShouldSaveMetadata) this.SaveMetadata(basicEvent);
            this.Validate(basicEvent);
            if (this.ShouldBePreprocessed) this.Preprocess(basicEvent);
            this.Search(basicEvent);
            this.ProcessEvent(basicEvent);
            if (this.ShouldBeEventStored) this.Store(basicEvent);
            if (this.ShouldSaveMetadata) this.UpdateMetadata(basicEvent);
        }

        protected virtual void Preprocess(T basicEvent)
        {
        }
        protected virtual void ProcessEvent(T basicEvent)
        {
        }
        protected virtual void Search(T basicEvent)
        {
        }
        protected virtual void Store(T basicEvent)
        {
        }
        protected virtual Guid SaveMetadata(T basicEvent)
        {
            return Guid.Empty;
        }
        protected virtual void UpdateMetadata(T basicEvent)
        {
        }
        protected virtual void Validate(T basicEvent)
        {
        }
}
```

As you can see, we have extended our **AbstractPipeline** to make a unified pipeline process. First, we added a type parameter to the class definition. It defines passed parameter of all functions used in the processing function. It allows us to use specific properties in overridden functions.

Secondly, we have added all possible functions participating in the event processing and made the **Process** function from them. It will allow us to write less code in derived classes.

We have changed all derived pipelines. Let us see how they appear now:

```
public class IoTPipeline : AbstractPipeline<IIoTEventData>
{
        public ICommunicationClient<IoTData, string> SystemCApiClient { get; set;}
        public IoTPipeline()
        {
            this.ShouldBeEventStored = false;
            this.ShouldBePreprocessed = false;
        }
        protected override void ProcessEvent(IIoTEventData basicEvent)
        {
              this.RegisterStep(basicEvent, "EVENT_PROCESSING");
              var data = new IoTData(basicEvent.Source, basicEvent.Action,
                                     basicEvent.Value);
              this.SystemCApiClient.ExecuteRequest(data);
        }
        protected override void Validate(IIoTEventData basicEvent)
        {
            if (basicEvent.Action == null)
                throw new PipelineProcessingException("Action of the event
                                                          cannot be null");
            if (basicEvent.Value == null)
                throw new PipelineProcessingException("Value of the event
                                                          cannot be null");
        }
}
```

In the current **IoTPipeline** implementation, we should implement only the required functions for concrete event type processing like **Validate** and **ProcessEvent**. Also, in the constructor, we should set Boolean properties to disable calls to specific functions.

We have two interesting situations with **FileUploadPipeline**: Type A and Type B. We have two ways to implement them: implement a generic **FileUploadPipeline** with the required methods for the two of them or make a separate pipeline for each. We have chosen the first approach, which is as follows:

```
public class FileUploadPipeline : AbstractPipeline<IUploadEventData>
{
        public ICommunicationClient<UploadFileInfo, int> UploadFileClient {
                                                              get; set; }
        public ICommunicationClient<string, string>
                             TargetSystemSearchApiClient { get; set; }
        public ICommunicationClient<string, string>
                             TargetSystemStoreApiClient { get; set; }
        public ICommunicationClient<string, byte[]> DownloadFileClient {
                                                              get; set; }

        protected override void Preprocess(IUploadEventData basicEvent)
        {
            this.RegisterStep(basicEvent, "EVENT_PREPROCESSING");
            this.DownloadFileClient.ExecuteRequest(basicEvent.FileUrl);
        }
        protected override void ProcessEvent(IUploadEventData basicEvent)
        {
            if (this.UploadFileClient == null)
                return;

            this.RegisterStep(basicEvent, "EVENT_PROCESSING");
            this.UploadFileClient.ExecuteRequest(new UploadFileInfo
            {
                FileName = basicEvent.FileName,
                Content = new byte[0]
            });
        }
        protected override void Search(IUploadEventData basicEvent)
        {
            this.RegisterStep(basicEvent, "EVENT_SEARCH");
            this.TargetSystemSearchApiClient.ExecuteRequest(basicEvent.
                                                              FileName);
        }
        protected override void Store(IUploadEventData basicEvent)
        {
            this.RegisterStep(basicEvent, "EVENT_STORE");
            this.TargetSystemStoreApiClient.ExecuteRequest(basicEvent.
                                                              FileName);
```

```
        }
        protected override Guid SaveMetadata(IUploadEventData basicEvent)
        {
            this.RegisterStep(basicEvent, "SAVE_METADATA");
            return Guid.NewGuid();
        }
        protected override void UpdateMetadata(IUploadEventData basicEvent)
        {
            this.RegisterStep(basicEvent, "UPDATE_PROCESSING");
        }
        protected override void Validate(IUploadEventData basicEvent)
        {
            if (basicEvent.FileName == null)
                throw new PipelineProcessingException("Filename of the
                                                   event cannot be null");
            if (basicEvent.FileType == null)
                throw new PipelineProcessingException("File Type of the
                                                   event cannot be null");
            if (basicEvent.FileUrl == null)
                throw new PipelineProcessingException("File Url of the
                                                   event cannot be null");
        }
}
```

We have implemented one generic **FileUploadPipeline**, which can be used to create file upload pipelines with various configurations. It has all the required functions implemented, and you simply need to configure it before use.

ExceptionHandlingPipeline remains unchanged, except that it now accepts type parameters. The compiler checks if **AbstractPipeline** (which is passed in through **Pipeline** property) matches this type of parameter. Look at the given code:

```
public class ExceptionHandlingPipeline<T> : AbstractPipeline<T> where T
                                                          : IBasicEvent
{
        private AbstractPipeline<T> internalPipeline;
        private Logger loggingClient;

        public ExceptionHandlingPipeline()
        {
```

```
        this.RegisterStepExecution += RegisterStepExecutionHandler;
    }
    public Logger LoggingClient
    {
        set
        {
            this.loggingClient = value;
            this.loggingClient.StartSession(Guid.NewGuid());
        }
    }
    public AbstractPipeline<T> Pipeline
    {
        set
        {
            if (this.internalPipeline != null)
                this.internalPipeline.RegisterStepExecution -=
                                            RegisterStepExecutionHandler;
            this.internalPipeline = value;
            this.internalPipeline.RegisterStepExecution +=
                                            RegisterStepExecutionHandler;
        }
    }
    public override void Process(T basicEvent)
    {
        try
        {
            this.RegisterStep(basicEvent, "PROCESSING_STARTED");
            this.internalPipeline.Process(basicEvent);
            this.RegisterStep(basicEvent, "PROCESSING_FINISHED");
        }
        catch { // exception handling code }
        finally
        {
            this.loggingClient.EndSession();
        }
    }
```

```
        private void RegisterStepExecutionHandler(IBasicEvent basicEvent,
string step)
        {
            var message = $"Executing step: {step} for event: {basicEvent.
Id}-{basicEvent.Source}-{basicEvent.Type}";
            this.loggingClient.Log(message);
        }
    }
```

The last pipeline is ReportPipeline. It is a smallest one:

```
public class ReportPipeline : AbstractPipeline<ReportEvent>
{
        public AbstractPipeline<IUploadEventData> UploadPipeline { get; set; }
        public AbstractPipeline<IIoTEventData> IoTTPipeline { get; set; }
        public override void Process(ReportEvent basicEvent)
        {
            this.UploadPipeline.Process(basicEvent);
            this.IoTTPipeline.Process(basicEvent);
        }
}
```

The main change is that we have changed its internal list of pipelines with two public properties. The problem is that we cannot cast **Class<B>** and **Class<C>** to **Class<A>**. It is the nature of generics, so in this case, it was easier to add properties instead of attempting workarounds.

Factories have not changed, except that they now accept a generic type parameter. Look at the following code:

```
public abstract class AbstractFactory<T> where T: IBasicEvent
{
        public abstract AbstractPipeline<T> GetPipeline(BasicEvent basicEvent);
}
```

The last crucial change happened to **FactoryCreator**. Now it is more **FactoryExecutor** instead of Creator:

```
public static class FactoryCreator
{
        private static AbstractFactory<IIoTEventData> iotFactory;
        private static AbstractFactory<IUploadEventData> fileUploadFactory;
        private static AbstractFactory<ReportEvent> reportFactory;
```

```
        static FactoryCreator()
        {
            iotFactory = new IoTFactory();
            fileUploadFactory = new FileUploadFactory();
            reportFactory = new ReportFactory();
        }
        public static void Execute(BasicEvent basicEvent)
        {
            switch (basicEvent.Source)
            {
                case Constants.IOT_EVENT_SOURCE:
                    {
                      iotFactory.GetPipeline(basicEvent).Process(basicEvent
                                                          as BaseIoTEvent);
                        break;
                    }
                case Constants.FILE_EVENT_SOURCE:
                    {
                                 fileUploadFactory.GetPipeline(basicEvent).
                                   Process(basicEvent as BaseUploadEvent);
                        break;
                    }
                case Constants.REPORT_EVENT_SOURCE:
                    {
                   reportFactory.GetPipeline(basicEvent).Process(basicEvent
                                                            as ReportEvent);
                        break;
                    }
                default:
                        throw new NotImplementedException($"Scenario for
                              {basicEvent.Source} is not implemented");
            }
        }
}
```

We have added **Execute** method and removed **GetPipeline** method, as it is easier to manage pipelines with different generic type parameters in one class instead of making them public.

So, for now, we are calling **Process** method of the returned pipeline, which works.

Template method design pattern provides an opportunity to design a general workflow that can be tweaked by additional properties. In our case, we have used it to specify a main pipeline process in which we can enable/disable specific actions like create/update metadata, preprocess events, and so on. Unfortunately, in some cases, this approach can become a bottleneck when you have more than 2-3 cases to generalize. The amount of logic and Boolean properties will become larger and larger, and at the end, you will have a class filled with an enormous amount of spaghetti code.

In the next section, we will show you how to modularize pipeline processing strategies.

Strategy

Strategy is a behavioral design pattern that allows you to split different control branches into separate classes and switch them at runtime.

Functionality split

In our case, we want to select a specific strategy based on the source and type of event to be processed. In the preceding section, we made one generalized pipeline process. However, in hundreds of cases, it will not work well because we will have a lot of exceptional cases, special attributes, conditions, and so on. As a result, the code will become a mess. To deal with it, we can introduce strategy pattern to our code, which will help modularize our class hierarchy.

Let us create separate **Strategy** classes for each case to be processed. Refer to the following *Figure 6.5*:

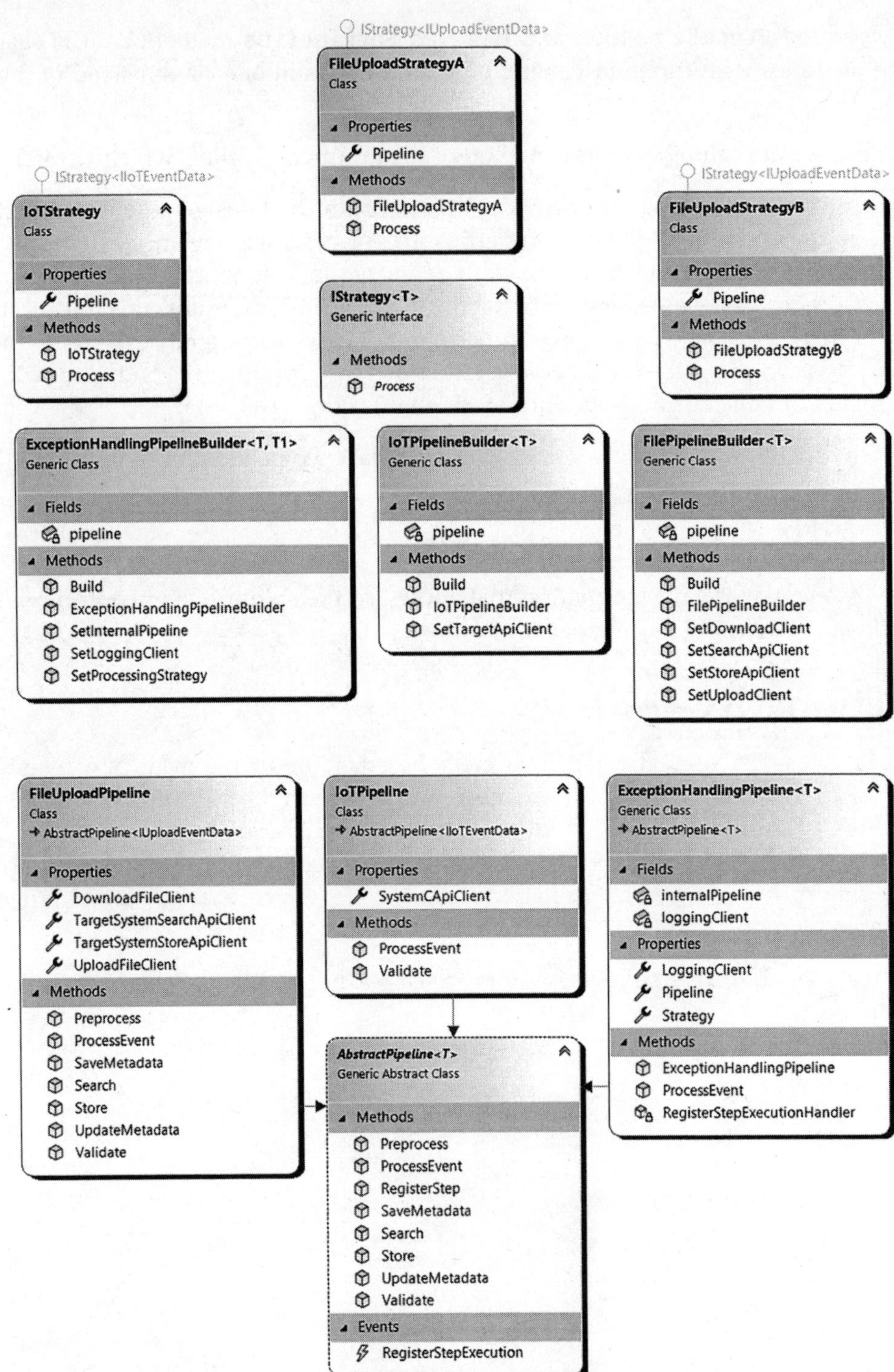

Figure 6.5: Strategy diagram

It may not be noticeable, but we have removed the **Process** method from our **AbstractPipeline** and all our derived pipelines. From this moment, each pipeline has methods that allow an event to be processed but do not have any method to combine them together.

In the center, we have placed the **IStrategy<T>** interface with its derived classes. Each strategy has a constructor which accepts **AbstractPipeline<T>** instance and provided method **Process**, which from this moment contains pipeline execution sequence. As all of our pipelines are wrapped into **ExceptionHandlingPipeline**, we decided this pipeline should have a generic **Strategy** property. We will call the **Process** method to execute the underlying pipeline.

Code

The main entity that our solution will be based on is an **IStrategy<T>** interface:

```
public interface IStrategy<T>
{
        public void Process(T basicEvent);
}
```

It is very simple and contains only one method, **Process**. It is called when we need to process the event.

Next, we will look at our **IStrategy** derived classes:

```
public class FileUploadStrategyA: IStrategy<IUploadEventData>
{
        public AbstractPipeline<IUploadEventData> Pipeline { get; set; }
        public FileUploadStrategyA(AbstractPipeline<IUploadEventData> pipeline)
        {
            this.Pipeline = pipeline;
        }
        public  void Process(IUploadEventData basicEvent)
        {
            this.Pipeline.SaveMetadata(basicEvent);
            this.Pipeline.Validate(basicEvent);
            this.Pipeline.Preprocess(basicEvent);
            this.Pipeline.Search(basicEvent);
            this.Pipeline.ProcessEvent(basicEvent);
            this.Pipeline.Store(basicEvent);
            this.Pipeline.UpdateMetadata(basicEvent);
```

```
        }
}
public class FileUploadStrategyB: IStrategy<IUploadEventData>
{
     public AbstractPipeline<IUploadEventData> Pipeline { get; set; }
     public FileUploadStrategyB(AbstractPipeline<IUploadEventData> pipeline)
        {
            this.Pipeline = pipeline;
        }
        public void Process(IUploadEventData basicEvent)
        {
            this.Pipeline.Validate(basicEvent);
            this.Pipeline.Preprocess(basicEvent);
            this.Pipeline.Search(basicEvent);
            this.Pipeline.ProcessEvent(basicEvent);
        }
}
public class IoTStrategy: IStrategy<IIoTEventData>
{
        public AbstractPipeline<IIoTEventData> Pipeline { get; set; }
        public IoTStrategy(AbstractPipeline<IIoTEventData> pipeline)
        {
            this.Pipeline = pipeline;
        }
        public void Process(IIoTEventData basicEvent)
        {
            this.Pipeline.SaveMetadata(basicEvent);
            this.Pipeline.Validate(basicEvent);
            this.Pipeline.Search(basicEvent);
            this.Pipeline.ProcessEvent(basicEvent);
            this.Pipeline.UpdateMetadata(basicEvent);
        }
}
```

They are also very simple. Each has a constructor that accepts a specific pipeline and method **Process**, which calls **Pipeline** methods. A generic type parameter is used to define the type of event that will be passed to pipelines.

We have modified **AbtractPipeline**. So from this moment, it does not contain any generic **Process** method and only defines a virtual empty method overwritten in derived classes:

```
public abstract class AbstractPipeline<T> where T : IBasicEvent
{
        public event RegisterStepExecutionDelegate RegisterStepExecution;
        public virtual void RegisterStep(T basicEvent, string step)
        {
            if (this.RegisterStepExecution != null)
                this.RegisterStepExecution(basicEvent, step);
        }
        public virtual void Preprocess(T basicEvent)
        {
        }
        public virtual void ProcessEvent(T basicEvent)
        {
        }
        public virtual void Search(T basicEvent)
        {
        }
        public virtual void Store(T basicEvent)
        {
        }
        public virtual Guid SaveMetadata(T basicEvent)
        {
            return Guid.Empty;
        }
        public virtual void UpdateMetadata(T basicEvent)
        {
        }
        public virtual void Validate(T basicEvent)
        {
        }
}
```

For example, we can look at **FileUploadPipeline**, which overwrites methods needed to complete the pipeline:

```
public class FileUploadPipeline : AbstractPipeline<IUploadEventData>
{
        public ICommunicationClient<UploadFileInfo, int> UploadFileClient
                                                             { get; set; }
        public ICommunicationClient<string, string>
                                    TargetSystemSearchApiClient { get; set; }
        public ICommunicationClient<string, string>
                                    TargetSystemStoreApiClient { get; set; }
        public ICommunicationClient<string, byte[]> DownloadFileClient
                                                             { get; set; }
        public override void Preprocess(IUploadEventData basicEvent)
        {
            this.RegisterStep(basicEvent, "EVENT_PREPROCESSING");
            this.DownloadFileClient.ExecuteRequest(basicEvent.FileUrl);
        }
        public override void ProcessEvent(IUploadEventData basicEvent)
        {
            if (this.UploadFileClient == null)
                return;
            this.RegisterStep(basicEvent, "EVENT_PROCESSING");
            this.UploadFileClient.ExecuteRequest(new UploadFileInfo
            {
                FileName = basicEvent.FileName,
                Content = new byte[0]
            });
        }
        public override void Search(IUploadEventData basicEvent)
        {
            this.RegisterStep(basicEvent, "EVENT_SEARCH");
            this.TargetSystemSearchApiClient.ExecuteRequest(basicEvent.
                                                            FileName);
        }
        public override void Store(IUploadEventData basicEvent)
        {
            this.RegisterStep(basicEvent, "EVENT_STORE");
                 this.TargetSystemStoreApiClient.ExecuteRequest(basicEvent.
                                                            FileName);
```

```
        }
        public override Guid SaveMetadata(IUploadEventData basicEvent)
        {
            this.RegisterStep(basicEvent, "SAVE_METADATA");
            return Guid.NewGuid();
        }
        public override void UpdateMetadata(IUploadEventData basicEvent)
        {
            this.RegisterStep(basicEvent, "UPDATE_PROCESSING");
        }
        public override void Validate(IUploadEventData basicEvent)
        {
            if (basicEvent.FileName == null)
                throw new PipelineProcessingException("Filename of the event
                                                        cannot be null");
            if (basicEvent.FileType == null)
               throw new PipelineProcessingException("File Type of the event
                                                        cannot be null");
            if (basicEvent.FileUrl == null)
                throw new PipelineProcessingException("File Url of the event
                                                        cannot be null");
        }
}
```

They have the same functionality as before, but without the **Process** method in **AbstractPipeline**. This functionality cannot be executed directly. It is possible only with the help of **Strategy** classes.

As we already have **ExceptionHandlingPipeline**, we decided to reuse it:

```
public class ExceptionHandlingPipeline<T> : AbstractPipeline<T> where T
                                                        : IBasicEvent
{
        private AbstractPipeline<T> internalPipeline;
        private Logger loggingClient;
        public IStrategy<T> Strategy { get; set; }
        public ExceptionHandlingPipeline()
        {
            this.RegisterStepExecution += RegisterStepExecutionHandler;
```

```
    }
    public Logger LoggingClient
    {
        set
        {
            this.loggingClient = value;
            this.loggingClient.StartSession(Guid.NewGuid());
        }
    }
    public AbstractPipeline<T> Pipeline
    {
        set
        {
            if (this.internalPipeline != null)
                this.internalPipeline.RegisterStepExecution -=
                                    RegisterStepExecutionHandler;

            this.internalPipeline = value;
            this.internalPipeline.RegisterStepExecution +=
                                    RegisterStepExecutionHandler;
        }
    }
    private void RegisterStepExecutionHandler(IBasicEvent basicEvent,
                                    string step)
    {
        var message = $"Executing step: {step} for event: {basicEvent.
                    Id}-{basicEvent.Source}-{basicEvent.Type}";
        this.loggingClient.Log(message);
    }
    public override void ProcessEvent(T basicEvent)
    {
        try
        {
            this.RegisterStep(basicEvent, "PROCESSING_STARTED");
            this.Strategy.Process(basicEvent);
            this.RegisterStep(basicEvent, "PROCESSING_FINISHED");
        }
        catch (gRpcCommunicationException)
```

```
            {
                this.RegisterStep(basicEvent, "PROCESSING_FAILED");
                Console.WriteLine("gRpc communication error received");
            }
            catch (HttpCommunicationException)
            {
                this.RegisterStep(basicEvent, "PROCESSING_FAILED");
                Console.WriteLine("Http communication error received");
            }
            catch (FileCommunicationException)
            {
                this.RegisterStep(basicEvent, "PROCESSING_FAILED");
                Console.WriteLine("File communication error received");
            }
            catch (PipelineProcessingException)
            {
                this.RegisterStep(basicEvent, "PROCESSING_FAILED");
                Console.WriteLine("Pipeline business error received");
            }
            finally
            {
                this.loggingClient.EndSession();
            }
}
```

The new property **Strategy** has been added, which will be set in the **ExceptionHandlingPipelineBuilder** class. Instead of using the **Process** method, we are now using **ProcessEvent** method, in which we call the **Process** method of **Strategy** class instance. This will execute the desired pipeline of event processing.

ExceptionHandlingPipelineBuilder is responsible for setting up **Strategy** property:

```
public class ExceptionHandlingPipelineBuilder<T,T1>
                   where T: ExceptionHandlingPipeline<T1>, new()
                   where T1 : IBasicEvent
{
        private T pipeline = default;
        public ExceptionHandlingPipelineBuilder()
        {
```

```
            this.pipeline = new T();
        }
        public ExceptionHandlingPipelineBuilder<T, T1>
              SetLoggingClient(ILoggingDestination loggingDestination)
        {
            this.pipeline.LoggingClient = new Logger(loggingDestination);
            return this;
        }
        public ExceptionHandlingPipelineBuilder<T, T1>
                              SetProcessingStrategy(IStrategy<T1> strategy)
        {
            this.pipeline.Strategy = strategy;
            return this;
        }
        public ExceptionHandlingPipelineBuilder<T, T1>
             SetInternalPipeline(AbstractPipeline<T1> internalPipeline)
        {
            this.pipeline.Pipeline = internalPipeline;
            return this;
        }
        public ExceptionHandlingPipeline<T1> Build()
        {
            return this.pipeline;
        }
}
```

And it is set in **PipelineCreationFacade** class as:

```
public static class PipelineCreationFacade
{
        public static AbstractPipeline<IUploadEventData>
             BuildFileUploadPipelineA(ICommunicationClient<UploadFileInfo,
             int> fileUploadClient,
            ICommunicationClient<string, byte[]> fileDownloadClient,
               ICommunicationClient<string, string> searchApiClient,
            ICommunicationClient<string, string> storeApiClient
            )
        {
            var typeAPipelineBuilder = new
```

```
FilePipelineBuilder<FileUploadPipeline>();
            var pipeline = typeAPipelineBuilder.
                SetUploadClient(fileUploadClient).
                SetDownloadClient(fileDownloadClient).
                SetSearchApiClient(searchApiClient).
                SetStoreApiClient(storeApiClient).
                Build();
            var strategy = new FileUploadStrategyA(pipeline);
            return BuildExceptionHandlingPipeline(pipeline, strategy);
        }
        public static AbstractPipeline<IUploadEventData>
          BuildFileUploadPipelineB(ICommunicationClient<UploadFileInfo,
          int> fileUploadClient,
            ICommunicationClient<string, byte[]> fileDownloadClient,
                ICommunicationClient<string, string> searchApiClient,
            ICommunicationClient<string, string> storeApiClient
            )
        {
            var typeAPipelineBuilder = new
                                 FilePipelineBuilder<FileUploadPipeline>();
            var pipeline = typeAPipelineBuilder.
                SetUploadClient(fileUploadClient).
                SetDownloadClient(fileDownloadClient).
                SetSearchApiClient(searchApiClient).
                SetStoreApiClient(storeApiClient).
                Build();
            FileUploadStrategyB strategy =
                                          new FileUploadStrategyB(pipeline);
            return BuildExceptionHandlingPipeline(pipeline, strategy);
        }
        public static AbstractPipeline<IIoTEventData>
          BuildIoTPipeline(ICommunicationClient<IoTData, string> apiClient)
        {
            var typeCPipelineBuilder =
                                      new IoTPipelineBuilder<IoTPipeline>();
            var pipeline = typeCPipelineBuilder.
                SetTargetApiClient(apiClient).
                Build();
```

```
            IoTStrategy strategy = new IoTStrategy(pipeline);
            return BuildExceptionHandlingPipeline(pipeline, strategy);
        }
        private static AbstractPipeline<T>
                    BuildExceptionHandlingPipeline<T>(AbstractPipeline<T>
                                                            internalPipeline,
            IStrategy<T> processingStrategy) where T : IBasicEvent
        {
            var exceptionPipelineBuilder =
    new ExceptionHandlingPipelineBuilder<ExceptionHandlingPipeline<T>, T>();
            return exceptionPipelineBuilder.
                SetLoggingClient(GetFileLogger()).
                SetInternalPipeline(internalPipeline).
                SetProcessingStrategy(processingStrategy).
                Build();
        }
        private static ILoggingDestination GetFileLogger()
        {
            var fileLogger = new DashboardLogger();
            return new DateLoggingDecorator(
                        new LoggingDestinationDecorator(fileLogger));
        }
}
```

PipelineCreationFacade knows how to configure concrete pipeline and passes it to the **BuildExceptionHandlingPipeline** method.

Some supporting changes were added. We have changed **FactoryCreator**:

```
public static class FactoryCreator
{
        private static AbstractFactory<IIoTEventData> iotFactory;
        private static AbstractFactory<IUploadEventData> fileUploadFactory;
        static FactoryCreator()
        {
            iotFactory = new IoTFactory();
            fileUploadFactory = new FileUploadFactory();
}
public static void Execute(BasicEvent basicEvent)
```

```
        {
            switch (basicEvent.Source)
            {
                case Constants.IOT_EVENT_SOURCE:
                    {
                        iotFactory.GetPipeline(basicEvent).
                             ProcessEvent(basicEvent as BaseIoTEvent);
                        break;
                    }
                case Constants.FILE_EVENT_SOURCE:
                    {
                        fileUploadFactory.GetPipeline(basicEvent).
                          ProcessEvent(basicEvent as IUploadEventData);
                        break;
                    }
                case Constants.REPORT_EVENT_SOURCE:
                    {
                        fileUploadFactory.GetPipeline(basicEvent).
                          ProcessEvent(basicEvent as IUploadEventData);
                        iotFactory.GetPipeline(basicEvent).
                             ProcessEvent(basicEvent as IIoTEventData);
                        break;
                    }
                default:
                    throw new NotImplementedException($"Scenario for
                          {basicEvent.Source} is not implemented");
            }
        }
}
```

We have removed **ReportFactory** as it is not required anymore and added two pipelines execution in the **"REPORT"** case instead.

To support this, we added new cases to **FileUploadFactory**:

```
public class FileUploadFactory: AbstractFactory<IUploadEventData>
{
    public override AbstractPipeline<IUploadEventData> GetPipeline(BasicEvent
            basicEvent)
        {
            return basicEvent.Type switch
```

```
            {
            Constants.A_EVENT_TYPE => PipelineDirector.BuildTypeAPipeline(),
            Constants.B_EVENT_TYPE => PipelineDirector.BuildTypeBPipeline(),
            Constants.R_EVENT_TYPE => PipelineDirector.BuildTypeBPipeline(),
                _ => throw new NotImplementedException()
            };      }
}
```

And IoTFactory

```
public class IoTFactory: AbstractFactory<IIoTEventData>
{
    public override AbstractPipeline<IIoTEventData> GetPipeline(BasicEvent
                                                                basicEvent)
     {
            return basicEvent.Type switch
            {
            Constants.C_EVENT_TYPE => PipelineDirector.BuildTypeCPipeline(),
            Constants.R_EVENT_TYPE => PipelineDirector.BuildTypeCPipeline(),
                _ => throw new NotImplementedException()
            };
     }
}
```

The event of Type **"TypeR"** returns concrete pipelines, which we are using to process the **ReportEvent** instance.

The result of execution looks the same as in the preceding chapter, see the following *Figure 6.6*:

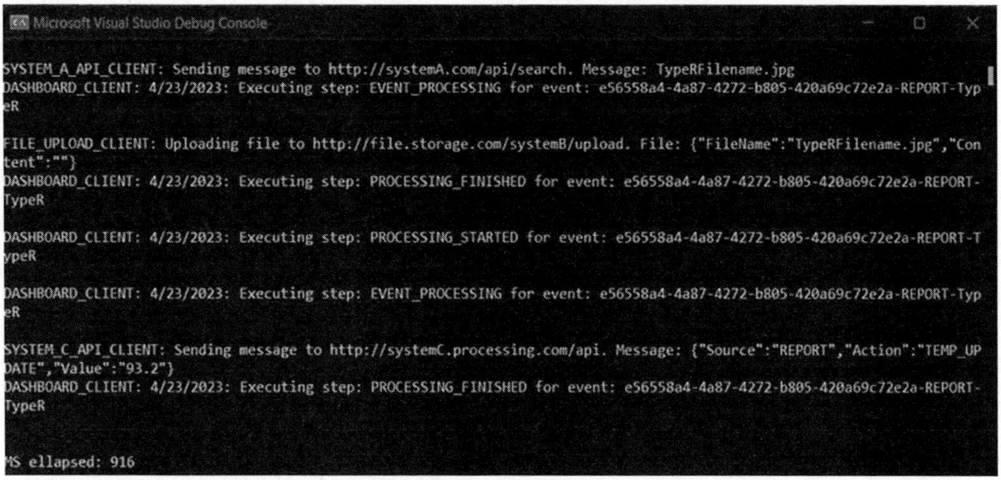

```
Microsoft Visual Studio Debug Console

SYSTEM_A_API_CLIENT: Sending message to http://systemA.com/api/search. Message: TypeRFilename.jpg
DASHBOARD_CLIENT: 4/23/2023: Executing step: EVENT_PROCESSING for event: e56558a4-4a87-4272-b805-420a69c72e2a-REPORT-Typ
eR

FILE_UPLOAD_CLIENT: Uploading file to http://file.storage.com/systemB/upload. File: {"FileName":"TypeRFilename.jpg","Con
tent":""}
DASHBOARD_CLIENT: 4/23/2023: Executing step: PROCESSING_FINISHED for event: e56558a4-4a87-4272-b805-420a69c72e2a-REPORT-
TypeR

DASHBOARD_CLIENT: 4/23/2023: Executing step: PROCESSING_STARTED for event: e56558a4-4a87-4272-b805-420a69c72e2a-REPORT-T
ypeR

DASHBOARD_CLIENT: 4/23/2023: Executing step: EVENT_PROCESSING for event: e56558a4-4a87-4272-b805-420a69c72e2a-REPORT-Typ
eR

SYSTEM_C_API_CLIENT: Sending message to http://systemC.processing.com/api. Message: {"Source":"REPORT","Action":"TEMP_UP
DATE","Value":"93.2"}
DASHBOARD_CLIENT: 4/23/2023: Executing step: PROCESSING_FINISHED for event: e56558a4-4a87-4272-b805-420a69c72e2a-REPORT-
TypeR

MS ellapsed: 916
```

Figure 6.6: *Result of execution*

Strategy design pattern provides an opportunity to customize a generalized algorithm. In our case, we have used the strategy design pattern to customize our general pipeline processing procedure, which we have defined in the **`AbstractPipeline`** class. It provides the possibility to switch algorithms in real-time or at startup time using configuration, input parameters, and, in our case, message properties. For example, we can take insurance premium calculation: there are a lot of components that should be calculated based on person and car properties. Each of these components can vary and could be taken based on configuration.

In the next section of this chapter, we will continue to modularize the event processing pipeline.

Chain of responsibility

The chain of responsibility design pattern is a behavioral design pattern. It allows you to pass messages through a chain of handlers. We need it to modularize our processing pipeline. Each method call can be treated like an action resided in its own class. It implies that the configuration of a specific processing pipeline can be done in real time by creating a chain of specific methods which should participate in event processing.

Modularizing the pipeline

The design of such a chain of responsibility will look as shown in *Figure 6.7*:

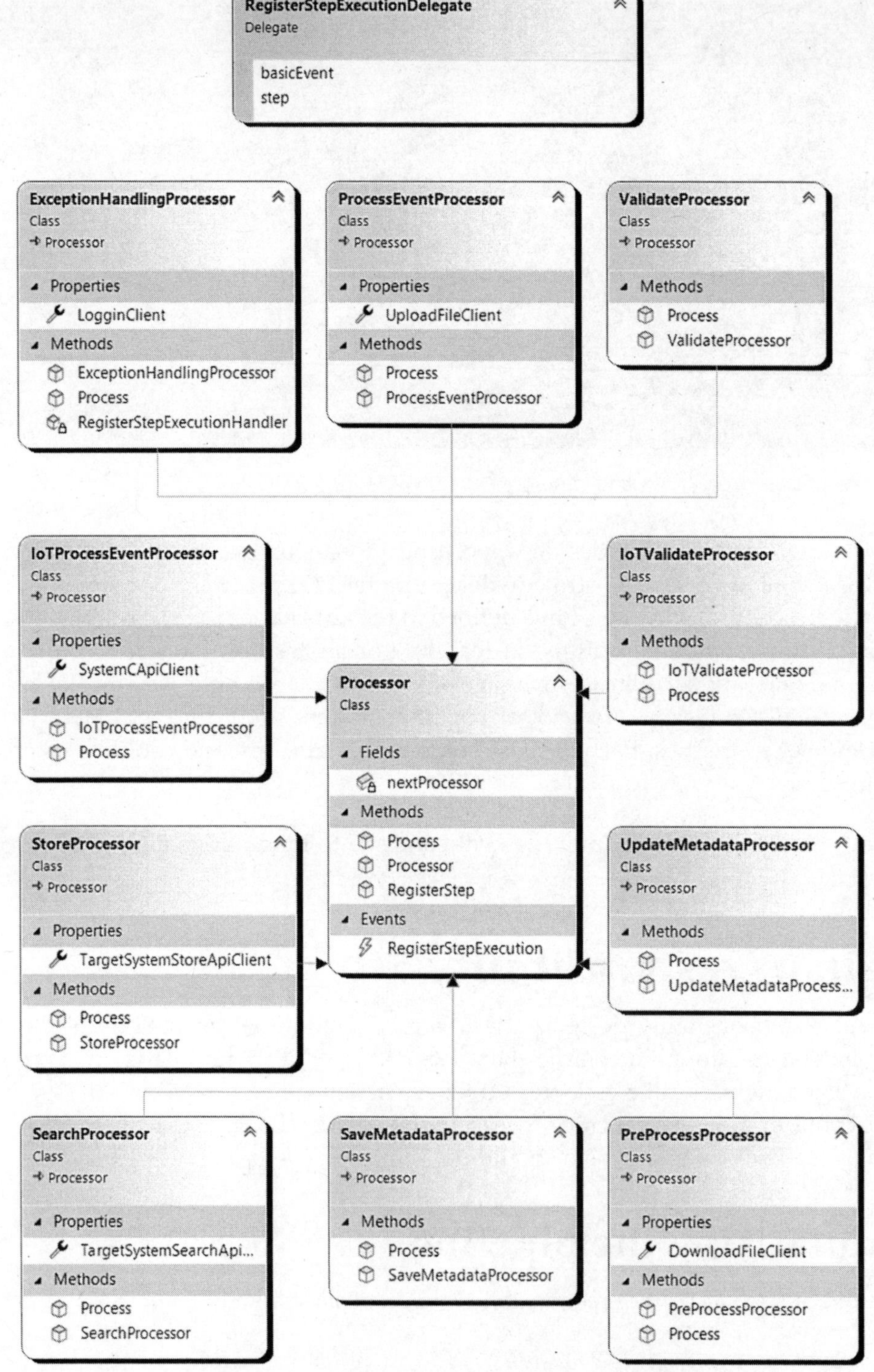

Figure 6.7: Chain of responsibility design pattern diagram

In this figure, we can see that we should create one **Processor** class, which will be the base class for all derived processors and a bunch of concrete processors.

In the next *Figure 6.7(a)*, you will see the left part of *Figure 6.7* with concrete processors classes:

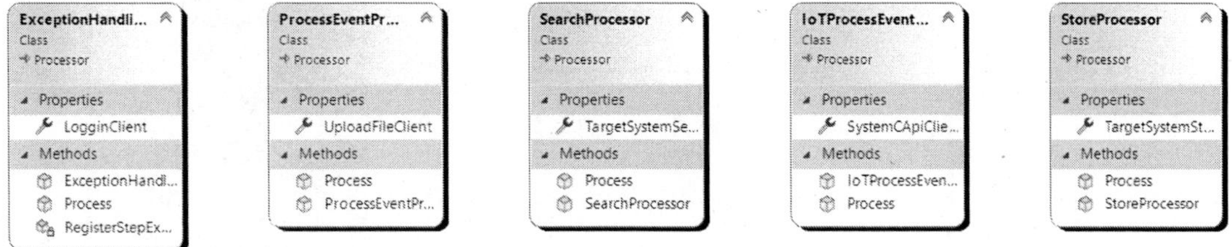

Figure 6.7(a): *Chain of responsibility design pattern diagram. Concrete processors. Part 1*

And *Figure 6.7(b)* will demonstrate the right part of the *Figure 6.7*:

Figure 6.7(b): *Chain of responsibility design pattern diagram. Concrete processors. Part 2*

Also, we have moved the **RegisterStep** functionality to this **Processor**.

Let us see what we have removed, look at *Figure 6.8*:

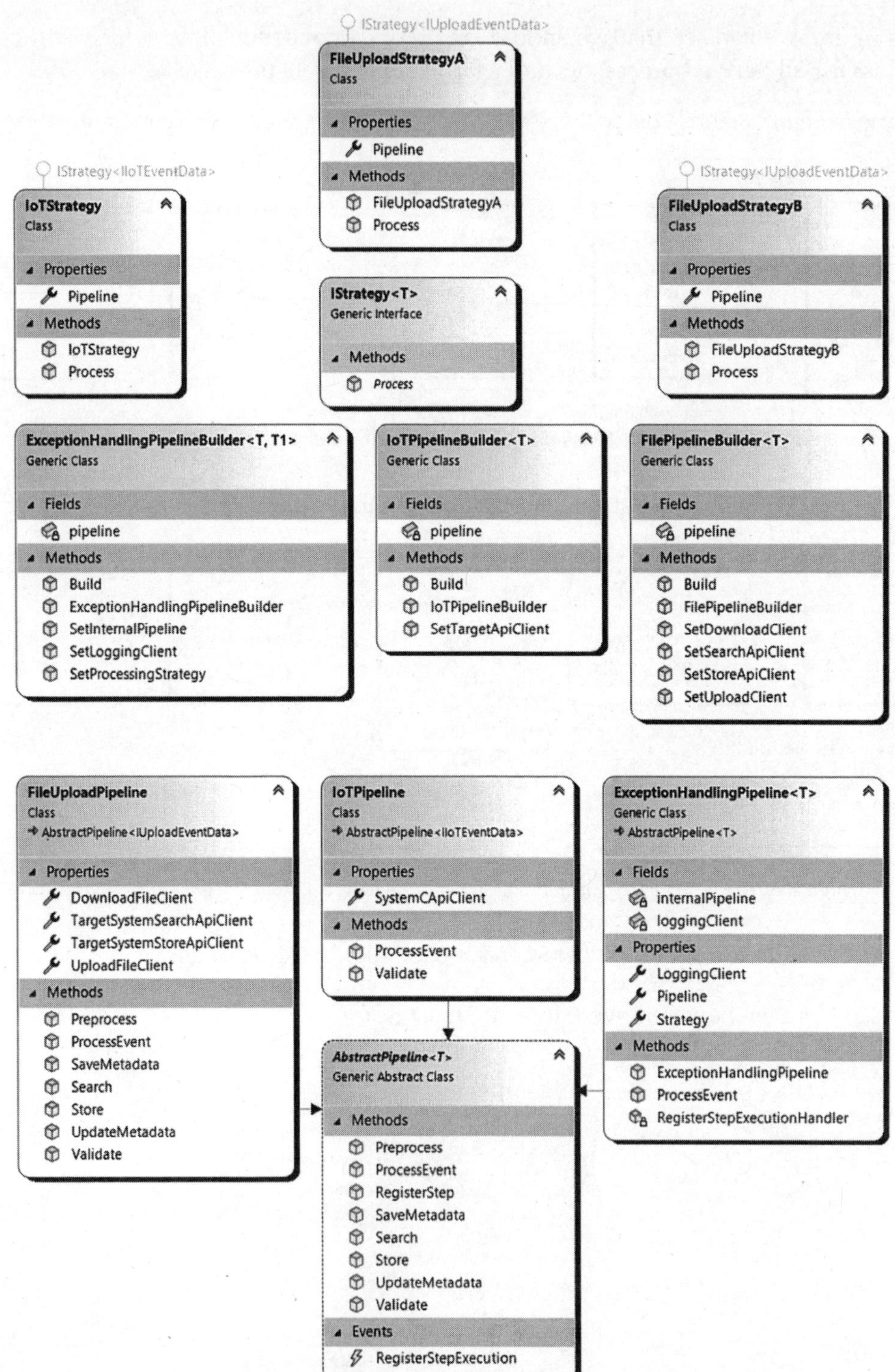

Figure 6.8: Removed classes diagram

All these classes should be removed from the project.

We also need to change **PipelineDirector** and **Factories** to work with **Processor** instances instead of **AbstractPipeline** derived classes.

Code

Let us start with the **Processor** class:

```
public class Processor
{
        private Processor nextProcessor;
        public event RegisterStepExecutionDelegate RegisterStepExecution;
        public Processor(Processor nextProcessor)
        {
            this.nextProcessor = nextProcessor;
        }
        public virtual void RegisterStep(IBasicEvent basicEvent, string step)
        {
            if (this.RegisterStepExecution != null)
                this.RegisterStepExecution(basicEvent, step);
        }
        public virtual void Process(IBasicEvent request)
        {
            if (this.nextProcessor != null)
                this.nextProcessor.Process(request);
        }
}
```

Processor has very limited functionality on its own. It accepts an internal processor as an input parameter and provides the possibility to log steps with a preconfigured logger. It also executes **Process** function of the passed **Processor** instance.

The next one is **ExceptionHandlingProcessor**. It provides the same capabilities as **ExceptionHandlingPipeline** before:

```
public class ExceptionHandlingProcessor : Processor
{
        public Logger LogginClient { get; set; }
        public ExceptionHandlingProcessor(Processor nextProcessor, Logger
```

```
                              loggingClient) : base(nextProcessor)
{
    this.RegisterStepExecution += RegisterStepExecutionHandler;
nextProcessor.RegisterStepExecution += RegisterStepExecutionHandler;
    this.LogginClient = loggingClient;
    this.LogginClient.StartSession(Guid.NewGuid());
}
public override void Process(IBasicEvent basicEvent)
{
    try
    {
        this.RegisterStep(basicEvent, "PROCESSING_STARTED");
        base.Process(basicEvent);
        this.RegisterStep(basicEvent, "PROCESSING_FINISHED");
    }
    catch (gRpcCommunicationException)
    {
        this.RegisterStep(basicEvent, "PROCESSING_FAILED");
        Console.WriteLine("gRpc communication error received");
    }
    catch (HttpCommunicationException)
    {
        this.RegisterStep(basicEvent, "PROCESSING_FAILED");
        Console.WriteLine("Http communication error received");
    }
    catch (FileCommunicationException)
    {
        this.RegisterStep(basicEvent, "PROCESSING_FAILED");
        Console.WriteLine("File communication error received");
    }
    catch (PipelineProcessingException)
    {
        this.RegisterStep(basicEvent, "PROCESSING_FAILED");
        Console.WriteLine("Pipeline business error received");
    }
```

```
            finally
            {
                this.LogginClient.EndSession();
            }
        }
          private void RegisterStepExecutionHandler(IBasicEvent basicEvent,
                                                          string step)
        {
             var message = $"Executing step: {step} for event: {basicEvent.
                         Id}-{basicEvent.Source}-{basicEvent.Type}";
            this.LogginClient.Log(message);
        }
}
```

It executes **base.Process** method, which in turn executes internal processor function **Process**.

Then we can review each of the **Processors**, but let us limit it to one because all of them have the same structure and similar functionality:

```
public class IoTProcessEventProcessor : Processor
{
        public ICommunicationClient<IoTData, string> SystemCApiClient
                                                        { get; set; }
        public IoTProcessEventProcessor(Processor nextProcessor,
       ICommunicationClient<IoTData, string> client) : base(nextProcessor)
        {
            this.SystemCApiClient = client;
        }
        public override void Process(IBasicEvent request)
        {
            if (this.SystemCApiClient == null)
                return;
            var uploadData = request as IIoTEventData;
            if (uploadData == null)
                throw new ArgumentException(nameof(request));
            this.RegisterStep(request, "EVENT_PROCESSING");
              var data = new IoTData(uploadData.Source, uploadData.Action,
```

```
                                                   uploadData.Value);
            this.SystemCApiClient.ExecuteRequest(data);
            base.Process(request);
        }
}
```

As you may recall, each step could have its own **ICommunicationClient** instance, so **Processor** can also have such an instance that it executes in the **Process** function. It executes the **RegisterStep** functionality in the same way as in preceding chapters.

It is time to look at **Factories**:

```
public abstract class AbstractFactory<T> where T: IBasicEvent
{
        public abstract Processor GetPipeline(BasicEvent basicEvent);
}
```

AbstractFactory GetPipeline method has changed its signature. Now it should return **Processor** instance:

```
public class IoTFactory: AbstractFactory<IIoTEventData>
{
        public override Processor GetPipeline(BasicEvent basicEvent)
        {
            return basicEvent.Type switch
            {
            Constants.C_EVENT_TYPE => PipelineDirector.BuildTypeCPipeline(),
            Constants.R_EVENT_TYPE => PipelineDirector.BuildTypeCPipeline(),
                _ => throw new NotImplementedException()
            };
        }
}
public class FileUploadFactory: AbstractFactory<IUploadEventData>
{
        public override Processor GetPipeline(BasicEvent basicEvent)
        {
            return basicEvent.Type switch
            {
            Constants.A_EVENT_TYPE => PipelineDirector.BuildTypeAPipeline(),
```

```
            Constants.B_EVENT_TYPE => PipelineDirector.BuildTypeBPipeline(),
            Constants.R_EVENT_TYPE => PipelineDirector.BuildTypeBPipeline(),
                _ => throw new NotImplementedException()
            };
    }
}
```

Our concrete factories now return Processor instances. Also, we still have **TypeR** type of event for composite event processing. The **PipelineDirector** looks like this after changes we have made:

```
public static class PipelineDirector
{
        private static Configuration config = Configuration.Instance;
        private static SystemAApiClient systemASearchClient =
                                    new (config.ASystemSearchApi);
        private static SystemAApiClient systemAStoreClient =
                                    new (config.ASystemStoreApi);
        private static FileUploadClient fileUploadAClient =
                                    new (config.ASystemUploadUrl);
        private static FileUploadClient fileUploadBClient =
                                    new (config.BSystemUploadUrl);
        private static FileDownloadClient fileDownloadClient = new ();
        private static SystemCApiClient systemCApiClient =
                                    new (config.CSystemApi);
        private static DashboardNotificationClient dashboardClient =
                                    new(config.DashboardLoggingUrl);

        public static Processor BuildTypeAPipeline()
        {
            return PipelineCreationFacade.
                    BuildFileUploadPipelineA(fileUploadAClient,
                    fileDownloadClient, systemASearchClient,
                    systemAStoreClient);
        }
        public static Processor BuildTypeBPipeline()
        {
            return PipelineCreationFacade.
             BuildFileUploadPipelineB(fileUploadBClient, fileDownloadClient,
             systemASearchClient, null);
        }
```

```
        public static Processor BuildTypeCPipeline()
        {
            return PipelineCreationFacade.BuildIoTPipeline(systemCApiClient);
        }
}
```

PipelineDirector returns **Processor** instances and uses the same **PipelineCreationFacade** to make them.

And the most interesting part is **PipelineCreationFacade**. Now it looks like this:

```
public static class PipelineCreationFacade
{
        public static ProcessorBuildFileUploadPipelineA(
            ICommunicationClient<UploadFileInfo, int> fileUploadClient,
            ICommunicationClient<string, byte[]> fileDownloadClient,
            ICommunicationClient<string, string> searchApiClient,
            ICommunicationClient<string, string> storeApiClient
            )
        {
            Processor proc = new ExceptionHandlingProcessor(
            new SaveMetadataProcessor(
                new ValidateProcessor(
                    new PreProcessProcessor(
                        new SearchProcessor(
                            new ProcessEventProcessor(
                            new StoreProcessor(
                            new UpdateMetadataProcessor(null),
                            storeApiClient),
                            fileUploadClient),searchApiClient),
                            fileDownloadClient))),
                            GetFileLogger());
            return proc;
}
public static Processor BuildFileUploadPipelineB(
      ICommunicationClient<UploadFileInfo, int> fileUploadClient,
      ICommunicationClient<string, byte[]> fileDownloadClient,
      ICommunicationClient<string, string> searchApiClient,
      ICommunicationClient<string, string> storeApiClient
    )
{
```

```
            Processor proc = new ExceptionHandlingProcessor
             (new ValidateProcessor(
                new PreProcessProcessor(
                   new SearchProcessor(
                      new ProcessEventProcessor(
                      null, fileUploadClient),searchApiClient),
                      fileDownloadClient)), GetFileLogger());
      return proc;
}
public static Processor BuildIoTPipeline(
             ICommunicationClient<IoTData, string> apiClient)
{
     Processor processor = new ExceptionHandlingProcessor(
          new SaveMetadataProcessor(
                new IoTValidateProcessor(
                      new IoTProcessEventProcessor(
                            new UpdateMetadataProcessor(null),
                      apiClient))), GetFileLogger());
          return processor;
        }
        private static Logger GetFileLogger()
        {
            var fileLogger = new FileLogger();
                return new Logger(LoggingDestinationDecorator(fileLogger));
        }
}
```

Each public method creates a chain of specific processors to process incoming events. This chain is wrapped into the **ExceptionHandlingProcessor** instance, which handles all things related to logging and exception handling.

In the result of code execution, we will receive the same picture as in the preceding chapters, see *Figure 6.9*:

```
SYSTEM_A_API_CLIENT: Sending message to http://systemA.com/api/search. Message: TypeBFilename.jpg
FILE_UPLOAD_CLIENT: Uploading file to http://file.storage.com/systemB/upload. File: {"FileName":"TypeBFilename.jpg","Con
tent":""}

DOWNLOAD_CLIENT: Downloading file from  http://typeB.file.url.
SYSTEM_A_API_CLIENT: Sending message to http://systemA.com/api/search. Message: TypeB2Filename.jpg
FILE_UPLOAD_CLIENT: Uploading file to http://file.storage.com/systemB/upload. File: {"FileName":"TypeB2Filename.jpg","Co
ntent":""}

SYSTEM_C_API_CLIENT: Sending message to http://systemC.processing.com/api. Message: {"Source":"IOT","Action":"TEMP_UPDAT
E","Value":"92.2"}

SYSTEM_C_API_CLIENT: Sending message to http://systemC.processing.com/api. Message: {"Source":"IOT","Action":"TEMP_UPDAT
E","Value":"92.2"}

SYSTEM_C_API_CLIENT: Sending message to http://systemC.processing.com/api. Message: {"Source":"IOT","Action":"TEMP_UPDAT
E","Value":"92.2"}

DOWNLOAD_CLIENT: Downloading file from  http://typeR.file.url.
SYSTEM_A_API_CLIENT: Sending message to http://systemA.com/api/search. Message: TypeRFilename.jpg
FILE_UPLOAD_CLIENT: Uploading file to http://file.storage.com/systemB/upload. File: {"FileName":"TypeRFilename.jpg","Con
tent":""}
SYSTEM_C_API_CLIENT: Sending message to http://systemC.processing.com/api. Message: {"Source":"REPORT","Action":"TEMP_UP
DATE","Value":"93.2"}

MS ellapsed: 866
```

***Figure 6.9:** Result of execution in console*

Logs are also generated. Refer to the following *Figure 6.10*:

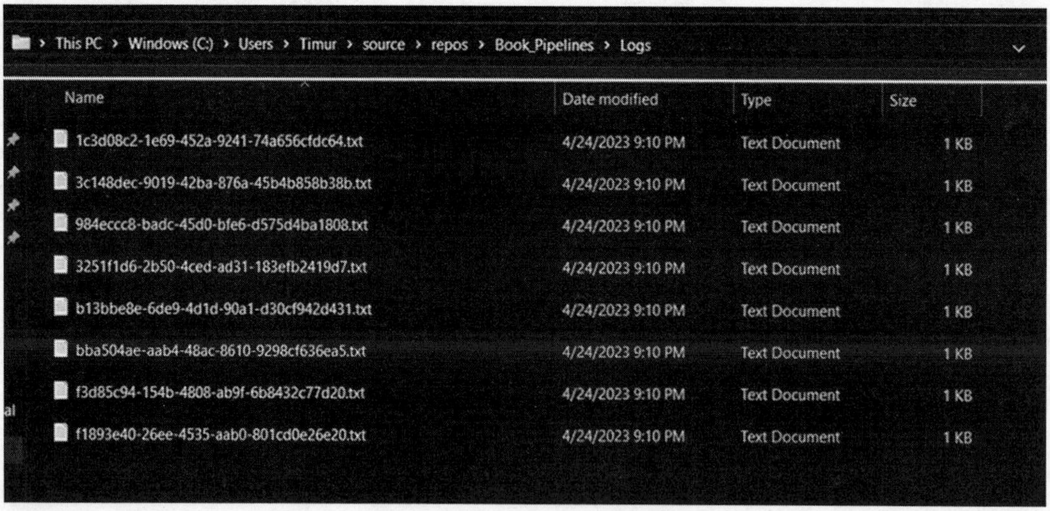

This PC › Windows (C:) › Users › Timur › source › repos › Book_Pipelines › Logs

Name	Date modified	Type	Size
1c3d08c2-1e69-452a-9241-74a656cfdc64.txt	4/24/2023 9:10 PM	Text Document	1 KB
3c148dec-9019-42ba-876a-45b4b858b38b.txt	4/24/2023 9:10 PM	Text Document	1 KB
984eccc8-badc-45d0-bfe6-d575d4ba1808.txt	4/24/2023 9:10 PM	Text Document	1 KB
3251f1d6-2b50-4ced-ad31-183efb2419d7.txt	4/24/2023 9:10 PM	Text Document	1 KB
b13bbe8e-6de9-4d1d-90a1-d30cf942d431.txt	4/24/2023 9:10 PM	Text Document	1 KB
bba504ae-aab4-48ac-8610-9298cf636ea5.txt	4/24/2023 9:10 PM	Text Document	1 KB
f3d85c94-154b-4808-ab9f-6b8432c77d20.txt	4/24/2023 9:10 PM	Text Document	1 KB
f1893e40-26ee-4535-aab0-801cd0e26e20.txt	4/24/2023 9:10 PM	Text Document	1 KB

***Figure 6.10:** Logs of execution*

This behavioral design pattern provides the opportunity to decouple your actions from each other. Every action can be separated from others, has a unique configuration, and provides unique functionality. In large systems, it always seems like a positive aspect until you need to add some generalized functionality. There are always some exceptions, special cases, and nuances that can ruin your architecture.

There are some nuances with functions which return values that are needed further. It is a standard case for a pipeline. It can be solved easily by creating a special context class, which will be initialized before chain execution and is passed to all chain members as an input parameter of the **`Process`** function. Then, you can set your return value to this context's property and use it later in another action.

Synergy of the patterns

In this chapter, we will not need any Design or Code sections as we have rewritten the same functionality step-by-step, displaying different capabilities of different design patterns, which could help you manage your class hierarchy more easily.

Conclusion

Template method design pattern is very good at unification; however, problems arise when you have a lot of special and corner cases. All that should be placed in one function, and all conditions should be there, too.

Strategy design pattern provides you with the possibility to separate each strategy into a class and configure how it should work independently from other strategies. It still has some limitations because each strategy is based on the contract that the base class of pipeline provides. In this case, we are moving outside the logic of calling generalized methods.

Most of the modularity is achieved by using the chain of responsibility design pattern. Each action resides in its class and is separated from others. You do not need to have a generalized class that has some common functionality. Create a class for your action and include it in the responsible chain. You will get a clear, separate design that provides maximum independence from other classes.

In the next chapter, we will review the following behavioral design pattern: Observer, Visitor and State. Each of them is unique in their ability to gather information from objects and manage their data.

Join our book's Discord space

CHAPTER 7
Behavioral Design Patterns: Observer, Visitor, and State

Introduction

This chapter explores object behavioral design patterns using Observer, Visitor, and State.

These three patterns help in everyday work to gather information from underlying objects and manage them.

Structure

This chapter covers the following topics:

- Observer
  - o System notifications mechanism
  - o Code
- Visitor
  - o Collecting processing information
  - o Code
- State
  - o Designing stateful system
  - o Code

- Synergy of the patterns

Objectives

At the end of this chapter, you will be able to describe Observer, Visitor, and State design patterns and apply them to real-world problems.

Let us dive in!

Observer

The idea of the Observer design pattern is to be able to be notified when something happens in an object that you are interested in.

System notifications mechanism

We need to create a Publisher and Subscriber and adapt them to our current pipeline design.

Let us design it! Refer to the following *Figure 7.1*:

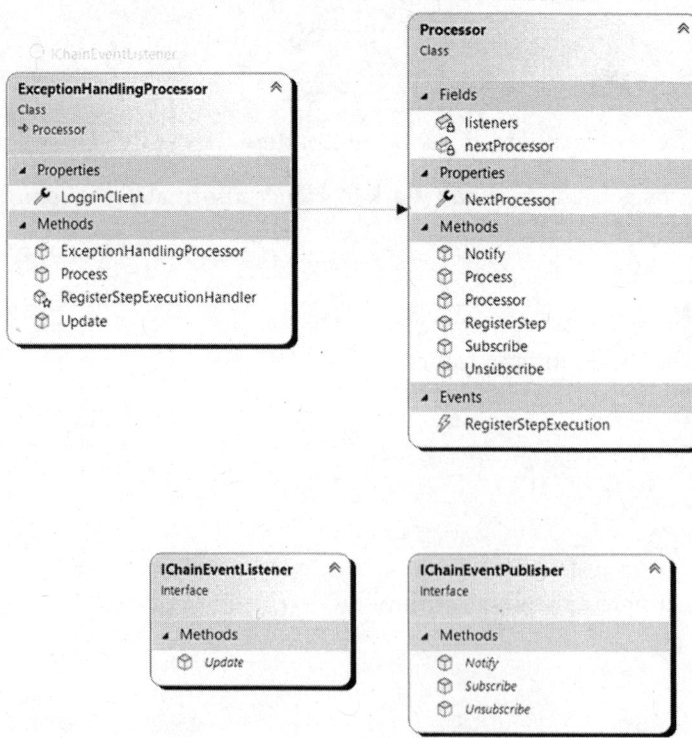

Figure 7.1: *Observer design pattern diagram*

IChainEventListener has only one method: **Update**. It is responsible for notifying subscribers about an event that has happened. **IChainEventPublisher** has more functionality with **Subscribe**, **Unsubscribe**, and **Notify** methods, which are responsible for subscribing to an event, unsubscribing, and notifying **IChainEventListeners** members about an event that has happened.

Code

The most simple and understandable entity is **IChainEventListener**. Let us look at the following code:

```
public interface IChainEventListener
{
        void Update(IBasicEvent basicEvennt, string message);
}
```

The single method accepts **IBasicEvent** and message string as parameters.

The second interface is **IChainEventPublisher**:

```
public interface IChainEventPublisher
{
        void Subscribe (IChainEventListener subscriber);
        void Unsubscribe (IChainEventListener subscriber);
        void Notify(IBasicEvent basicEvent, string message);
}
```

The names of the methods talk to itself:

```
public class Processor: IChainEventPublisher
{
   // Other functionality

        private List<IChainEventListener> listeners =
                                new List<IChainEventListener>();
        public Processor NextProcessor { get => nextProcessor; }

        public void Subscribe(IChainEventListener subscriber)
        {
            this.listeners.Add(subscriber);
        }

        public void Unsubscribe(IChainEventListener subscriber)
        {
            this.listeners.Remove(subscriber);
```

```
        }

        public void Notify(IBasicEvent basicEvent, string message)
        {
            this.listeners.ForEach(x =>
            {
                x.Update(basicEvent, message);
            });
        }
}
```

At this moment, the base **Processor** class implements the **IChainEventPublisher** interface. It provides an opportunity to **Subscribe** and to **Notify** subscribers about events happening:

```
public class ExceptionHandlingProcessor : Processor, IChainEventListener
{
        public Logger LogginClient { get; set; }

        public ExceptionHandlingProcessor(Processor nextProcessor,
                            Logger loggingClient) : base(nextProcessor)
        {
            this.RegisterStepExecution += RegisterStepExecutionHandler;
            var tmpProcess = nextProcessor;
            do
            {
                tmpProcess.Subscribe(this);
                tmpProcess = tmpProcess.NextProcessor;
            } while (tmpProcess.NextProcessor != null);

            this.LogginClient = loggingClient;
            this.LogginClient.StartSession(Guid.NewGuid());
        }

        protected void RegisterStepExecutionHandler(IBasicEvent basicEvent,
                                                    string step)
        {
            var message = $"Executing step: {step} for event: {basicEvent.
                        Id}-{basicEvent.Source}-{basicEvent.Type}";
```

```
            LogginClient.Log(message);
        }

        // Other functionality

        public void Update(IBasicEvent basicEvent, string message)
        {
            RegisterStepExecutionHandler(basicEvent, message);
        }
}
```

So, in *Chapter 6, Chain of responsibility* section, we made it slightly wrong. We specifically made one error that ruined our intent to log all messages. In this section, we will fix this error with the help of Observer design pattern.

In the constructor, we are going through all processors and subscribing to their events in the **`do while loop`**. In the **`Update`** function, which is derived from **`IChainEventListener`**, we are calling **`RegisterStepExecutionHandler`** function, which in turn uses **`LoggingClient`** to log messages. This **`LoggingClient`** is set by **`PipelineCreationFacade`**.

That is all the code we need to implement the **`Observer`** pattern.

In the result of execution, we will receive the following result for all pipelines:

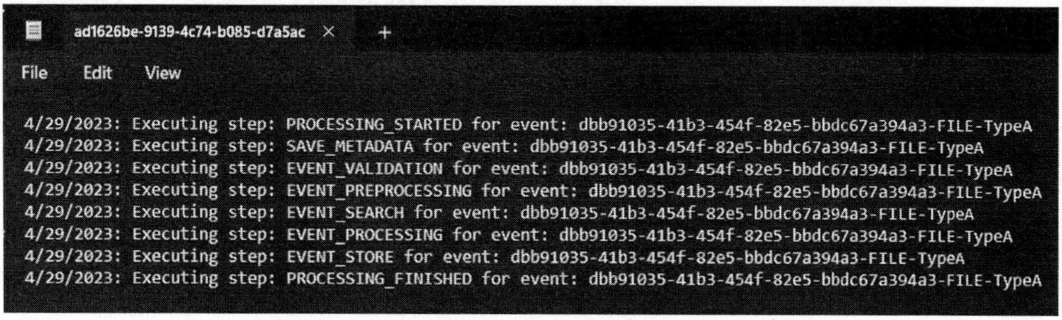

```
ad1626be-9139-4c74-b085-d7a5ac
File   Edit   View

4/29/2023: Executing step: PROCESSING_STARTED for event: dbb91035-41b3-454f-82e5-bbdc67a394a3-FILE-TypeA
4/29/2023: Executing step: SAVE_METADATA for event: dbb91035-41b3-454f-82e5-bbdc67a394a3-FILE-TypeA
4/29/2023: Executing step: EVENT_VALIDATION for event: dbb91035-41b3-454f-82e5-bbdc67a394a3-FILE-TypeA
4/29/2023: Executing step: EVENT_PREPROCESSING for event: dbb91035-41b3-454f-82e5-bbdc67a394a3-FILE-TypeA
4/29/2023: Executing step: EVENT_SEARCH for event: dbb91035-41b3-454f-82e5-bbdc67a394a3-FILE-TypeA
4/29/2023: Executing step: EVENT_PROCESSING for event: dbb91035-41b3-454f-82e5-bbdc67a394a3-FILE-TypeA
4/29/2023: Executing step: EVENT_STORE for event: dbb91035-41b3-454f-82e5-bbdc67a394a3-FILE-TypeA
4/29/2023: Executing step: PROCESSING_FINISHED for event: dbb91035-41b3-454f-82e5-bbdc67a394a3-FILE-TypeA
```

Figure 7.2: *Result of execution*

In this section, we have reviewed the classical implementation of the **`Observer`** pattern.

Earlier, we had implemented it modernly with the **`event`** concept that C# provides. If we were to make a comparison of these approaches, then C# does not require us to make a special interface for publishers and consumers. All it needs is a defined delegate for an event and event declaration with a supporting function to execute concrete events on request.

The declaration of the delegate itself looks like this:

```
public delegate void RegisterStepExecutionDelegate(IBasicEvent basicEvent,
string step);
```

Next, you need to define an event:

```
public event RegisterStepExecutionDelegate RegisterStepExecution;
```

And subscribe to it:

```
tmpProcess.RegisterStepExecution += RegisterStepExecutionHandler;
```

Then, you will need to define an execution function for an event:

```
public virtual void RegisterStep(IBasicEvent basicEvent, string step)
{
            if (RegisterStepExecution != null)
                RegisterStepExecution(basicEvent, step);
}
```

Call the execution function from the derived class:

```
RegisterStep(request, "EVENT_VALIDATION");
```

In this case, **Delegate** plays the role of a contract between the publisher and subscriber. **Event**, in turn, implements the functionality of a publisher. It allows subscribing, unsubscribing, and publishing information to event listeners.

Independently from implementation, this design pattern provides a unified approach to how event distribution is happening in modern OOP languages.

Visitor

Visitor is a behavioral design pattern that allows you to separate the algorithm from the objects over which it operates.

Collecting processing information

In our case, we want to gather processing information from each instance of **Processor** after the pipeline has been completed. To accomplish this, we need to add a new class called **ProcessorVisitor**, which will contain methods to gather information from each concrete class of **Processor** derived classes. Then, we need to extend the base **Processor** class with the new method **Accept(ProcesorVisitor visitor)** and override it in each derived class. **ExceptionHandlingProcessor** will be responsible for gathering the information. **PipelineCreationFacade** will inject the instance of **ProcessorVisitor** to a processing chain through the constructor of **ExceptionHandlingProcessor**.

Let us look at it in the following *Figure 7.3*:

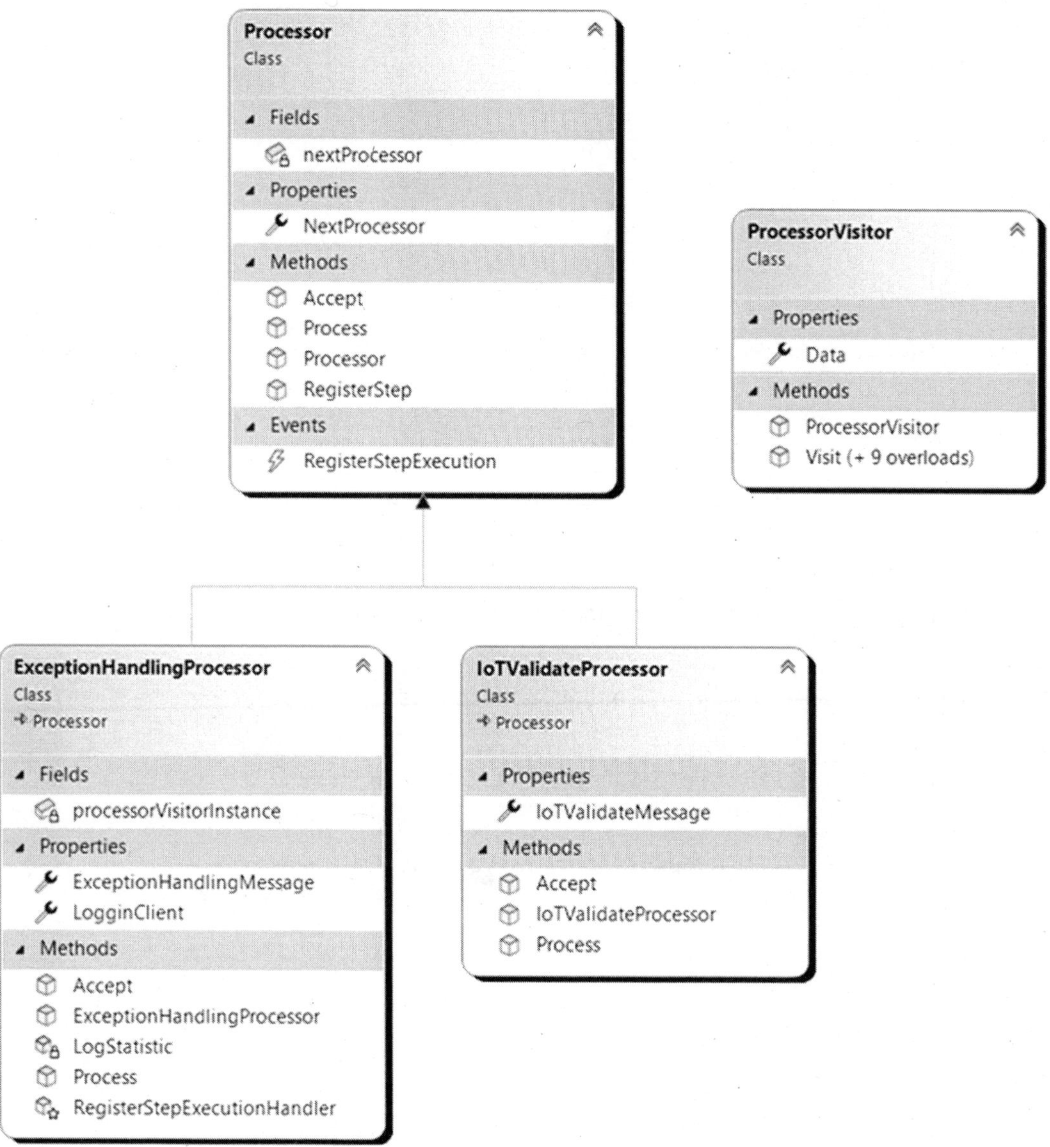

Figure 7.3: *Visitor design pattern diagram*

In this figure, you can see **ProcessorVisitor** class definition. **Data** property represents container for storing information collected from processors. The **Visit** method with nine overloads provides the functionality to collect needed information from specific **Processor**. As an example, we have added two processors to the figure: **ExceptionHandling** and **IoTValidate** processors. Each of them has **`Accept`** method which will be responsible for calling the appropriate **`ProcessorVisitor`** method.

Code

Let us start our code review by checking **ProcessorVisitor** code:

```
public class ProcessorVisitor
{
        public ProcessorVisitor()
        {
            this.Data = new List<string>();
        }

        public List<string> Data { get; set; }

        public void Visit(ExceptionHandlingProcessor processor)
        {
            this.Data.Add(processor.ExceptionHandlingMessage);
        }

        public void Visit(IoTProcessEventProcessor processor)
        {
            this.Data.Add(processor.IoTProcessEventMessage);
        }
        public void Visit(IoTValidateProcessor processor)
        {
            this.Data.Add(processor.IoTValidateMessage);
        }

        // Other 6 Visit functions
}
```

There is not much functionality. Each function is responsible for processing one concrete **Processor** type, and it simply copies to the **Data** property value of the string literal defined in this **Processor**. The name of this literal differs from **Processor** to **Processor** to imitate different information that we are collecting.

To call the **Visit** function on the **Processor**, we need some method which will call it. We have one in the **Processor** base class:

```
public class Processor
{
        private Processor nextProcessor;
        public Processor NextProcessor { get => nextProcessor; }

        public event RegisterStepExecutionDelegate RegisterStepExecution;

        public Processor(Processor nextProcessor)
        {
            this.nextProcessor = nextProcessor;
        }

        public virtual void RegisterStep(IBasicEvent basicEvent, string step)
        {
            if (RegisterStepExecution != null)
                RegisterStepExecution(basicEvent, step);
        }

        public virtual void Process(IBasicEvent request)
        {
            if (nextProcessor != null)
            {
                nextProcessor.Process(request);
            }
        }

        public virtual void Accept(ProcessorVisitor visitor)
        {
            if(nextProcessor != null)
            {
                nextProcessor.Accept(visitor);
            }
        }
}
```

The **`Accept`** method of the base class accepts **`ProcessVisitor`** as a parameter and passes it to nextProcessor's **`Accept`** method:

```
public class IoTValidateProcessor : Processor
{
        public string IoTValidateMessage { get { return "some special
                                        IoTValidateProccessor message"; } }
    public IoTValidateProcessor(Processor nextProcessor) : base(nextProcessor)
        {
        }
        public override void Accept(ProcessorVisitor visitor)
        {
            visitor.Visit(this);
            base.Accept(visitor);
        }
        public override void Process(IBasicEvent request)
        {
            RegisterStep(request, "EVENT_VALIDATION");
            var basicEvent = request as IIoTEventData;

            if (basicEvent.Action == null)
                throw new PipelineProcessingException("Action of the event
                                                        cannot be null");
            if (basicEvent.Value == null)
                throw new PipelineProcessingException("Value of the event
                                                        cannot be null");

            base.Process(request);
        }
}
```

Concrete **Processor** calls the **Visit** method of **ProcessorVisitor's** instance and passes itself as a parameter. After this, it calls the base **Accept** method, which calls the underlying nextProcessor's **Accept** method.

ExceptionHandlingProcessor is responsible for starting the execution of this chain after the processing pipeline is completed:

```
public class ExceptionHandlingProcessor : Processor
{
        private ProcessorVisitor processorVisitorInstance;
        public string ExceptionHandlingMessage { get { return "some special
                                ExceptionHandlingProccessor message"; } }
```

```
        public Logger LogginClient { get; set; }
        public ExceptionHandlingProcessor(Processor nextProcessor,
                    Logger loggingClient, ProcessorVisitor
                    processorVisitorInstance) : base(nextProcessor)
        {
            // other constructor stuff
            this.processorVisitorInstance = processorVisitorInstance;
        }
        // Other functionality
        private void LogStatistic()
        {
            string message = string.Join(Environment.NewLine,
                                     processorVisitorInstance.Data);
            LogginClient.Log(message);
        }
        public override void Accept(ProcessorVisitor visitor)
        {
            visitor.Visit(this);
            base.Accept(visitor);
        }
        public override void Process(IBasicEvent basicEvent)
        {
            try
            {
                RegisterStep(basicEvent, "PROCESSING_STARTED");
                base.Process(basicEvent);
                Accept(processorVisitorInstance);
                LogStatistic();
                RegisterStep(basicEvent, "PROCESSING_FINISHED");
            }
            // Catch blocks
            finally
            {
                LogginClient.EndSession();
            }
        }
}
```

As you can see, we have added **Accept** method, which is the same in all other **Processors**, and it calls this method after **base.Process()** method execution is completed in the **Process** method. It starts the execution of the chain of visits. Then we call the **LogStatistic** method, which passes **Data** property content to a **LoggingClient**.

ExceptionHandlingPipeline receives **ProcessorVisitor** instance through **constructor.** An instance of **ProcessorVisitor** is created and passed into **ExceptionHandlingPipeline** by **PipelineCreationFacade**:

```
public static Processor BuildIoTPipeline(
                        ICommunicationClient<IoTData, string> apiClient)
{
          Processor processor = new ExceptionHandlingProcessor(
           new SaveMetadataProcessor(
              new IoTValidateProcessor(
                  new IoTProcessEventProcessor(
                      new UpdateMetadataProcessor(null), apiClient))),
                    GetFileLogger(), new Chain.ProcessorVisitor());

          return processor;
      }
```

BuildIoTPipeline method is part of the **PipelineCreationFacade**, and as you can see, the last parameter for **ExceptionHandlingProcessor** is the **ProcessorVisitor** instance. For each instance of the processing chain, we are creating a new instance of the **ProcessorVisitor** class.

Let us execute the code and check the result. See the following *Figure 7.4*:

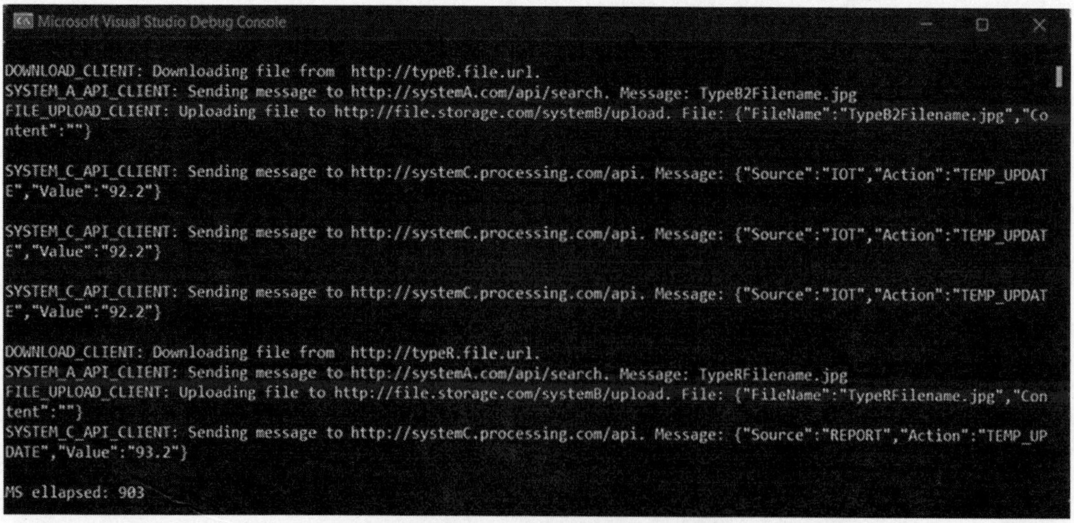

```
Microsoft Visual Studio Debug Console

DOWNLOAD_CLIENT: Downloading file from  http://typeB.file.url.
SYSTEM_A_API_CLIENT: Sending message to http://systemA.com/api/search. Message: TypeB2Filename.jpg
FILE_UPLOAD_CLIENT: Uploading file to http://file.storage.com/systemB/upload. File: {"FileName":"TypeB2Filename.jpg","Co
ntent":""}

SYSTEM_C_API_CLIENT: Sending message to http://systemC.processing.com/api. Message: {"Source":"IOT","Action":"TEMP_UPDAT
E","Value":"92.2"}

SYSTEM_C_API_CLIENT: Sending message to http://systemC.processing.com/api. Message: {"Source":"IOT","Action":"TEMP_UPDAT
E","Value":"92.2"}

SYSTEM_C_API_CLIENT: Sending message to http://systemC.processing.com/api. Message: {"Source":"IOT","Action":"TEMP_UPDAT
E","Value":"92.2"}

DOWNLOAD_CLIENT: Downloading file from  http://typeR.file.url.
SYSTEM_A_API_CLIENT: Sending message to http://systemA.com/api/search. Message: TypeRFilename.jpg
FILE_UPLOAD_CLIENT: Uploading file to http://file.storage.com/systemB/upload. File: {"FileName":"TypeRFilename.jpg","Con
tent":""}
SYSTEM_C_API_CLIENT: Sending message to http://systemC.processing.com/api. Message: {"Source":"REPORT","Action":"TEMP_UP
DATE","Value":"93.2"}

MS ellapsed: 903
```

Figure 7.4: *Visitor design pattern execution result*

The code execution result looks the same. Now, it takes some additional 30-40ms to execute the chain of visitors and put additional information into log. See the following *Figure 7.5*:

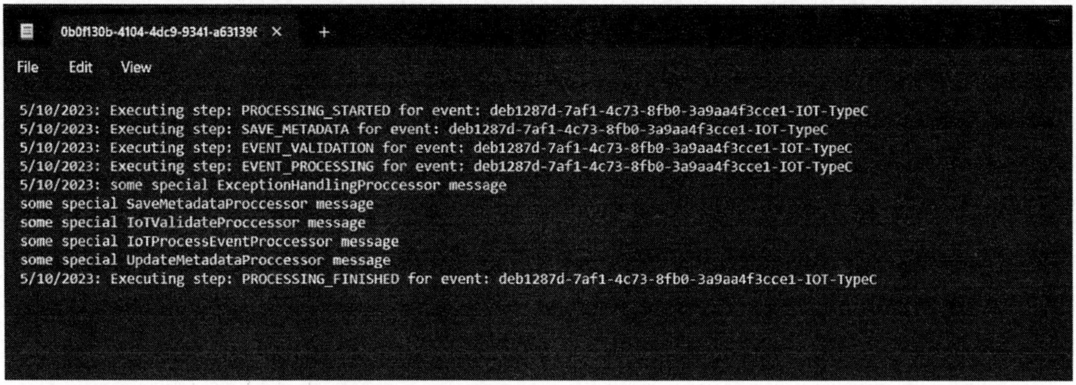

```
0b0f130b-4104-4dc9-9341-a63139(   ×   +
File   Edit   View

5/10/2023: Executing step: PROCESSING_STARTED for event: deb1287d-7af1-4c73-8fb0-3a9aa4f3cce1-IOT-TypeC
5/10/2023: Executing step: SAVE_METADATA for event: deb1287d-7af1-4c73-8fb0-3a9aa4f3cce1-IOT-TypeC
5/10/2023: Executing step: EVENT_VALIDATION for event: deb1287d-7af1-4c73-8fb0-3a9aa4f3cce1-IOT-TypeC
5/10/2023: Executing step: EVENT_PROCESSING for event: deb1287d-7af1-4c73-8fb0-3a9aa4f3cce1-IOT-TypeC
5/10/2023: some special ExceptionHandlingProccessor message
some special SaveMetadataProccessor message
some special IoTValidateProccessor message
some special IoTProcessEventProccessor message
some special UpdateMetadataProccessor message
5/10/2023: Executing step: PROCESSING_FINISHED for event: deb1287d-7af1-4c73-8fb0-3a9aa4f3cce1-IOT-TypeC
```

Figure 7.5: *Log result of Visitor design pattern*

This is how it looks in the new log file. At the bottom of the log, you can see one new message with data from each **`Processor`**.

Visitor design pattern provides you with an opportunity to decouple some part of functionality from your main classes. In our case, it is copying some information from processing classes. However, in other cases, it can be a much more complex part of functionality. Also, this design pattern could be applied when you cannot extend existing classes in any way (inheritance or class definition extension). You can use **`Extension Methods`** concept in C# to extend existing 3rd party classes. The usage of these functions will look like you are working with a native class itself. Then, you will not be required to create, initialize, and use additional service classes.

State

This design pattern allows you to structure your state machine in an OOP way instead of making a spaghetti code with switches and if/else statements.

Designing stateful system

Let us step back from pipelines and make an audio player to demonstrate the State design pattern principles.

In our example, we will design an audio player with play/stop, fast forwarding and rewind, and on/off functionality. Refer to the following *Figure 7.6*:

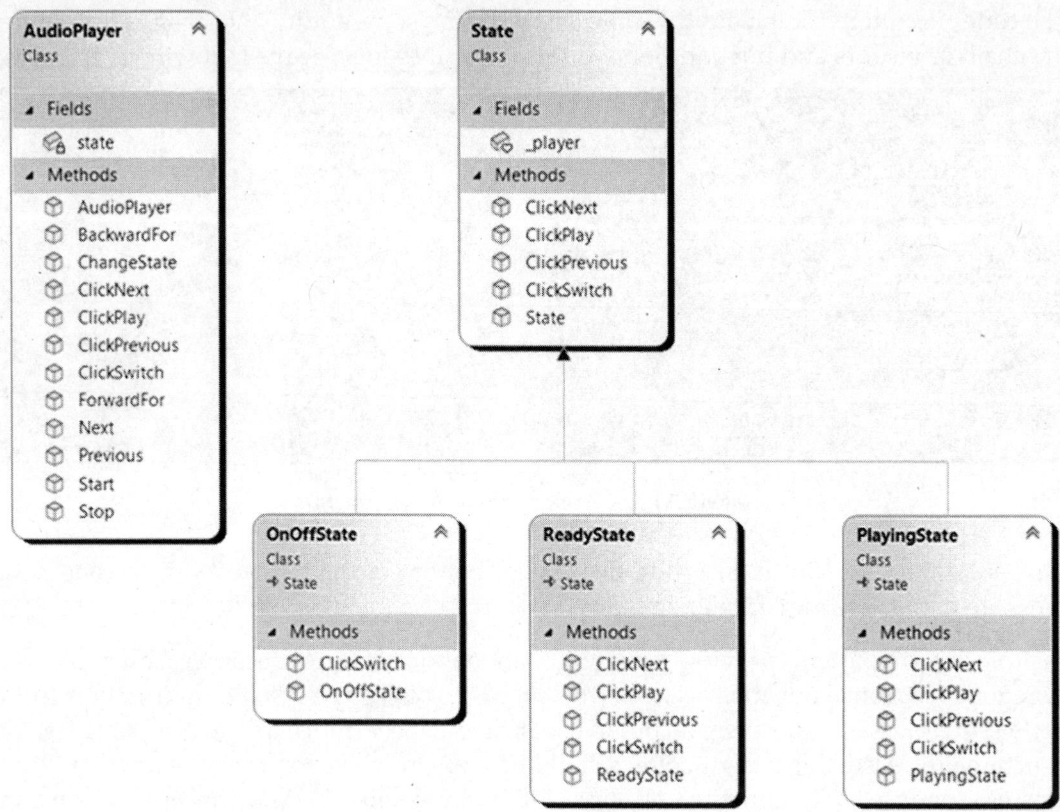

Figure 7.6: *State design pattern diagram*

In this figure, you can see that we have added the **AudioPlayer** class, which defines a set of functionality. Some of them, like **ClickNext, ClickPlay, ClickSwitch** are for controlling the player from the UI. Others, like **ForwardFor, Next, Previous, Start, Stop,** and **ChangeState** are for controlling the player from state.

We have defined one base **State** class, which defined the functionality needed to make a State Machine of AudioPlayer controller and three derived states to do concrete work.

Let us see how it works in code.

Code

We will start with the **AudioPlayer** code:

```
public class AudioPlayer
{
        private State state;
        public AudioPlayer()
```

```
        {
            this.state = new ReadyState(this);
        }
        public void  ChangeState(State state)
        {
            this.state = state;
        }
        public void ClickSwitch() => this.state.ClickSwitch();
        public void ClickPlay() => state.ClickPlay();
        public void ClickNext() => this.state.ClickNext();
        public void ClickPrevious() => state.ClickPrevious();
        public void Stop() => Console.WriteLine("Stopping...");
        public void ForwardFor(int sec) => Console.WriteLine($"Fast
                                          forwarding for {sec} sec");
          public void BackwardFor(int sec) => Console.WriteLine($"Rewinding
                                                 for {sec} sec");
        public void Start() => Console.WriteLine($"Starting playing");
       public void Next() => Console.WriteLine($"Switching to next record");
        public void Previous() => Console.WriteLine($"Switching to
                                                 previous record");
}
```

Functions are simple and are here to demonstrate the usage. As already mentioned, one part is for UI controlling code, and the second is used by **State** derived classes:

```
public class State
{
        internal AudioPlayer _player;
        public State(AudioPlayer player)
        {
            _player = player;
        }
        public virtual void ClickSwitch()
        {
        }
        public virtual void ClickPlay()
        {
        }
```

```
        public virtual void ClickNext()
        {
        }
        public virtual void ClickPrevious()
        {
        }
}
```

The next is **State** class, which defines the **State** derived classes functionality. This base class has no functionality and is neutral.

The following classes define the needed functionality for **AudioPlayer** controlling from **State** side:

```
public class OnOffState: State
{
        public OnOffState(AudioPlayer player): base(player)
        {
        }
        public override void ClickSwitch()
        {
            Console.WriteLine("Switching device ON");
            _player.ChangeState(new ReadyState(_player));
        }
}
```

OnOffState is responsible for managing switch functionality:

```
public class PlayingState: State
{
        public PlayingState(AudioPlayer player): base(player)
        {
        }

        public override void ClickSwitch()
        {
            Console.WriteLine("Switching device off");
            _player.ChangeState(new OnOffState(_player));
        }
```

```
        public override void ClickPlay()
        {
            _player.Stop();
            _player.ChangeState(new ReadyState(_player));
        }

        public override void ClickNext()
        {
            _player.ForwardFor(5);
        }

        public override void ClickPrevious()
        {
            _player.BackwardFor(5);
        }
}
```

`PlayingState` is responsible for managing the player when in Playing state:

```
public class ReadyState: State
{
        public ReadyState(AudioPlayer player): base(player)
        {
        }

        public override void ClickSwitch()
        {
            Console.WriteLine("Switching device off");
            _player.ChangeState(new OnOffState(_player));
        }

        public override void ClickPlay()
        {
            _player.Start();
            _player.ChangeState(new PlayingState(_player));
        }

        public override void ClickNext()
        {
```

```
            _player.Next();
        }

        public override void ClickPrevious()
        {
            _player.Previous();
        }
}
```

ReadyState is responsible for the player when it is switched on.

Some functions like **ClickPlay** in **ReadyState** change state and interact with a Player, while some interact with a Player like **ClickNext** and **ClickPrevious**.

All of them are somehow responsible for Player control and call specific functionality on the instance of Player.

To test it, we have made a simple piece of code:

```
AudioPlayer player = new AudioPlayer();
            player.ClickPlay();
            player.ClickNext();
            player.ClickSwitch();
            player.ClickSwitch();
            player.ClickNext();
            player.ClickPrevious();
            player.ClickPlay();
```

It gave us the following output, as shown in *Figure 7.7*:

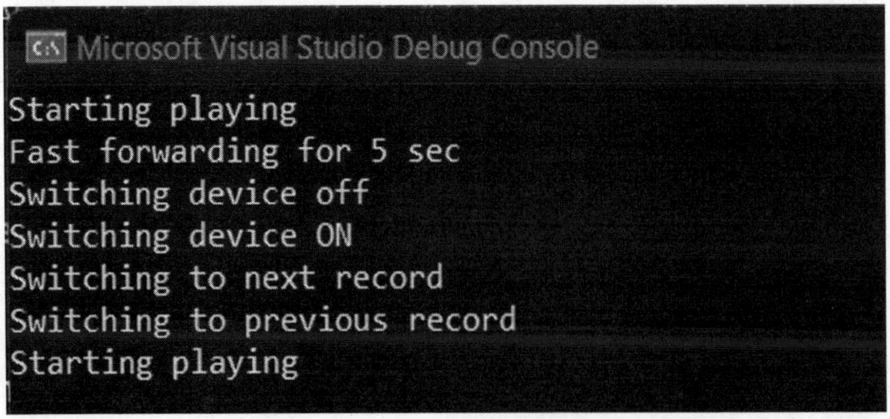

```
Microsoft Visual Studio Debug Console
Starting playing
Fast forwarding for 5 sec
Switching device off
Switching device ON
Switching to next record
Switching to previous record
Starting playing
```

***Figure 7.7:** AudioPlayer execution result*

The State design pattern is very useful when making a controlling code for some devices. All your switches and if's could be easily distributed across `State` derived classes and provide you with a clear structure of possible states. Each `State` usually contains a few lines of code, which is easily manageable and maintainable. The only minus we have found is that it is not easy to build a graph of transitions. So, if you have many states, maybe you need to use some other solution to achieve your goals. For example, you can try to use the *State Machine* concept. In our solution, AudioPlayer was responsible for both tasks: getting input from UI and executing device commands. It could split into two parts with the help of Proxy, Adapter, or Facade design patterns.

Conclusion

In this chapter, we have applied State and Visitor design patterns to our pipelines to get structured processing loggers and to show how we can implement events with only OOP structures.

Visitor design pattern is used widely in tasks where developers need to build a structure from many objects. It can be serializers, compilers, etc.

The Observer design pattern is widely used in programming languages core as events concept implementation. Nowadays, most OOP languages have events as a mechanism that allows objects to be notified of activities happening in other objects. In UI development, it is a core concept allowing our program to know when a user tries to call an action using UI elements like buttons, text boxes, etc.

In the next chapter, we will start to explore behavioral design patterns. Command and Mediator design patterns will be the first design patterns we will review. With their help, we will show how the core of the processing engine can be transformed into a modular and independent system of connected classes.

Join our book's Discord space

Join the book's Discord Workspace for Latest updates, Offers, Tech happenings around the world, New Release and Sessions with the Authors:

https://discord.bpbonline.com

CHAPTER 8
Behavioral Design Patterns: Mediator and Command

Introduction

This chapter explores object behavioral design using Mediator and Command. These two design patterns help in everyday work to distribute and execute an action per request.

Structure

The chapter covers the following topics:

- Mediator
    - Making a communication bus
    - Code
- Command
    - Code

Objectives

At the end of this chapter, you will be able to describe Mediator and Command design patterns and apply them to real-world problems.

Let us dive in!

Mediator

The idea of the mediator design pattern is to provide a communication bus that will distribute messages across different objects in the system.

Making a communication bus

We will apply Mediator design pattern to our events processing pipelines.

Let us design it! Refer to the following *Figure 8.1*:

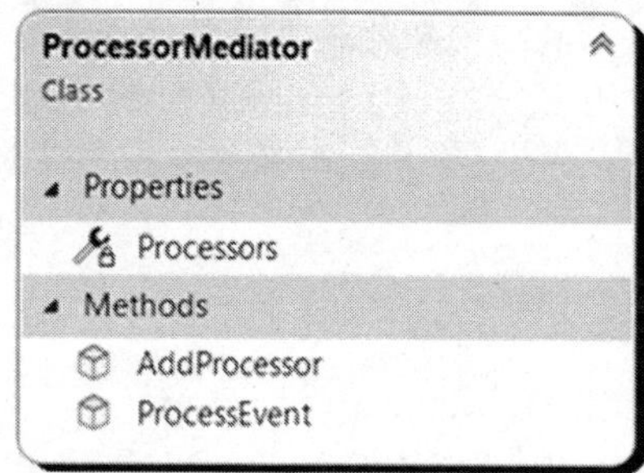

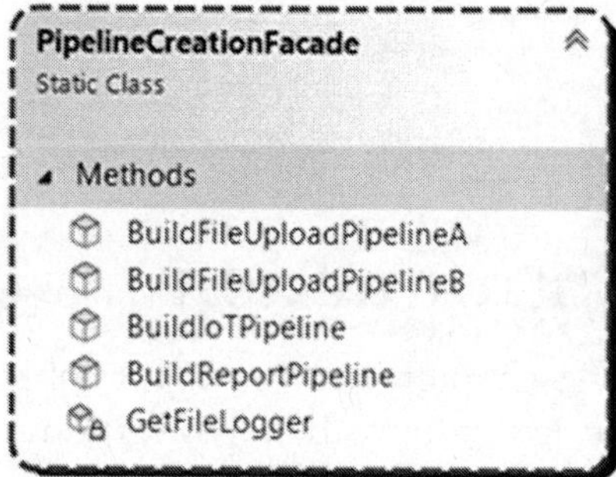

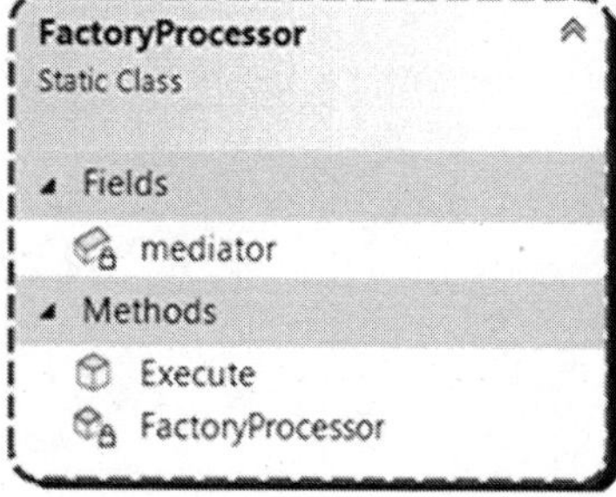

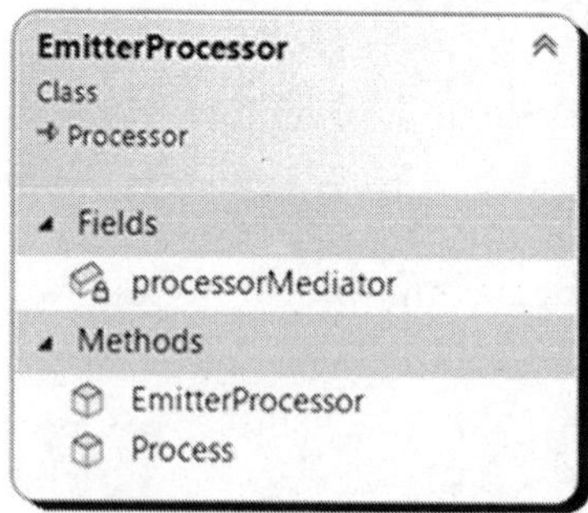

Figure 8.1: *Mediator design pattern diagram*

To apply Mediator design pattern, we need to make a **`ProcessorMediator`**, which will be responsible for events distribution. Then, change a **`FactoryProcessor`** class and force it to use **`ProcessorMediator`** to process events instead of Factories. **`PipelineCreationFacade`** should be extended, and the method **`BuildReportPipeline`** should be added. The last step is to add **EmitterProcessor**, which will be responsible for generating two events from **ReportEvent** instance and pushing them back to the mediator to be processed by appropriate pipelines.

Code

Let us start with **ProcessorMediator** as it is a core class in this pattern:

```
public class ProcessorMediator
{
        private Dictionary<string, List<Processor>> Processors { get; set;
                        } = new Dictionary<string, List<Processor>>();
        public void ProcessEvent(IBasicEvent basicEvent)
        {
            this.Processors[basicEvent.Type].ForEach(processor =>
                                       processor.Process(basicEvent));
        }
        public void AddProcessor(string source, Processor processor)
        {
            if (this.Processors.ContainsKey(source))
            {
                this.Processors[source].Add(processor);
            }
            else
            {
               this.Processors.Add(source, new List<Processor> { processor });
            }
        }
    }
```

It has a dictionary of processors, and each chain of processors has been bound to a concrete event type. It has two methods: **ProcessEvent** which is used for event processing and **AddProcessor**, which is responsible for adding new **Processor** instances to a dictionary.

Next, we will review the **FactoryProcessor** class:

```
public static class FactoryProcessor
{
        static ProcessorMediator mediator = new ProcessorMediator();
```

```
        static FactoryProcessor()
        {
            mediator.AddProcessor("TypeA", PipelineDirector.BuildTypeAPipeline());
            mediator.AddProcessor("TypeB", PipelineDirector.BuildTypeBPipeline());
            mediator.AddProcessor("TypeC", PipelineDirector.BuildTypeCPipeline());
            mediator.AddProcessor("TypeR",
                            PipelineDirector. BuildTypeRPipeline(mediator));
        }
        public static void Execute(BasicEvent basicEvent)
        {
            mediator.ProcessEvent(basicEvent);
        }
}
```

It contains the **ProcessorMediator** instance, which is initialized by calling the **AddProcessor** method for four pipeline processors. We have defined it as a static class because **FactoryProcessor** will not change its state during runtime. There is no need to create separate instances of the class, and the initialization can be called only once per run.

It has **Execute** method which calls the **ProcessEvent** of **ProcessorMediator** instance.

The next candidate to review is **PipelineCreationFacade**:

```
public static class PipelineCreationFacade
{
        public static Processor BuildFileUploadPipelineA
            (ICommunicationClient<UploadFileInfo, int> fileUploadClient,
             ICommunicationClient<string, byte[]> fileDownloadClient,
             ICommunicationClient<string, string> searchApiClient,
             ICommunicationClient<string, string> storeApiClient
            )
        {
            Processor proc = new ExceptionHandlingProcessor(
             new SaveMetadataProcessor(
                new ValidateProcessor(
                    new PreProcessProcessor(
                        new SearchProcessor(
                            new ProcessEventProcessor(
                                new StoreProcessor(
                                    new UpdateMetadataProcessor(null),
```

```
                                storeApiClient),
                            fileUploadClient),
                        searchApiClient),
                    fileDownloadClient))), GetFileLogger(), new Chain.
                                            ProcessorVisitor());
    return proc;
}
public static Processor BuildFileUploadPipelineB(
  ICommunicationClient<UploadFileInfo, int> fileUploadClient,
  ICommunicationClient<string, byte[]> fileDownloadClient,
  ICommunicationClient<string, string> searchApiClient,
  ICommunicationClient<string, string> storeApiClient
    )
{
Processor proc = new ExceptionHandlingProcessor(new ValidateProcessor(
        new PreProcessProcessor(
            new SearchProcessor(
                new ProcessEventProcessor(
                    null, fileUploadClient),
                searchApiClient),
            fileDownloadClient)), GetFileLogger(),
    new Chain.ProcessorVisitor());
    return proc;
}
public static Processor BuildIoTPipeline(
               ICommunicationClient<IoTData, string> apiClient)
{
    Processor processor = new ExceptionHandlingProcessor(
     new SaveMetadataProcessor(
        new IoTValidateProcessor(
            new IoTProcessEventProcessor(
                new UpdateMetadataProcessor(null),
                apiClient))), GetFileLogger(),
                      new Chain.ProcessorVisitor());
                      return processor;
}
public static Processor BuildReportPipeline(ProcessorMediator mediator)
```

```
    {
        Processor processor =
            new ExceptionHandlingProcessor(
                new EmitterProcessor(null,mediator),
            GetFileLogger(), new Chain.ProcessorVisitor());
        return processor;
    }

    private static Logger GetFileLogger()
    {
        var fileLogger = new FileLogger();
        return new Logger(
                    new DateLoggingDecorator(
                        new LoggingDestinationDecorator(fileLogger)));
    }
}
```

We have extended it and added the **BuildReportPipeline** method in which we are using **EmitterProcessor** class as a part of the pipeline:

```
public class EmitterProcessor : Processor
{
    private ProcessorMediator processorMediator;
    public EmitterProcessor(Processor nextProcessor,
                ProcessorMediator mediator) : base(nextProcessor)
    {
        this.processorMediator = mediator;
    }
    public override void Process(IBasicEvent request)
    {
        RegisterStep(request, "EMITTER_EMIT_EVENT");
        var reportEvent = request as ReportEvent;
        var iotEvent = new ReportEvent(reportEvent);
        iotEvent.Type = "TypeC";
        var fileEvent = new ReportEvent(reportEvent);
        fileEvent.Type = "TypeB";
```

```
            processorMediator.ProcessEvent(fileEvent);
            processorMediator.ProcessEvent(iotEvent);
        }
}
```

EmitterProcessor class is used to push back two events in answer to **ReportEvent** instance processing.

If we use **ProcessorMediator** class, we do not need to use factories. So, **FileFactory** and **IoTFactory** with **AbstractFactory** classes were removed from the project.

In the end, we are using the same code as in the preceding chapters to test our processing:

```
public static void Main()
{
            Stopwatch watch = new Stopwatch();
            watch.Start();
            // Events definition
            List<BasicEvent> eventList = new List<BasicEvent> {
                                                    event1, event2,
                    event3, event4, event5, event6, reportEvent };
            eventList.ForEach(eventObj =>
            {
                FactoryProcessor.Execute(eventObj);
                Console.WriteLine();
            });
            watch.Stop();
            Console.WriteLine($"MS ellapsed: {watch.ElapsedMilliseconds}");
}
```

The result looks the same as in the preceding chapters. Refer to the following *Figure 8.2*:

```
Microsoft Visual Studio Debug Console
SYSTEM_A_API_CLIENT: Sending message to http://systemA.com/api/search. Message: TypeBFilename.jpg
FILE_UPLOAD_CLIENT: Uploading file to http://file.storage.com/systemB/upload. File: {"FileName":"TypeBFilename.jpg","Con
tent":""}

DOWNLOAD_CLIENT: Downloading file from  http://typeB.file.url.
SYSTEM_A_API_CLIENT: Sending message to http://systemA.com/api/search. Message: TypeB2Filename.jpg
FILE_UPLOAD_CLIENT: Uploading file to http://file.storage.com/systemB/upload. File: {"FileName":"TypeB2Filename.jpg","Co
ntent":""}

SYSTEM_C_API_CLIENT: Sending message to http://systemC.processing.com/api. Message: {"Source":"IOT","Action":"TEMP_UPDAT
E","Value":"92.2"}

SYSTEM_C_API_CLIENT: Sending message to http://systemC.processing.com/api. Message: {"Source":"IOT","Action":"TEMP_UPDAT
E","Value":"92.2"}

SYSTEM_C_API_CLIENT: Sending message to http://systemC.processing.com/api. Message: {"Source":"IOT","Action":"TEMP_UPDAT
E","Value":"92.2"}

DOWNLOAD_CLIENT: Downloading file from  http://typeR.file.url.
SYSTEM_A_API_CLIENT: Sending message to http://systemA.com/api/search. Message: TypeRFilename.jpg
FILE_UPLOAD_CLIENT: Uploading file to http://file.storage.com/systemB/upload. File: {"FileName":"TypeRFilename.jpg","Con
tent":""}
SYSTEM_C_API_CLIENT: Sending message to http://systemC.processing.com/api. Message: {"Source":"REPORT","Action":"TEMP_UP
DATE","Value":"93.2"}

MS ellapsed: 874
```

Figure 8.2: *Result of ProcessMediator execution*

In our case, the Mediator design pattern plays the role of a bus, which knows how to distribute events between **`Processors`**. Also, it provides an interface by which any part of the program can communicate with **`Processors`** (only one way in our case) without knowing what **`Processors`** are and what interface they have. It is more important that **`Processors`** can communicate with each other by sending different events to **`ProcessMediator`**, as we did with the **`ReportEvent`**. We split the instance into two separate events and submitted them back to **`ProcessMediator`** to be processed by **`IoT`** and **`FileUpload`** processors.

Usually, such a design pattern is used in chat-like apps. A good example of this pattern usage is the *.NET SignalR* framework which provides the possibility to integrate web sockets and similar technologies into your app. The most basic example in the SignalR tutorial is a chat based on the Mediator design pattern.

Command

The Command design pattern is a behavioral design pattern that allows you to turn a request into a standalone object that contains information about the event, a function that should be called, and the function's arguments. This allows users to decouple event processing from event handlers and to parameterize objects with operations, delay the execution of an operation or queue it, and support undoable operations.

Turn pipeline into a CommandIn. In our scenario, we will apply Command design pattern to our pipelines. The main entities are **`CommandInvoker`**, **`ICommand`** interface, and concrete **`Commands`** derived from the **`ICommand`** interface. Refer to the following *Figure 8.3*:

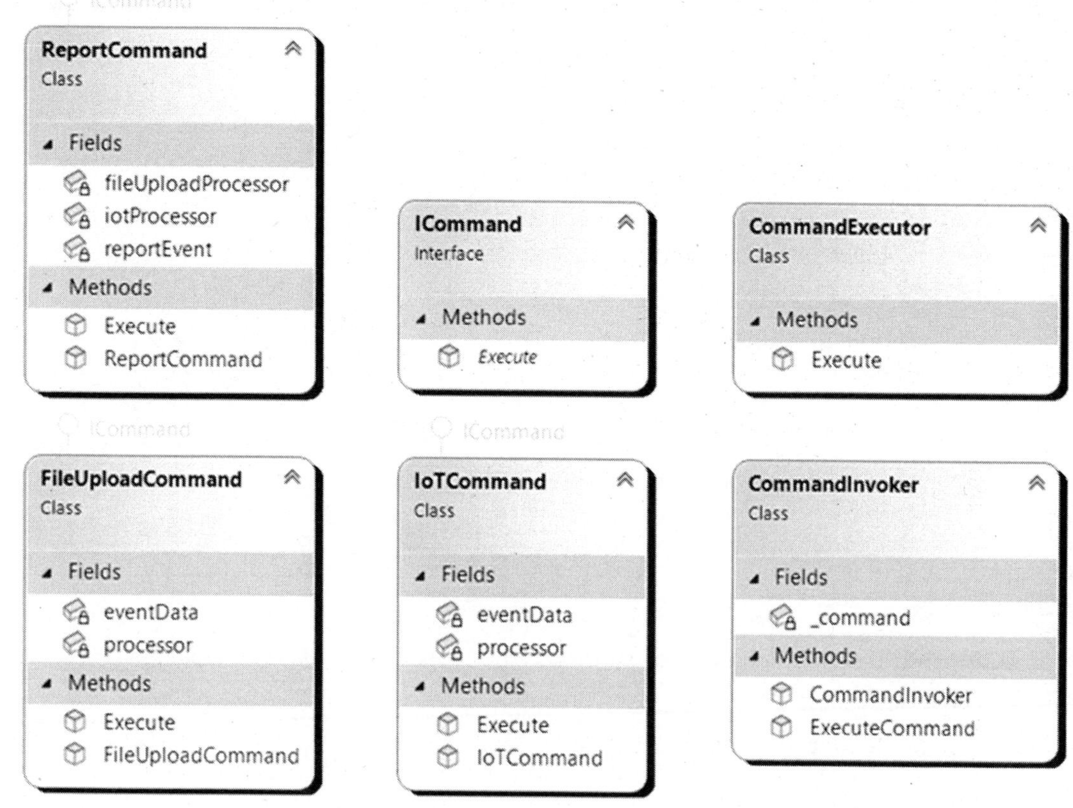

Figure 8.3: Command design pattern diagram

`CommandInvoker` is responsible for keeping an instance of the **`ICommand`** derived class and execute it per request. We have added **`CommandExecutor`**, which uses **`CommandInvoker`** internally to execute the command. **`ICommand`** interface defines only one method: **`Execute`**, which executes concrete functionality defined in derived classes. Each of the concrete commands: **`ReportCommand`**, **`FileUploadCommand`**, and **`IoTCommand`** has a constructor which accepts required processors and an event instance on which the processor should be executed.

Code

Let us review the **`ICommand`** interface:

```
public interface ICommand
{
        void Execute();
}
```

It has only method Execute, which is used by **CommandInvoker**:

```
public class CommandInvoker
{
        private ICommand _command;
        public CommandInvoker(ICommand command)
        {
            _command = command;
        }
        public void ExecuteCommand()
        {
            _command.Execute();
        }
}
```

CommandInvoker is responsible for keeping an instance of **ICommand** class and executing it by request.

An **ICommand** instance is passed through the constructor and is executed in the **ExecuteCommand** function call:

```
public class ReportCommand : ICommand
{
        private readonly Processor fileUploadProcessor;
        private readonly Processor iotProcessor;
        private readonly ReportEvent reportEvent;
        public ReportCommand(Processor fileUploadProcessor, Processor
                                       iotProcessor, ReportEvent reportEvent)
        {
            this.fileUploadProcessor = fileUploadProcessor;
            this.iotProcessor = iotProcessor;
            this.reportEvent = reportEvent;
        }
        public void Execute()
        {
            this.fileUploadProcessor.Process(reportEvent);
            this.iotProcessor.Process(reportEvent);
        }
}
```

Concrete command **ReportCommand** executes two processors: one for upload and one for IoT pipeline. All processors and event instances are passed through the constructor. **Execute** method is responsible for executing pipelines.

All other commands are similar to **ReportCommand**, except for accepting only one **Processor** instance as an input parameter:

```
public class FileUploadCommand : ICommand
{
        private readonly Processor processor;
        private readonly IUploadEventData eventData;
        public FileUploadCommand(Processor processor, IUploadEventData
                                                          eventData)
        {
            this.processor = processor;
            this.eventData = eventData;
        }
        public void Execute()
        {
            this.processor.Process(eventData);
        }
}
public class IoTCommand : ICommand
{
        private readonly Processor processor;
        private readonly IIoTEventData eventData;
        public IoTCommand(Processor processor, IIoTEventData eventData)
        {
            this.processor = processor;
            this.eventData = eventData;
        }
        public void Execute()
        {
            this.processor.Process(eventData);
        }
}
```

The last one is **CommandExecutor**:

```
public class CommandExecutor
{
```

```
        public void Execute(IBasicEvent basicEvent)
        {
            ICommand command = basicEvent.Type switch
            {
                "TypeA" => new FileUploadCommand(PipelineDirector.
                BuildTypeAPipeline(), basicEvent as IUploadEventData),
                "TypeB" => new FileUploadCommand(PipelineDirector.
                   BuildTypeBPipeline(), basicEvent as IUploadEventData),
                "TypeC" => new IoTCommand(PipelineDirector.
                      BuildTypeCPipeline(), basicEvent as IIoTEventData),
                "TypeR" => new ReportCommand(PipelineDirector.
                   BuildTypeBPipeline(), PipelineDirector.
                   BuildTypeCPipeline(),  basicEvent as ReportEvent),
                _ => throw new InvalidOperationException("Not supported type")
            };
            CommandInvoker commandInvoker = new CommandInvoker(command);
            commandInvoker.ExecuteCommand();
        }
}
```

It provides functionality to match the correct **`Processor`** with an event and execute the selected pipeline through **`CommandInvoker`**.

In the result of the execution of our standard code for testing, we will receive the same output as in the preceding chapters. Refer to the following *Figure 8.4*:

```
Microsoft Visual Studio Debug Console
SYSTEM_A_API_CLIENT: Sending message to http://systemA.com/api/search. Message: TypeBFilename.jpg
FILE_UPLOAD_CLIENT: Uploading file to http://file.storage.com/systemB/upload. File: {"FileName":"TypeBFilename.jpg","Con
tent":""}

DOWNLOAD_CLIENT: Downloading file from  http://typeB.file.url.
SYSTEM_A_API_CLIENT: Sending message to http://systemA.com/api/search. Message: TypeB2Filename.jpg
FILE_UPLOAD_CLIENT: Uploading file to http://file.storage.com/systemB/upload. File: {"FileName":"TypeB2Filename.jpg","Co
ntent":""}

SYSTEM_C_API_CLIENT: Sending message to http://systemC.processing.com/api. Message: {"Source":"IOT","Action":"TEMP_UPDAT
E","Value":"92.2"}

SYSTEM_C_API_CLIENT: Sending message to http://systemC.processing.com/api. Message: {"Source":"IOT","Action":"TEMP_UPDAT
E","Value":"92.2"}

SYSTEM_C_API_CLIENT: Sending message to http://systemC.processing.com/api. Message: {"Source":"IOT","Action":"TEMP_UPDAT
E","Value":"92.2"}

DOWNLOAD_CLIENT: Downloading file from  http://typeR.file.url.
SYSTEM_A_API_CLIENT: Sending message to http://systemA.com/api/search. Message: TypeRFilename.jpg
FILE_UPLOAD_CLIENT: Uploading file to http://file.storage.com/systemB/upload. File: {"FileName":"TypeRFilename.jpg","Con
tent":""}
SYSTEM_C_API_CLIENT: Sending message to http://systemC.processing.com/api. Message: {"Source":"REPORT","Action":"TEMP_UP
DATE","Value":"93.2"}

MS ellapsed: 893
```

Figure 8.4: *Result of Command design pattern execution*

As we are not applying the Command design pattern over the Mediator, no new abstraction layer is added, and the execution time is the same as in the preceding chapters.

To make this run, we have changed our standard test code:

```
public static void Main()
{
        CommandExecutor commandExecutor = new CommandExecutor();
        Stopwatch watch = new Stopwatch();
        watch.Start();
        // Events definition
        List<BasicEvent> eventList = new List<BasicEvent> { event1,
                                                            event2,… }
        eventList.ForEach(eventObj =>
        {
            commandExecutor.Execute(eventObj);
            Console.WriteLine();
        });
        watch.Stop();
        Console.WriteLine($"MS ellapsed: {watch.ElapsedMilliseconds}");
}
```

`CommandExecutor` variable initialization was added in the third line, and instead of the **`ProcessorMediator`** call, we are calling the **`commandExecutor.Execute`** method. Those are the only changes required to test the Command design pattern.

Command design pattern provides an abstraction over an action that can be executed per request. This pattern is mostly used in UI applications, which provides the possibility to execute the same action through the menus/buttons/keyboard shortcuts. In this case, a developer can pass **`ICommand`** interface instance with encapsulated action to various methods which will use **`CommandInvoker`** to invoke a command without knowing anything about underlying functionality. In our case, it is not so noticeable as we do not have many possibilities to execute the functionality. Still, we hope that our example was clear enough for you to understand the main point of this design pattern.

Conclusion

In this chapter, we do not have any synergy between presented patterns as they are interchangeable.

Mediator design pattern provides us the opportunity to create an abstraction that allows different classes and types to communicate with each other. It provides some sort of

Service Bus in which we can push the event, and then interested parties can receive and process it. This pattern truly shines in distributed systems when many clients interact with each other by sending and receiving messages. In our case, the example is stripped down, however, we have examined the main points of this pattern with pushing/receiving and resending messages through the Mediator class.

Command design pattern is slightly different. It shines in UI applications when the same action can be executed by different classes, but the result and functionality should be the same. Command design pattern provides an abstraction and allows to hide underlying functionality from code that does not need to know how action should be called and what data should be passed into.

In the next chapter, we will continue to explore Behavioral Design patterns and review Interpreter, Iterator, and Memento. Each of them solves a unique problem in their own way.

CHAPTER 9
Behavioral Design Patterns: Interpreter, Iterator, and Memento

Introduction

This chapter explores object behavioral design using Interpreter, Iterator, and Memento. These three design patterns provide functionality in different fields of software engineering. Memento helps us to save the state of the program. Iterator provides a standardized way of iterating over collection-like objects. Interpreter helps in solving problems with language processing tasks.

In this chapter, we will not modify our pipelines since these design patterns are partially not applicable and useless to our main project.

Structure

In this chapter, we will cover the following topics:

- Interpreter
    - Making a language processor
    - Code
- Iterator
    - Implementing the Enumeration concept

- Code
- Memorizing events
- Code

Objectives

At the end of this chapter, you will be able to describe Interpreter, Iterator, and Memento design patterns and apply them to real-world problems.

Let us dive in!

Interpreter

The idea of Interpreter design pattern is to provide structure to a grammatical representation of a language and an interpreter to execute/translate the grammar.

Making a language processor

We will apply the Interpreter design pattern to make a postfix notation calculator. It is a classical example of a parser and interpreter task.

Postfix math notations look like this: *A B C - +*. It can be translated to *A + B - C*. We will make a parser and interpreter (simple calculator) for such notation.

Let us design it! Refer to the following *Figure 9.1*:

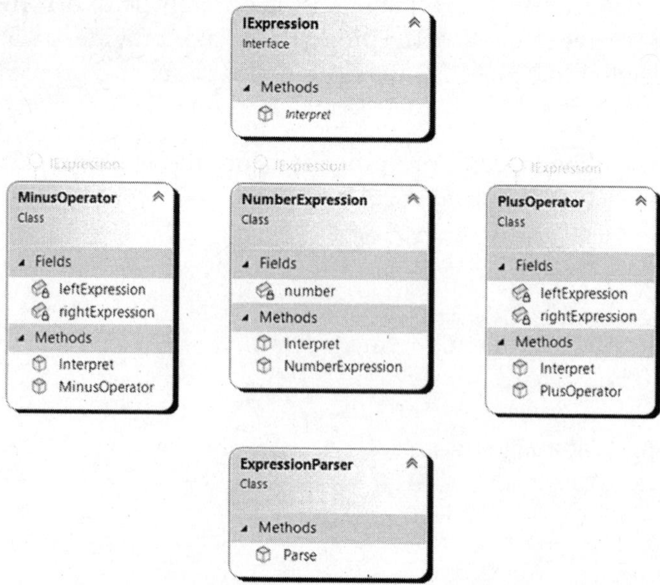

***Figure 9.1:** Interpreter design pattern diagram*

IExpression is a core interface. It defines the method Interpret, which makes the interpretation of an expression. In the case of **NumberExpression** class, it returns a number. In the case of **MinusOperator** and **PlusOperator** classes, it makes actual math operations over two **IExpression** instances.

ExpressionParser class is responsible for parsing a postfix expression into tokens and converting these tokens to actual expression structure.

Code

IExpression is a core interface, and we will review it first:

```
public interface IExpression
{
        int Interpret();
}
```

It defines only one operation and as we make a simple calculator, it returns **int** as a result of operation. It can be a simple number or the result of an operation:

```
public class MinusOperator : IExpression
{
        private IExpression leftExpression;
        private IExpression rightExpression;
        public MinusOperator(IExpression leftExpression, IExpression
                                                          rightExpression)
        {
            this.leftExpression = leftExpression;
            this.rightExpression = rightExpression;
        }
        public int Interpret()
        {
            return this.leftExpression.Interpret() - this.rightExpression.
                                                          Interpret();
        }
}
```

MinusOperator is an expression that operates over two expressions passed through a constructor and used in the Interpret method to return a result of this operation:

```
public class PlusOperator : IExpression
{
        private IExpression leftExpression;
        private IExpression rightExpression;
        public PlusOperator(IExpression leftExpression, IExpression
                                                                rightExpression)
        {
            this.leftExpression = leftExpression;
            this.rightExpression = rightExpression;
        }
        public int Interpret()
        {
            return this.leftExpression.Interpret() + this.rightExpression.
                                                                Interpret();
        }
}
```

PlusOperator looks the same, except for an operation that it applies to its operands.

NumberExpression represents a number in the code:

```
public class NumberExpression : IExpression
{
        private int number;
        public NumberExpression(int number)
        {
            this.number = number;
        }
        public int Interpret()
        {
            return this.number;
        }
}
```

The last one is **ExpressionParser**:

```
public class ExpressionParser
{
        public IExpression Parse(string expression)
        {
            Stack<IExpression> stack = new Stack<IExpression>();
            string[] tokens = expression.Split(' ');
            for (int i = 0; i < tokens.Length; i++)
            {
                switch (tokens[i])
                {
                    case "+":
                        IExpression rightPlus = stack.Pop();
                        IExpression leftPlus = stack.Pop();
                        IExpression plus = new PlusOperator(leftPlus,
                                                            rightPlus);
                        stack.Push(plus);
                        break;
                    case "-":
                        IExpression rightMinus = stack.Pop();
                        IExpression leftMinus = stack.Pop();
                        IExpression minus = new MinusOperator(leftMinus,
                                                              rightMinus);
                        stack.Push(minus);
                        break;
                    default:
                        stack.Push(new NumberExpression(int.
                                                Parse(tokens[i])));
                        break;
                }
            }
            return stack.Pop();
        }
}
```

It is the most difficult class in this pattern. The **Parse** method splits a string into tokens. Each token is a symbol. Symbols should be separated by space.

In postfix notation, numbers are typed before operators (it is slightly more complex if we include divide, multiple operators, and parentheses). In our case, we will not provide any validation methods, so the **`Parse`** method works only with correct expressions.

Our **`Parse`** method extracts numbers and pushes them on the stack. When it receives an operation symbol, it pops two previous numbers, creates **`IExpression`** with an operation symbol with numbers as input parameters, and pushes the newly created operation on the stack.

Let us see how this code works:

```
public static void Main()
{
            string expression = "2 3 1 - +";
            Parser parser = new Parser();
            IExpression expr = parser.Parse(expression);

            Console.WriteLine("The result is: " + expr.Interpret());
}
```

The code with a simple operation can be translated to 2 + 3 – 1, equal to 4.

The result of our code execution is given in the following *Figure 9.2*:

```
Microsoft Visual Studio Debug Console
The result is: 4

C:\Users\Timur\source\repos\Book_Pipelines\Book_Pipelines\bin\Debug\net6.0\Book_Pipelines.exe (process 18988) exited wit
h code 0.
Press any key to close this window . . .
```

***Figure 9.2:** Result of Interpreter design pattern execution*

If you are interested in an example of this pattern which includes divide, multiply operations and supports brackets, please visit **https://www.csharptutorial.net/csharp-design-patterns/csharp-interpreter-pattern/**.

Interpreter behavioral design pattern provides a well-known structure to solve problems with interpreting a **Domain Specific Language** (**DSL**).

Such languages are often called scripts and used internally in applications to automate their work. For example, it can be macros, some script language inside the application (Javascript?, Lua), or some specifically formatted strings which should be interpreted in a specific way inside the application.

Interpreter is a very specific pattern that is not used often. However, when you need to integrate scripting capabilities in your application, you think about Interpreter.

Iterator

Iterator design pattern provides you with a way to enumerate all elements of some object. It is mostly used for in-memory collections. However, there are cases when it provides asynchronous access to remote objects whose properties can be enumerated. Nowadays, enumerations can be found in most programming languages and they already have Enumeration as a concept embedded inside the framework/language.

Implementing the Enumeration concept

In this chapter, we will review the basic implementation of Enumeration concept from scratch using OOP features.

For this, we will need to define a few entities. Refer to the following *Figure 9.3*:

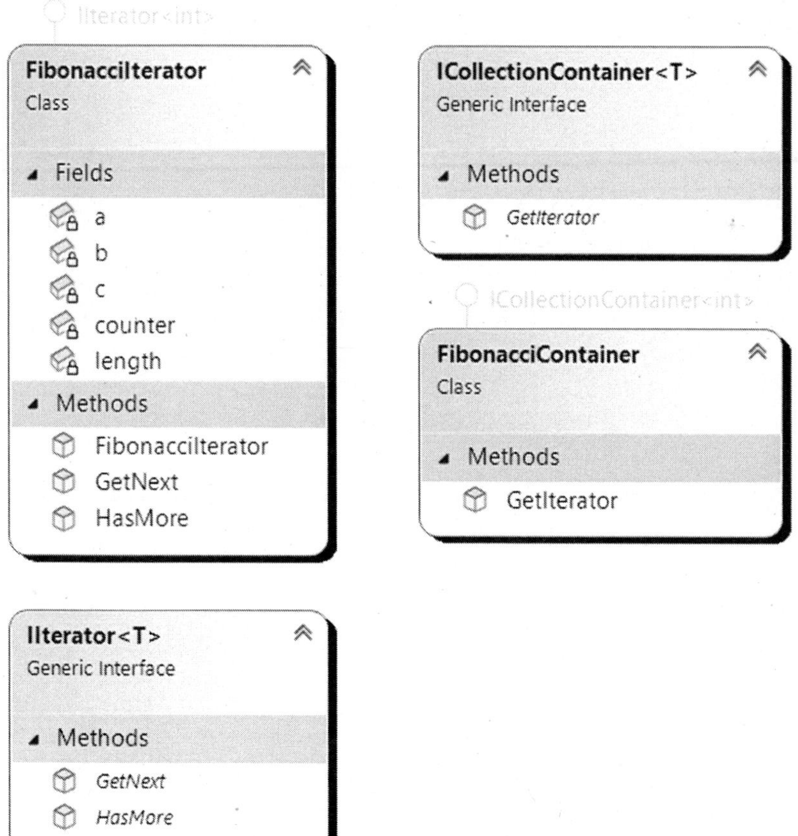

Figure 9.3: *Iterator design pattern diagram*

IIterator is the main interface for iterable collection of items. It has **GetNext** and **HasMore** methods, which are used by **ICollectionContainer**. It provides the method **GetIterator**, which returns an instance of the **IIterator** interface. In our case, it will be the **FibonnaciIterator** instance, which is derived from the **IIterator<int>** interface and returns a sequence of Fibonacci numbers.

Code

We will start with the **IIterator** interface:

```
public interface IIterator<T>
{
        public bool HasMore();
        public T GetNext();
}
```

It is a generic interface with generic type parameter **T**, which does not have any constraints.

This interface is implemented by the **FibonacciIterator** class:

```
public class FibonnaciIterator : IIterator<int>
{
        private readonly int length;
        private int counter = 0, a = 0, b = 1, c = 0;
        public FibonnaciIterator(int length)
        {
            this.length = length;
        }
        public int GetNext()
        {
            if(!HasMore()) throw new InvalidOperationException();
            int result = 0;
            if (counter > 0)
            {
                c = a + b;
                a = b;
                b = c;
                result = c;
            }
```

```
            counter++;
            return result;
        }
        public bool HasMore() => counter < length;
}
```

This iterator defines **T** as **int** and provides a simple iterative approach to calculate the sequence of Fibonacci numbers.

ICollectionContainer provides an interface with a method that allows you to get an iterator for a collection:

```
public interface ICollectionContainer<T>
{
        public IIterator<T> GetIterator();
}
public class FibonnaciContainer : ICollectionContainer<int>
{
        public IIterator<int> GetIterator()
        {
            return new FibonnacyIterator(25);
        }
}
```

FibonacciContainer returns the **FibonacciIterator** instance with the predefined length of sequence.

The demonstration code looks like this:

```
FibonnaciContainer fibonacy = new FibonnaciContainer();
for (var iter = fibonacy.GetIterator(); iter.HasMore();)
{
       var number = iter.GetNext();
       Console.WriteLine(number);
}
```

Figure 9.4 shows the result of code execution:

***Figure 9.4:** The result of Iterator design pattern code execution*

The concept of iterators can be found in many languages, for example, C#, Java, JavaScript, and many more. It is a useful design pattern that allows developers to enumerate any type of collection easily. In C#, it is possible to enumerate SQL query results, in-memory objects, XML and JSON nodes, etc.

We did this implementation from scratch to see how it can be implemented. However, .NET Core already has built-in types and C# keywords to support the implementation of Iterator over custom type. The main entities are **`IEnumerable`** and **`IEnumerator`**. All collections in C# are using these interfaces to provide the possibility to iterate over them using the **`foreach`** keyword.

Memorizing events

Memento design pattern is used when a developer needs to save and later restore the object state.

It does not matter in which system it is saved and in which the object has been restored. It can be used to save objects into string in one system and then sent to another system through HTTP, gRPC, etc, where it should be restored. Alternatively, it can be used with the Command pattern, for example, when you want to implement **`Undo`** command. This pattern can be applied in many ways through the application development lifecycle. Refer to the following *Figure 9.5*:

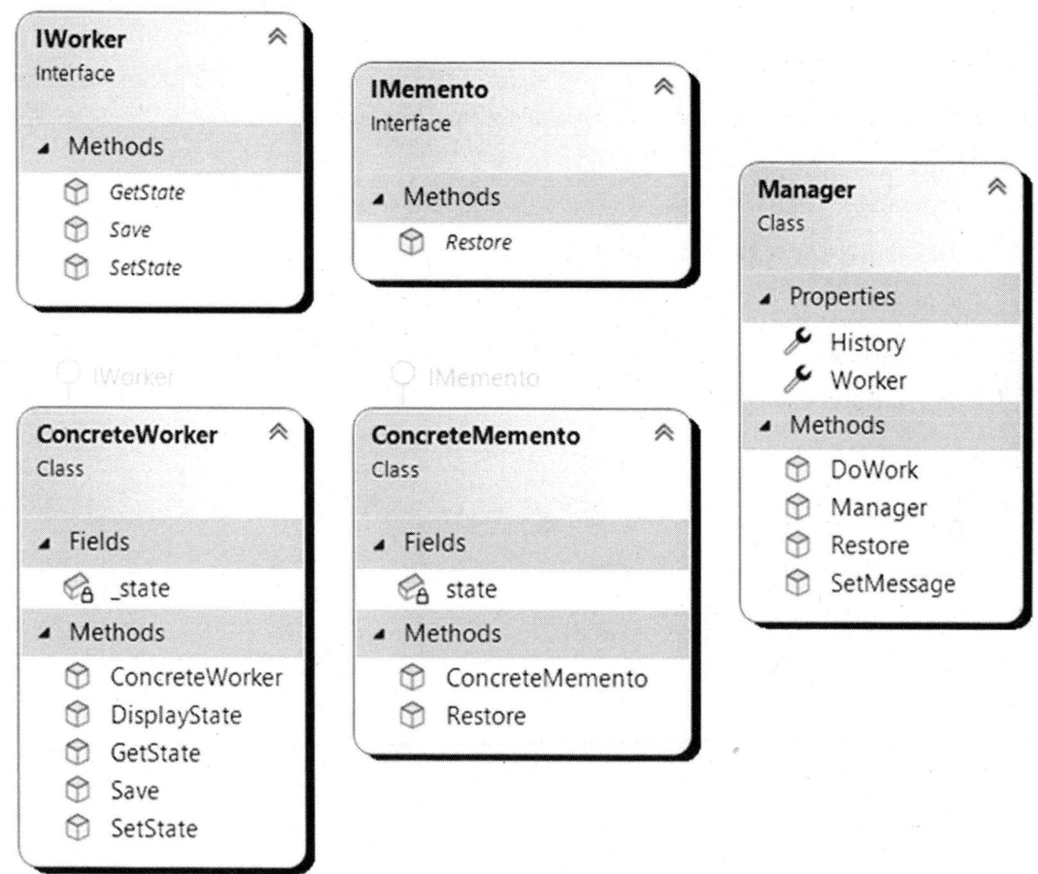

***Figure 9.5:** Memento design pattern diagram*

In our design, you can notice two interfaces: **`IWorker`** and **`IMemento`**. **`IWorker`** defines standard methods to support the Memento design pattern. It has **`GetState`**, **`Save,`** and **`SetState`** methods. **`IMememnto`** defines only one method: **`Restore`**. However, **`ConcreteMemento`** defines a constructor which will accept **`IWorker`** instance and save its state locally.

`ConcreteWorker` implements **`IWorker`** interface members and adds **`DisplayState`** functionality that imitates the work it should do.

`Manager` class defines three methods: **`DoWork`**, which calls **`DisplayState`** on the **`ConcreteWorker`** class instance. **`Restore`** is called by outside code to restore the previous state, and **`SetMessage`**, which is also called by outside code when it needs to change the message to be displayed.

Let us see how it looks in the code.

Code

IMemento interface is a core entity for this design pattern:

```
public interface IMemento
{
        void Restore(IWorker worker);
}
```

It has the method **Restore** which accepts **IWorker** and restores the state of it.

```
public interface IWorker
{
        public IMemento Save();

        public object GetState();

        void SetState(Object state);
}
```

IWorker interface provides methods for saving its own state in the **IMemento** derived instance, getting state of the worker, and setting state from the previously saved one:

```
public class ConcreteWorker : IWorker
{
        private string state;
        public ConcreteWorker(string state)
        {
            this.state = state;
        }
        public void DisplayState()
        {
            Console.WriteLine(this.state);
        }
        public IMemento Save()
        {
            return new ConcreteMemento(this);
        }
        public object GetState()
```

```
        {
            return this.state;
        }
        public void SetState(Object state)
        {
            this.state = state.ToString();
        }
}
```

ConcreteWorker implements **IWorker** interfaces and adds the required functionality:

```
public class ConcreteMemento : IMemento
{
        private object state;
        public ConcreteMemento(IWorker worker)
        {
            this.state = worker.GetState();
        }
        public void Restore(IWorker worker)
        {
            worker.SetState(this.state);
        }
}
```

ConcreteMemento, in turn, implements **IMemento** interface and provides the constructor with **IWorker** parameters, which allows it to save the current state of the worker:

```
public class Manager
{
        public List<IMemento> History { get; set; } = new List<IMemento>();
        public ConcreteWorker Worker { get; set; }
        public Manager(ConcreteWorker worker)
        {
            this.Worker = worker;
        }
        public void SetMessage(string message)
        {
            this.History.Add(Worker.Save());
            this.Worker.SetState(message);
        }
```

```
        public void DoWork()
        {
            this.Worker.DisplayState();
        }
        public void Restore()
        {
            var lastMemento = this.History.Last();
            this.History.Remove(lastMemento);
            lastMemento.Restore(Worker);
        }
}
```

Manager class is responsible for doing some work. To accomplish this, it provides an interface that contains a constructor and accepts **ConcreteWorker** as a parameter. **SetMessage** method allows the outside code to pass a new message to be displayed, and **DoWork** method displays the state in the console . In our case, execute the worker's and the **Restore** methods, which restores the worker's state from the history.

Let us see them in codes:

```
ConcreteWorker worker = new ConcreteWorker(String.Empty);
Manager manager = new Manager(worker);
manager.SetMessage("Hello!");
manager.DoWork();
manager.SetMessage("How are you?");
manager.DoWork();
manager.SetMessage("Good bye!");
manager.DoWork();
manager.Restore();
manager.DoWork();
manager.Restore();
manager.DoWork();
```

In this code, we create a **ConcreteWorker** instance and pass it to a newly created **Manager's** instance constructor. When we set a new message through **SetMessage** method of the manager, the **Save** method of the worker's instance is called, creating a new history record. The manager sets a new message to a worker state. On the next line, we are calling the **DoWork** function, which delegates all the work to a worker and displays a message in the console.

When we call **Restore** function on a manager's instance, we restore the state from **IMemento** history record to a worker's state.

The result of the code execution can be seen in *Figure 9.6*:

```
Microsoft Visual Studio Debug Console
Hello!
How are you?
Good bye!
How are you?
Hello!

C:\Users\Timur\source\repos\Book_Pipelines\Book_Pipelines\bin\Debug\net6.0\Book_Pipelines.exe (process 12276) exited wit
h code 0.
Press any key to close this window . . .
```

***Figure 9.6:** The result of code execution of Memento design pattern*

Memento design pattern is mostly used in UI applications when a user works with local files or edits a document. It allows a developer to make a specific Memento for each type of menu item /action, which can change the specific piece of state of a document/file. To save the state of an object and send it to another system, save it to a file developer can use a technique called serialization. In .NET Core, there is a special namespace **`System.Text.Json`** in which he/she can find a lot of classes specific to JSON serialization.

Conclusion

In this chapter, we have reviewed three important design patterns. Some are used widely, like Iterator, and can be found in any programming language nowadays. Some are specific, like Interpreter, mainly for DSL processing. Memento design pattern is used frequently, however, it does not have a base implementation in the core library of any language. Most programming languages that have the capability to work with networks and network protocols like HTTP provide classes for object serialization into XML/JSON/base64. So, as a developer, you can save a state and restore it later.

In the next chapter, we will review SOLID principles. These principles are not design patterns; however, they could help developers prepare their code to design patterns adaptation.

Join our book's Discord space

Join the book's Discord Workspace for Latest updates, Offers, Tech happenings around the world, New Release and Sessions with the Authors:

https://discord.bpbonline.com

Chapter 10
The SOLID Principles

Introduction

For the last 50-70 years of the evolution of programming languages and software development, discipline developers have faced various problems while delivering stable, maintainable, performance code. Most of the time, the problem is not in the language/framework/library they use. The problems lie in the field of basic structures, algorithms, and structure of the code that developers are generating every day.

In this chapter, we will discuss the SOLID architectural principles, their history, and structure.

Structure

In this chapter, we will cover the following topics:

- What are these principles for
- Brief description of principles
- Single Responsibility Principle
- Open/Closed Principle
- Liskov Substitution Principle

- Interface Segregation Principle
- Dependency Inversion Principle
- Secondary principles
- How to use principles

Objectives

At the end of this chapter, you will be able to describe the SOLID principles and apply them to real code.

Let us dive in!

What are these principles for

In 2000, *Robert C. Martin* developed the SOLID principles in his essay, *Design principles and Design pattern*. In this essay, he acknowledged that software would change and develop in time and become more and more complex. In this case, software becomes rigid, immobile, fragile, and viscous. To fight these problems, Martin described architectural principles that can help developers to control software complexity.

The SOLID principles were invented to help developers manage their code structure and OOP hierarchy in the most stable and maintainable way. We will not talk about performance here as stability and maintainability of the code are often contradicting with it. However, most of the time, the time of development and possibility to discover the code for young developers is much more important than performance improvements for 10ms.

It depends on the product. The code that allows a spaceship to land on the Moon should be as performant as possible. On the other hand, any website application can be allowed to spend an additional 10ms on some requests.

Brief description of principles

The main goal of the principles is to reduce the complexity of software by reducing the number of dependencies between entities. It helps with changes in one area of code without impacting others. Following these principles allows us to create more readable, maintainable, and opened to extensions code.

Martin has mentioned five main principles and three secondary principles. The main principles are as follows:

- **Single Responsibility Principle:** Each module (entity, class, interface) should be responsible only for one role.
- **Open/Closed Principle:** Any software entity (class, module, function, etc.) should be open for extension but closed for modification.

- **Liskov Substitution Principle:** Objects of a base class should be replaceable with derived classes without breaking the application.
- **Interface Segregation Principle:** Code should not depend on entities it does not use.
- **Dependency Inversion Principle:** High-level modules should be unaffected by changes in low-level modules.

The secondary principles are:

- **Keep it simple, stupid (KISS):** A solution is better when it uses fewer dependencies, OOP features, etc.
- **Don't repeat yourself (DRY):** Software code repetition should be avoided by using abstractions. Data normalization should be used to avoid redundancy.
- **Separation of concerns (SoC):** Application should be separated into units, and overlapping between unit functions should be minimal.

Single Responsibility Principle

The **Single Responsibility Principle** (**SRP**) is the first SOLID principle and declares that *a class should have one, and only one, reason to change*. It forces us to create classes that are responsible only for one role.

The violation of this principle is one of the most common mistakes that developers make while developing their applications.

Then, we can find the following code in our production build:

```
public class Employee
{
    public string EmployeeName { get; set; }
    public int EmployeeID { get; set; }

    public Employee(string name, int Id)
    {
    }
    public void GenerateReport(Employee emp)
    {
       // Long and tedious code to generate a report
    }
}
```

In this case, our **Employee** class has two responsibilities: keeping the data about the **Employee** and generating a report for it. It violates the SRP.

From the first look, it is not a big problem to add a piece of code to generate a simple HTML. However, later, the developer may receive a request to add additional functionality to add PDF/JSON/XML report generation. It will require the developer to make a code that will complicate the initial class. It is also possible that the same functionality for report generation will be required to apply to other entities of class hierarchy like Department.

If we are keeping the report generation function inside the **Employee** class, then it will force us to create a code that is:

- Not scalable
- Not maintainable
- Hard to change
- Hard to test

The solution is to apply SRP to this code. Let us see what it should look like.

First, let us take a look at the updated **Employee** class:

```
public class Employee
{
    public string EmployeeName { get; set; }
    public int EmployeeID { get; set; }
    public Employee(string name, int Id)
    {
    }
}
```

It will serve its primary purpose to keep information about concrete **Employee**. Then, we will create a report generator class:

```
public class EmployeeReport
{
    public void GenerateReport(Employee emp)
    {
        // Code to generate report
    }
}
```

Our **EmployeeReport** class also serves a single purpose; the generation of report about concrete **Employee** instance is passed in as a parameter.

With such a design, each class will have its responsibility and role. Developers can extend **EmployeeReport** with any functions they like. They can add third-party report generation libraries, or create a deep report generation class hierarchy, which will have separate generator classes for each type of format the client requires. They will be able to create **DepartmentReport** generator and reuse the existing classes of generators to generate reports for a new entity. No code copy-pasting, long functions, spaghetti code, and additional testing will be required.

Such an approach will help developers to create a maintainable code that is almost bug free and open to extension.

SRP benefits can be summarized in the following list:

- Easier maintenance
- Reusability of the code
- Improved testability

Open/Closed Principle

The definition of **Open/Closed Principle** (OCP) is that *software entities (classes, modules, functions, etc.) should be open for extension but closed for modification.* You should be able to extend the functionality of a class without altering its source code.

The violation of this principle can lead to bugs in existing code, break backward compatibility and force developers to change a lot of existing code, which again will lead them to a lot of bugs.

Let us look at a simple example of refactoring that leads us to a better code!

In this example, we will have two shapes:

```
public class Circle
{
    public double Radius { get; set; }
}
public class Rectangle
{
    public double Height { get; set; }
    public double Width { get; set; }
}
```

For these two classes, we want to create a **CommonAreaCalculator**:

```
public class CommonAreaCalculator
{
    public double TotalArea(object[] arrObjects)
    {
        double area = 0;
        foreach (var obj in arrObjects)
        {
            if (obj is Rectangle)
            {
                Rectangle rectangle = (Rectangle)obj;
                area += rectangle.Height * rectangle.Width;
            }
            else if (obj is Circle)
            {
                Circle circle = (Circle)obj;
                area += circle.Radius * circle.Radius * Math.PI;
            }
        }
        return area;
    }
}
```

This code works perfectly, however, it has one problem: if we need to add a new shape, we need to make changes to our **CommonAreaCalculator**. It violates the Open/Closed Principle, because we will be forced to modify the functionality of the function only because there is a new shape in our class hierarchy,

The easiest solution is to delegate **Area** calculation to shapes itself:

```
public abstract class Shape
{
    public abstract double Area();
}
```

We are defining base class **Shape**, which has abstract method **Area**. It should be overwritten in the derived classes:

```
public class Circle : Shape
{
```

```
    public double Radius { get; set; }
    public override double Area()
    {
        return Radius * Radius * Math.PI;
    }
}
public class Rectangle : Shape
{
    public double Height { get; set; }
    public double Width { get; set; }

    public override double Area()
    {
        return Height * Width;
    }
}
```

Now, the **CommonAreaCalculator** will look different:

```
public class AreaCalculator
{
    public double TotalArea(Shape[] arrShapes)
    {
        double area = 0;
        foreach (var shape in arrShapes)
        {
            area += shape.Area();
        }
        return area;
    }
}
```

With such a design, we have closed our classes for future modifications. For example, take a look at **CommonAreaCalculator**: it does not need to be extended to include one more shape in calculations. It is open for extension as any shape can be created deriving from common class and passed as part of array of shapes.

By following the Open/Closed principle, we can be sure that our class hierarchy is robust against possible changes in requirements in the near future. This principle makes our software easier to maintain, modify, and extend. It promotes reusability and modularity, which helps in the automatic testing of our codebase.

Liskov Substitution Principle

This principle was introduced in 1987 by *Barbara Liskov* and states that: *if a program is using a base class, it should be able to use any of its subclasses without the program knowing it*. In other words, the **Liskov Substitution Principle** (**LSP**) ensures that base class behavior will not be changed by derived classes, and it helps to maintain correct behavior of the whole application in case derived classes are used instead of a base class.

If developers follow this principle, they will create maintainable, flexible, and understandable code.

The simplest example we can look at is in the animal world.

First, we will create a Bird class:

```
public class Bird
{
    public virtual void Fly()
    {
        Console.WriteLine("Flying …");
    }
}
```

Now, we are introducing the **`Penguin`** class:

```
public class Penguin: Bird
{
    public override void Fly()
    {
        throw new NotImplementedException("Fly is not implemented!");
    }
}
```

This seems to be logical. Penguins cannot fly, so an exception is thrown.

However, this code violates LSP as the behavior of code will be changed if we use the Penguin class instance as the object with which our program is working. Developers can separate the code to support such birds, create additional control flow, and so on, but the code will become less understandable and less maintainable.

To fix this, we can introduce a new entity, **`IFlyable`** interface:

```
public class Bird
{
    // Other functionality of the Bird class
}
public interface IFlyable
{
    void Fly();
}
public class Sparrow : Bird, IFlyable
{
    public void Fly()
    {
        Console.WriteLine("Flying …");
    }
}
public class Penguin : Bird
{
    // Penguins can't fly so they don't implement IFlyable
}
```

With these changes, only birds that have the ability to fly could be passed as the parameter to methods that require Fly functionality. Also, we can reuse **IFlyable** interface with other classes like **Airplane**, **Rockets**, and so on.

This allows developers to preserve LSP, the code will be much more maintainable and understandable, and they can create more general code based on abilities and not on the types of objects. Such an approach leads developers to write less error-prone and robust code.

Interface Segregation Principle

The main idea of **Interface Segregation Principle** (**ISP**) is that no entity should be forced to depend on interfaces they do not use.

This principle improves the reusability and maintainability of your codebase by introducing modularity of functionality. Using this principle, each entity should know only the bare minimum to be implemented. The approach forced by this principle improves the cohesiveness of the classes, therefore enhancing the design of an application.

If developers violate the principle, the base classes/interfaces become overloaded. Derived classes are forced to implement functionality they do not know/do not need to know about. The codebase becomes less modular and more confusing. Coupling of the codebase is growing, and this increases the complexity of it. The simplest of changes become harder to implement.

For example, we will look at implementing a **multifunctional device (MFD)**. We will create an interface which requires to have all the functionality at once:

```
public interface IMachine
{
    void Fax(Document d);
    void Scan(Document d);
    void Print(Document d);
    void Copy(Document d);
}
```

A typical implementation is as follows:

```
public class MultiFunctionPrinter: IMachine
{
    public void Fax(Document d)
    {
        // Faxing implementation here
    }
    public void Scan(Document d)
    {
        // Scanning implementation here
    }
    public void Print(Document d)
    {
        // Printing implementation here
    }
    public void Copy(Document d)
    {
        // Copying implementation here
    }
}
```

It is fine if organizations that will use our application have only MFD. However, developers will soon receive a ticket that the application does not work correctly with some devices. It can be a simple printer or fax. As developers implemented only the general MFD class for any of the devices that the application is connected to, the other functionality is also enabled and confuses users. In this case, developers can implement specific drivers for separate devices, for example, a Printer. With the current approach, it will look like this:

```
public class SimplePrinter: IMachine
{
    public void Print(Document d)
    {
        // Printing implementation here
    }
    public void Scan(Document d)
    {
        // Does nothing or throws an exception, violating ISP
    }
    public void Fax(Document d)
    {
        // Does nothing or throws an exception, violating ISP
    }
    public void Copy(Document d)
    {
        // Does nothing or throws an exception, violating ISP
    }
}
```

It seems that 75% of functionality is useless for such devices but developers are forced to provide an implementation of redundant methods. The **`Printer`** class should not know about the Fax, Copy, etc. functionality and their parameters.

Let us apply ISP to **`IMachine`** interface and derived classes:

```
public interface IPrinter
{
    void Print(Document d);
}
public interface IScanner
{
    void Scan(Document d);
}
public interface IFaxMachine
```

```
{
    void Fax(Document d);
}
public interface ICopyMachine
{
    void Copy(Document d);
}
```

We have split the **IMachine** interface into separate entities, and now we need to combine them into classes to make a device of our/users dream:

```
public class MultiFunctionPrinter : IPrinter, IScanner, IFaxMachine, ICopyMachine
{
    public void Print(Document d)
    {
        // Printing implementation here
    }
    public void Scan(Document d)
    {
        // Scanning implementation here
    }
    public void Fax(Document d)
    {
        // Faxing implementation here
    }
    public void Copy(Document d)
    {
        // Copying implementation here
    }
}
public class SimplePrinter : IPrinter
{
    public void Print(Document d)
    {
        // Printing implementation here
    }
}
```

As you can see, each class has the required functionality without redundant code. Such an approach forces us to modularize our codebase, decreasing coupling and increasing cohesion. The first means that our classes become smaller, more granular, and independent from other application parts, facilitating future changes. Cohesion means that created entities are focused on a task that they should do.

Dependency Inversion Principle

The **Dependency Inversion Principle** (**DIP**) states that:

- High-level modules should not depend on low-level modules. Both should depend on abstractions.
- Abstractions should not depend on details. Details should depend on abstractions.

The main idea of this principle is to force developers to write code with less coupling, thereby increasing reusability and flexibility, making the system more robust and maintainable.

Violation of this principle leads developers to making a coupled code that is hard to change and maintain, as any change in the control flow or structure could require a lot of changes in the codebase.

Let us continue our journey with **`Printers`**:

```
public class Document
{
    public string Content { get; set; }
}
public class Printer
{
    public void Print(Document document)
    {
        // Code to print the document
    }
}
public class Editor
{
    private Printer _printer;
    public Editor()
    {
        _printer = new Printer();
```

```
    }
    public void PrintDocument(Document document)
    {
        _printer.Print(document);
    }
}
```

Right now, we have an implementation of **Print** functionality from our developers. In this implementation, there are a few problems:

- **Editor** class is dependent on the concrete class **Printer**.
- **Editor** class is responsible for instantiating the **Printer** class.
- If we want to change the **Printer** class to **PdfPrinter**, we need to change the **Editor** class.

We have made a code review and decided that our developers should refactor this code using DIP. In the result, we have received the following code:

```
public interface IPrinter
{
    void Print(Document document);
}
public class Printer : IPrinter
{
    public void Print(Document document)
    {
        // Code to print the document
    }
}
public class Editor
{
    private IPrinter _printer;
    public Editor(IPrinter printer)
    {
        _printer = printer;
    }
    public void PrintDocument(Document document)
    {
```

```
        _printer.Print(document);
    }
}
```

Let us summarize the changes:

- **Editor** class now depends on abstraction through **IPrinter** interface.
- **IPrinter** instance is passed through constructor params.
- We can easily switch **IPrinter** implementation from the outside code.

For example, we can create a new **Printer** that can print the PDF file and pass it through the constructor of **Editor** class:

```
public class PdfPrinter : IPrinter
{
    public void Print(Document document)
    {
        // Code to print the document to PDF
    }
}
var editor = new Editor(new PdfPrinter());
```

This is the simplest example of DIP. In the real world, developers are creating much more complex systems in which DIP does exist as part of a framework, and most classes are registered and instantiated with the help of it. In such a system, DIP helps to reduce the complexity of the system, of object instantiation and configuration and promotes modularity and flexibility.

The advantages of DIP can be summarized in the following list:

- **Flexibility:** High-level modules are now dependent on low-level modules through abstraction. The details and concrete classes are hidden from them. These give developers the flexibility to change low-level modules without affecting high-level modules and use additional configuration systems to switch between concrete classes for low-level modules on the fly.
- **Reusability:** Each low-level module can be used in multiple high-level modules without additional changes.
- **Modularity:** Granular modules are easier to use, change, and test.

Understanding and applying the DIP can result in software that is easier to manage, understand, and extend. It is a powerful principle in object-oriented design that helps to create more maintainable code.

Secondary principles

Secondary principles advice on how to write a good code. KISS principle promotes simplicity over complexity. It does not mean you must make the whole application in one file/function. It rather means that your code should not be overly complicated and should be clean and maintainable. You can implement KISS by using clean and concise code, avoiding unnecessary inheritance, using meaningful variable and method names, keeping functions small, and staying focused on a single task.

The violation of this principle leads developers to bloated, unmaintainable, overcomplicated code with intricate class hierarchy.

Let us review a simple example of violation of this principle and how we can fix the code:

```
public bool IsPalindrome(string input)
{
    string cleanedInput = "";
    foreach (char c in input)
    {
        if (char.IsLetter(c))
        {
            cleanedInput += char.ToLower(c);
        }
    }
    int i = 0;
    int j = cleanedInput.Length - 1;
    while (i < j)
    {
        if (cleanedInput[i] != cleanedInput[j])
        {
            return false;
        }
        i++;
        j--;
    }
    return true;
}
```

Although this code works correctly, it looks a bit overcomplicated.

The solution is to use tools that language provides to you to simplify your code. Now, the code looks clean and short:

```
public bool IsPalindrome(string input)
{
    string cleanedInput = new string(input.Where(c => Char.IsLetter(c)).
ToArray()).ToLower();
    string reversedInput = new string(cleanedInput.Reverse().ToArray());
    return cleanedInput == reversedInput;
}
```

Sometimes, refactored solutions can be slower than the original. It is a typical tradeoff between performance and maintainability. If your project does not require real-time performance- maintainable and clean code always has higher priority.

DRY principle states that developers should not repeat themselves. This principle leads developers to write code based on abstractions and common functions. As a result, they receive a clean class hierarchy and code that is easy to maintain and support.

The violation of this principle leads developers to write code that is repeated in different places. In this case, basic OOP capabilities are not used as inheritance can be replaced by copy-paste. As a result, the codebase is hard to change, maintain, and understand.

In this simple code example, we have two functions: **OrderProcess** and **OrderReturn**. In each of these methods, the same code pieces are used:

```
public void OrderProcess()
{
    // Validate order to be processed
    // Calculate total of order to be processed
    // Save order to be processed
}
public void OrderReturn()
{
    // Validate order to be returned
    // Calculate total of order to be returned
    // Save order to be returned
}
```

The problem with such a code are the changes that should be applied. Instead of changing one piece of code, developers should change 2-3-4 ... code blocks. It often leads to simple bugs, which are time-consuming to fix.

Our solution is straightforward: move common functionality to methods that can be used by both functions. We are also moving validations to separate functions because the code will be easier to read:

```
public void OrderProcess()
{
    OrderValidate();
    CalculateOrderTotal();
    SaveOrder();
}
public void ProcessReturn()
{
    OrderValidateReturn();
    CalculateOrderTotal();
    SaveOrder();
}
private void OrderValidate ()
{
    // Validate order
}
private void OrderValidateReturn ()
{
    // Validate return
}
private void CalculateOrderTotal ()
{
    // Calculate total
}
private void SaveOrder()
{
    // Save order
}
```

DRY principle provides many benefits to developers: clean code, common functions, and an easy-to-maintain codebase.

SoC principle implies the usage of the OOP concept to organize your application into entities that are responsible for different functionality aspects.

Clean code structure, layering, and clean class hierarchy are easy to maintain, support, and reuse.

The violation of this principle leads developers to write bloated classes in which responsibilities are mixed, and the same class becomes responsible for saving in the database and simultaneously displaying results in the console or generating HTML code.

Let us review an example of a violation of SoC:

```
public class CustomerService
{
    public void CustomerAdd(CustomerEntity customer)
    {
        // Add customer code
    }
    public void CustomerRemove(CustomerEntity customer)
    {
        // Remove customer code
    }
    public void CustomerDisplay(CustomerEntity customer)
    {
        // Display customer code
    }
}
```

In this code, we can see the above-mentioned situation. The **CustomerService** class is responsible for working with databases while simultaneously outputting customer information in a specific format to a device.

To fix that, we can separate these functionalities into two classes:

```
public class CustomerDatabaseService
{
    public void CustomerAdd(CustomerEntity customer)
    {
        // Add customer code
    }

    public void CustomerRemove(CustomerEntity customer)
    {
        // Remove customer code
    }
}
```

```
public class CustomerDisplayService
{
    public void CustomerDisplay(CustomerEntity customer)
    {
        // Display customer code
    }
}
```

In this case, each class works with the **CustomerEntity** class. At the same time, areas of responsibility are separated, and each is responsible for only one area.

One of the best examples of the SoC principle is the **Model-View-Controller** (**MVC**) pattern, which is a widely used pattern to develop UI applications.

In an MVC application, you would have:

- Models to manage data and business logic.
- Controllers to manage user input and application flow.
- Views to manage user interface and presentation.

Each of these parts has a different role, thus applying separation of concerns.

How to use principles

At first glance, these principles look easy to apply and use. This is almost true for the first 100 entities. However, after some time and a significant number of changes are made to the codebase, it becomes a hard task to make your codebase consistent, robust, and principled.

The secondary principles are the easiest to start with. They are not obligatory but can help to tidy up your codebase. After applying secondary principles, you will have a clean code structure, which can be refactored further using SOLID main principles. When you finish this task, you can think about possibly using some of the design patterns we reviewed in this book.

If you are starting your journey in writing code, secondary principles are all you need to make good progress. Do not overcomplicate your first-class hierarchy, as you will have many more problems on which you will spend your time.

Overengineering from the start and premature optimization are the cornerstones on which most failed projects are based. Secondary principles help you create a basic class hierarchy that can be later easily refactored and extended with SOLID and design patterns.

Conclusion

The SOLID principles de facto are a standard in today's world of software development. It is a guideline for OOP, whose purpose is to teach you how to make software designs more understandable, flexible, maintainable, testable, and robust. Here is a short description of each principle:

- **Single Responsibility Principle:** Every entity or function should have a single responsibility or single reason to change. This principle promotes cohesion and modularity, making the software more understandable and maintainable.
- **Open-Closed Principle:** Every entity should be open for extension but closed for modification. This principle promotes the possibility of adding new features or functionality without changing the existing code using interfaces or abstract classes.
- **Liskov Substitution Principle:** This principle states that *objects of a superclass should be replaceable with objects of its subclasses without breaking the application*. Any piece of code that uses the base class should be able to use any of its subclasses without knowing it, thus keeping the functionality of the program untouched.
- **Interface Segregation Principle:** Clients should not be forced to depend upon interfaces they do not use. It is better to have many specific interfaces rather than one large, common interface.
- **Dependency Inversion Principle:** High-level modules should not depend on low-level modules. Both should depend on abstractions.

SOLID principles provide an approach to designing a class hierarchy, promoting maintainability, reusability, and testability. By following these principles, developers will create code that is high-quality, scalable, and robust.

In the next chapter, we will review the **Inversion of Control** (**IoC**) functionality that .NET Core provides us. We will cover the basic functionality of IoC and adapt our pipelines to be used together with it.

Join our book's Discord space

Join the book's Discord Workspace for Latest updates, Offers, Tech happenings around the world, New Release and Sessions with the Authors:

https://discord.bpbonline.com

CHAPTER 11
Inversion of Control in .NET Core

Introduction

In this chapter, we will discuss the **Inversion of Control** (**IoC**) principle and how it is implemented in the .NET Core Framework.

For the last decade, IoC has become the most used principle in software development. From hobby projects to large systems that process millions of requests per minute, IoC is a must.

Structure

In this chapter, we will cover the following topics:

- Overview of IoC
- .NET Core provided services
- Design services for Dependency Injection
- Adopt pipelines to .NET IoC
- Code

Objectives

At the end of this chapter, you will be able to describe IoC and use it with design patterns and SOLID principles.

Overview of IoC

If you check over the internet, you will find that the first similar term was used in 1970s in *Jackson Structured methodology*, written by *Michael Anthony Jackson*. It may sound different; however, the etymology is similar: inversion program.

Nowadays, the methodology of IoC is described as *a principle/design pattern in software engineering that refers to a method of decoupling the conventional flow of control in a system*. It means that IoC takes the management of initialization away from developers. With IoC, we code against an abstraction instead of concrete classes. When specific business logic should be run, IoC takes the responsibility for initialization, injection, and invocation of the code provided by the developer. We are inverting control from the concrete class to the IoC framework and its configuration.

This pattern helps developers to increase modularity and make a class hierarchy or application itself extensible. Under the cover, this pattern uses the **Dependency Injection Principle** (**DIP**) and Service Locator design pattern.

We should first review the conceptual way in which IoC works at runtime to understand it better.

In normal or straight control, we have the following *Figure 11.1* at compile time:

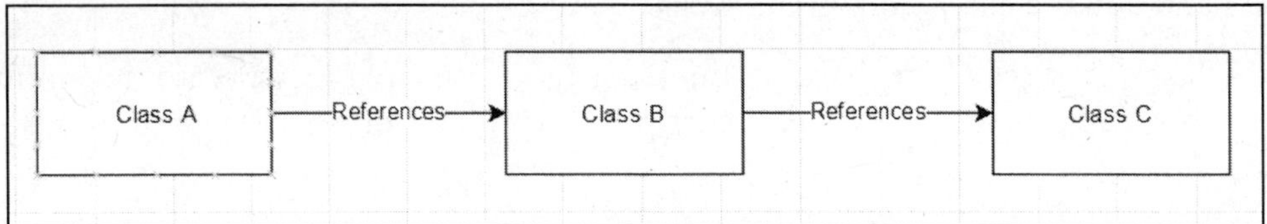

Figure 11.1: *Straight flow at compile time*

At runtime, nothing changes. It is still a direct reference to instances of classes. Refer to the following *Figure 11.2*:

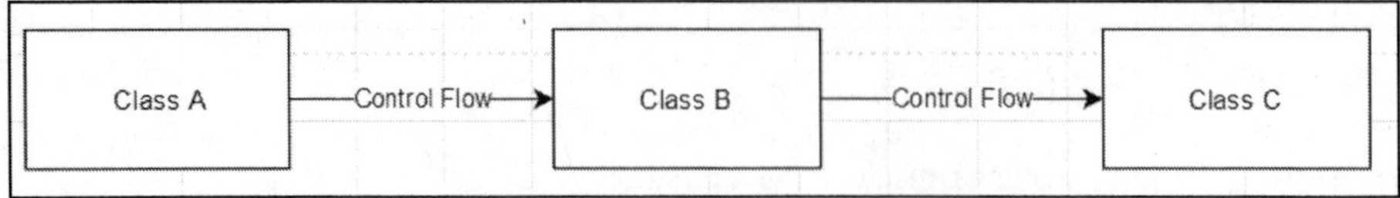

Figure 11.2: *Straight flow at runtime*

When flow is inversed, we will have a different figure at compile time. Refer to the following *Figure 11.3*:

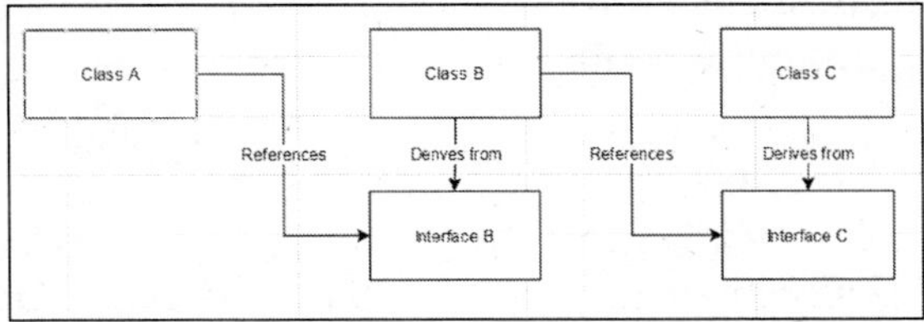

***Figure 11.3:** Inversed flow at compile time*

It looks different at runtime, as shown in *Figure 11.4*:

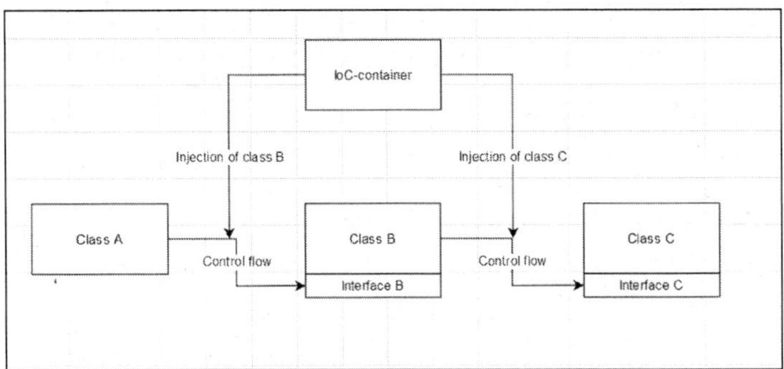

***Figure 11.4:** Inversed flow at runtime*

In *Figure 11.3* and *Figure 11.4*, we can look at IoC from different perspectives. At compile time, Class A and Class B have references to specific interfaces instead of classes. However, at runtime, dependencies are injected (passed as a parameter) through class constructor and then used by a class through a variable of interface. Such a class structure is responsible for the implementation of DIP. The second part is to have an IoC container instance, which is responsible for caching registered interfaces and classes. The third Service Locator orchestrates classes, interfaces, configuration, and injection.

Take a look at the following *Figure 11.5*:

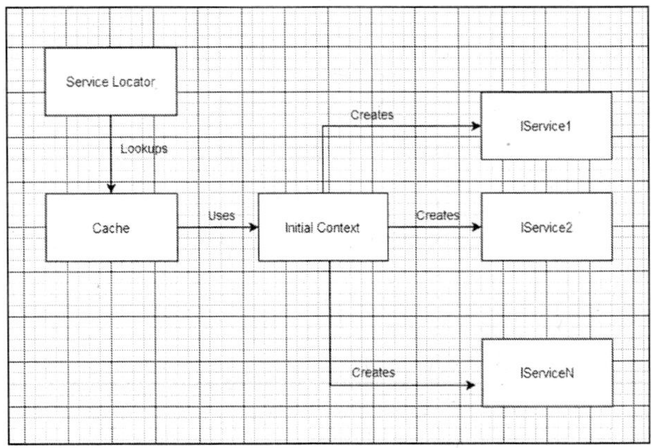

***Figure 11.5:** Conceptual IoC principle diagram*

- Service Locator is responsible for providing an API for outside code for requesting initialized entity from IoC container.
- Cache is a middleware responsible for keeping instances of objects and managing their lifetime.
- Initial Context (IoC container) is responsible for objects initialization with all the required dependencies.

.NET Core provided services

.NET Core has built-in support for DI and IoC. It provides the following capabilities:

- **Registration:** .NET Core provides a container that allows you to register your custom types.
- **Resolution:** .NET Core provides a service that helps to inject the required object into requested class.
- **Lifetime:** .NET Core is responsible for managing lifetime scopes of the DI objects.
- **Storage:** .NET Core provides a container class that keeps all objects in place.

The main package for IoC in .NET is **`Microsoft.Extensions.DependencyInjection`**. It is automatically added in the ASP.NET Core projects. However, in the console project, we should manually add it using NuGet Package Manager through Visual Studio or command line.

Here are some of the key classes and interfaces that .NET Core uses in its built-in IoC framework:

- **`IServiceCollection`:** This interface is a central part of .NET Core's IoC framework and is used for registering services for DI.
- **`ServiceProvider`:** It is a built-in class responsible for resolving and providing instances of registered services.
- **`IServiceProvider`:** This is an interface implemented by the **`ServiceProvider`** class. It provides a way to retrieve a service instance.
- **`ServiceDescriptor`:** This class describes a service type, its implementation, and lifetime. It is often used internally in the DI container, but may also be used manually when registering services.
- **`ServiceLifetime`:** This enumeration defines possible options for lifetime configuration of objects registered through IoC Container. The options are **`Singleton`**, **`Scoped`**, and **`Transient`**.

- **Microsoft.Extensions.DependencyInjection.ServiceCollectionServiceExtensions:** This is a static class that contains extension methods for adding services to **IServiceCollection**.

.NET Core's built-in IoC container is compact and does not support advanced features provided by other containers like **Autofac** or **Ninject**. However, it is sufficient for many applications and integrates seamlessly with .NET Core.

Design services for Dependency Injection

Let us write some code to understand the steps we need to take to use IoC in our console application.

We should define our dependency service class, which will provide functionality to our main class:

```
public class GenericDependency: IGenericDependency
{
        public void DoWork()
        {
            Console.WriteLine("Doing some work...");
        }
}
public interface IGenericDependency
{
        void DoWork();
}
```

Then, we define our main **Service** class, which will utilize **GenericDependency**:

```
public class GenericService
{

        private readonly IGenericDependency _genericDependency;
        public GenericService(IGenericDependency genericDependency)
        {
            _genericDependency = genericDependency;
        }

        public void DoSomeCoolStuff()
        {
```

```
            _genericDependency.DoWork();
        }
}
```

After we have implemented our DIP, we can register these entities in the .NET Core built-in IoC service and use it:

```
var container = new ServiceCollection();
container.AddScoped<IGenericDependency, GenericDependency>();
container.AddScoped<GenericService>();

// Build the IoC and get a provider
var provider = container.BuildServiceProvider();
var service = provider.GetService<GenericService>();
service.DoSomeCoolStuff();
```

By splitting this code into steps, we can make the following sequence:

- Initialize the container.
- Register entities in container.
- Make a provider by building the container.
- Request an instance of the **GenericService** from the provider.
- Call **GenericService** functionality.

In the result of the code execution, we will receive the following, as shown in *Figure 11.6*:

***Figure 11.6:** Execution of GenericService*

Adopt pipelines to .NET IoC

After exploring the basics of IoC in .NET Core, we can start refactoring our existing pipelines solution to a new reality. Let us remember what the result of the *Façade* section of *Chapter 5, Structural Design Patterns: Object Composition*, looked like. In that chapter, we had **AbstractPipeline** class and derived classes from it. We also had **AbstractFactory** with derived factories, which are responsible for pipelines creation. Refer to the following *Figure 11.7*:

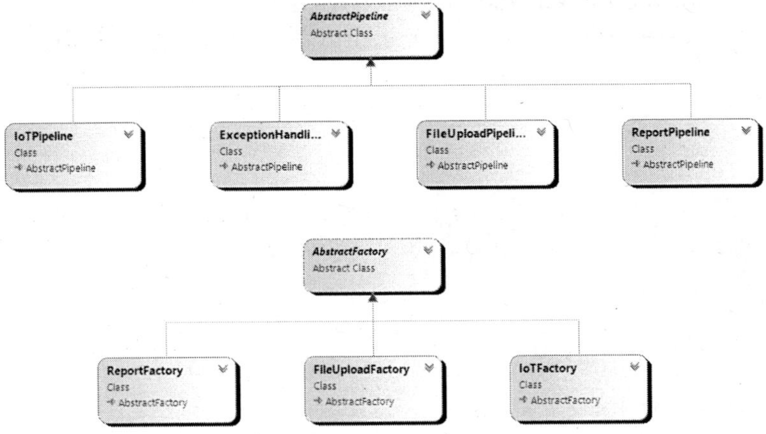

Figure 11.7: *Pipelines and Factories diagram from Chapter 5, Facade section.*

The sub-system of Communication clients will be required to be adapted to a new approach. Refer to the following *Figure 11.8*:

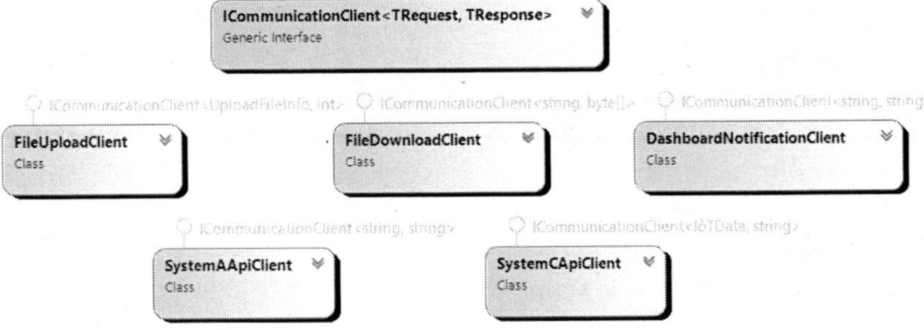

Figure 11.8: *Communication clients diagram from Chapter 5, Façade section*

The pipeline execution sub-system will also be required to be adapted to the IoC approach. Refer to the following *Figure 11.9:*

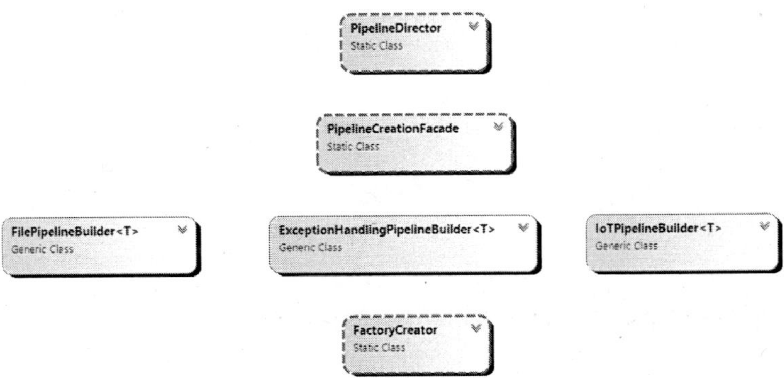

Figure 11.9: *Pipeline support classes from Chapter 5, Façade section*

Our task is to move the initialization of these classes to the IoC system and receive all needed services/classes from the IoC container instead of initializing them inside service classes.

Code

To make the code work with IoC, we need to make some adjustments to our existing codebase to support DI and IoC in the following list of classes:

- **`FactoryCreator`**
- **`FileFactory`**
- **`PipelineDirector`**
- **`PipelineCreationFacade`**
- **`FileUploadClient`**
- **`IoTFactory`**
- **`ReportFactory`**
- **`SystemAApiClient`**

Let us begin with the **`FactoryCreator`** class, which serves as our entrance point to event processing.

Before refactoring, it looked like this:

```
public static class FactoryCreator
{
        private static AbstractFactory iotFactory;
        private static AbstractFactory fileUploadFactory;
        private static AbstractFactory reportFactory;

        static FactoryCreator()
        {
            iotFactory = new IoTFactory();
            fileUploadFactory = new FileUploadFactory();
            reportFactory = new ReportFactory();
        }
        public static AbstractFactory GetPipelineFactory(BasicEvent basicEvent)
        {
            return basicEvent.Source switch
```

```
            {
                "IOT" => iotFactory,
                "FILE" => fileUploadFactory,
                "REPORT" => reportFactory,
                _ => throw new NotImplementedException("Cannot create a factory
                                                  for non known source"),
            };
        }
}
```

The problem with this class is its constructor and initialization of private variables. We are depending on them. According to the DIP, we should not initialize such private variables in the class constructor. We should allow to inject them through the constructor of class like:

```
public class FactoryCreator
{
        private IoTFactory iotFactory;
        private FileUploadFactory fileUploadFactory;
        private ReportFactory reportFactory;
        public FactoryCreator(IoTFactory iotFactory, FileUploadFactory
                        fileUploadFactory, ReportFactory reportFactory)
        {
            this.iotFactory = iotFactory;
            this.fileUploadFactory = fileUploadFactory;
            this.reportFactory = reportFactory;
        }
        public AbstractFactory GetPipelineFactory(BasicEvent basicEvent)
        {
            return basicEvent.Source switch
            {
                "IOT" => iotFactory,
                "FILE" => fileUploadFactory,
                "REPORT" => reportFactory,
                _ => throw new NotImplementedException("Cannot create a
                                    factory for non known source"),
            };
        }
}
```

`FileFactory` is the next class that we have to refactor:

```
public class FileUploadFactory: AbstractFactory
{
        public override AbstractPipeline GetPipeline(BasicEvent basicEvent)
        {
            return basicEvent.Type switch
            {
                "TypeA" => PipelineDirector.BuildTypeAPipeline(),
                "TypeB" => PipelineDirector.BuildTypeBPipeline(),
                _ => throw new NotImplementedException()
            };
        }
}
```

The main problem here is:

- This class depends on the **`PipelineDirector`**.
- **`PipelineDirector`** is a static class.

In the end, the **`FileUploadFactory`** should look like the following class:

```
public class FileUploadFactory: AbstractFactory
{
        private readonly PipelineDirector director;

        public FileUploadFactory(PipelineDirector director)
        {
            this.director = director;
        }
        public override AbstractPipeline GetPipeline(BasicEvent basicEvent)
        {
            return basicEvent.Type switch
            {
                "TypeA" => director.BuildTypeAPipeline(),
                "TypeB" => director.BuildTypeBPipeline(),
                _ => throw new NotImplementedException()
            };
        }
}
```

We have added the **PipelineDirector** as private variables. We have also added a constructor through which we can inject and use it to obtain a concrete **Pipeline**.

Our second problem was to refactor the **PipelineDirector**. Let us proceed with it:

```
public static class PipelineDirector
{
        private static Configuration config = Configuration.Instance;
        private static SystemAApiClient systemASearchClient =
                                     new (config.ASystemSearchApi);
        private static SystemAApiClient systemAStoreClient =
                                     new (config.ASystemStoreApi);
        private static FileUploadClient fileUploadAClient =
                                     new (config.ASystemUploadUrl);
        private static FileUploadClient fileUploadBClient =
                                     new (config.BSystemUploadUrl);
        private static FileDownloadClient fileDownloadClient = new ();
        private static SystemCApiClient systemCApiClient =
                                     new (config.CSystemApi);
        private static DashboardNotificationClient dashboardClient =
                                     new(config.DashboardLoggingUrl);

        public static AbstractPipeline BuildTypeAPipeline()
        {
            return PipelineCreationFacade.BuildFileUploadPipeline(true,
                                                  true, true,
                fileUploadAClient, fileDownloadClient, systemASearchClient,
                                                  systemAStoreClient);
        }
        public static AbstractPipeline BuildTypeBPipeline()
        {
            return PipelineCreationFacade.BuildFileUploadPipeline(true,
                                                  false, false,
                fileUploadBClient, fileDownloadClient, systemASearchClient, null);
        }
        public static AbstractPipeline BuildTypeCPipeline()
        {
            return PipelineCreationFacade.BuildIoTPipeline(true,
                                                  systemCApiClient);
        }
```

```
        public static AbstractPipeline BuildReportPipeline()
        {
            return new ReportPipeline(new List<AbstractPipeline>
                         {BuildTypeBPipeline(), BuildTypeCPipeline() });
        }
}
```

We should remove the static modifier from all members, remove the initialization of private variables, add the constructor, and define input parameters that can be injected by IoC:

```
public class PipelineDirector
{
        private SystemASearchApiClient systemASearchClient;
        private SystemAStoreApiClient systemAStoreClient;
        private FileAUploadClient fileUploadAClient;
        private FileBUploadClient fileUploadBClient;
        private FileDownloadClient fileDownloadClient;
        private SystemCApiClient systemCApiClient;
        private DashboardNotificationClient dashboardClient;
        private PipelineCreationFacade pipelineCreationFacade;
        public PipelineDirector(
             SystemASearchApiClient systemASearchClient,
             SystemAStoreApiClient systemAStoreClient,
             FileAUploadClient fileUploadAClient,
             FileBUploadClient fileUploadBClient,
             FileDownloadClient fileDownloadClient,
             SystemCApiClient systemCApiClient,
             DashboardNotificationClient dashboardClient,
             PipelineCreationFacade pipelineCreationFacade)
        {
            // private variables setters.
        }
        public AbstractPipeline BuildTypeAPipeline()
        {
            return pipelineCreationFacade.BuildFileUploadPipeline(
                true, true, true,fileUploadAClient, fileDownloadClient,
                systemASearchClient,systemAStoreClient);
        }
```

```
        public AbstractPipeline BuildTypeBPipeline()
        {
            return pipelineCreationFacade.BuildFileUploadPipeline(
                true, false, false, fileUploadBClient, fileDownloadClient,
                systemASearchClient, null);
        }
        // other's functions to build pipelines.
}
```

Now, this type can be registered in a container and initialized with all the required dependencies from the outside code.

We have moved the initialization of variables outside of the class by providing an instance constructor with the possibility to inject parameters. Also, we removed static modifiers from the class, constructor, and function to use this class in IoC.

Also, as you can notice, the types of private variables and parameters passed through the constructor are different. The class itself depends on an abstraction, but we are accepting concrete types because it is easier for us to implement the DIP.

The last type we need to review is our communication client with **TokenFactory**. For example, we will take **SystemAApiClient** because it faces a problem when used through the IoC container.

In our case, **SystemAApiClient** is used with two different URLs, creating a small problem as the IoC container does not know which instance to inject in the concrete case:

```
public class SystemAApiClient : ICommunicationClient<string, string>
{
        private string baseUrl = string.Empty;
        public SystemAApiClient(string baseUrl)
        {
            this.baseUrl = baseUrl;
        }
        public string ExecuteRequest(string data)
        {
            var token = TokenFactory.GetToken(SystemType.SystemAApi);

            Console.WriteLine($"SYSTEM_A_API_CLIENT: Sending message
                                    to {baseUrl}. Message: {data}");
            return string.Empty;
        }
}
```

This is an example of how our API client class looked before. The main problem is that the **TokenFactory** class is used to get a token. In **SystemAApiClient**, we should add a constructor and accept **TokenFactory** class as an input parameter:

```
public class SystemAApiClient : ICommunicationClient<string, string>
{
        private string baseUrl = string.Empty;
        private readonly TokenFactory tokenFactory;

        public SystemAApiClient(string baseUrl, TokenFactory tokenFactory)
        {
            this.baseUrl = baseUrl;
            this.tokenFactory = tokenFactory;
        }
        public string ExecuteRequest(string data)
        {
            var token = tokenFactory.GetToken(SystemType.SystemAApi);
                Console.WriteLine($"SYSTEM_A_API_CLIENT: Sending message to
                                        {baseUrl}. Message: {data}");
            return string.Empty;
        }
}
```

We have another problem with **SystemAApiClient**. As mentioned, it is used in two different methods with different URLs. It means that the IoC container should inject two different instances with different URLs and should somehow distinguish two instances for it. The next code example demonstrates the easiest solution for such a problem:

```
public class SystemASearchApiClient : SystemAApiClient
{
        public SystemASearchApiClient(string baseUrl, TokenFactory
                            tokenFactory) : base(baseUrl, tokenFactory)
        {

        }
}
public class SystemAStoreApiClient: SystemAApiClient
{
      public SystemAStoreApiClient(string baseUrl, TokenFactory tokenFactory):
                                              base(baseUrl, tokenFactory)
```

```
        {
        }
}
```

We have created two derived classes registered separately in the IoC container with different URLs. The **PipelineDirector'c** constructor accepts both and passes them to corresponding pipelines.

Before refactoring, our **TokenFactory** looked like this:

```
public static class TokenFactory
{
        private static Dictionary<SystemType,Token> tokens =
                                       new Dictionary<SystemType,Token>();
        public static Token GetToken(SystemType system)
        {
            if(tokens.ContainsKey(system) && tokens[system].ExpiresAt >
                                    DateTime.Now.AddMinutes(1))
            {
                return tokens[system];
            }
            // Imitating token request
            Thread.Sleep(200);
            tokens[system] = new Token
            {
                ExpiresAt = DateTime.Now.AddHours(2),
                TokenValue = Guid.NewGuid().ToString(),
                Type = system
            };

            return tokens[system];
        }
}
```

It is a static class whose idea is to save its state across different runs of pipelines. We should remove the static class and function modifiers, and register them in our IoC container:

```
public class TokenFactory
{
        private Dictionary<SystemType,Token> tokens =
                                    new Dictionary<SystemType,Token>();
```

```
        public Token GetToken(SystemType system)
        {
                if(tokens.ContainsKey(system) && tokens[system].ExpiresAt >
                                                DateTime.Now.AddMinutes(1))
            {
                return tokens[system];
            }
            // Imitating token request
            Thread.Sleep(200);
            tokens[system] = new Token
            {
                ExpiresAt = DateTime.Now.AddHours(2),
                TokenValue = Guid.NewGuid().ToString(),
                Type = system
            };

            return tokens[system];
        }
}
```

It was the simplest refactoring, and that covers everything for the current moment. At this point, we can register our classes in the IoC container and try to use it to run our application.

In the result of IoC container integration, we will have this piece of code at startup:

```
var container = new ServiceCollection();
Configuration config = Configuration.Instance;
container.AddSingleton<TokenFactory>();
container.AddScoped(x => new SystemASearchApiClient(
                config.ASystemSearchApi, x.GetService<TokenFactory>()));
container.AddScoped(x => new SystemAStoreApiClient(
                config.ASystemStoreApi, x.GetService<TokenFactory>()));
container.AddScoped(x => new FileAUploadClient(
                config.ASystemUploadUrl, x.GetService<TokenFactory>()));
container.AddScoped(x => new FileBUploadClient(
                config.BSystemUploadUrl, x.GetService<TokenFactory>()));
container.AddScoped<FileDownloadClient>();
container.AddScoped(x => new SystemCApiClient(
```

```
                    config.CSystemApi, x.GetService<TokenFactory>()));
container.AddScoped(x => new DashboardNotificationClient(
                config.DashboardLoggingUrl,
                x.GetService<TokenFactory>()));
container.AddScoped<PipelineCreationFacade>();
container.AddScoped<PipelineDirector>();
container.AddScoped<IoTFactory>();
container.AddScoped<FileUploadFactory>();
container.AddScoped<ReportFactory>();
container.AddScoped<FactoryCreator>();
            // Build the IoC and get a provider
var provider = container.BuildServiceProvider();
var factory = provider.GetService<FactoryCreator>();
            // Events definition
List<BasicEvent> eventList = new List<BasicEvent> { event1, event2,
                            event3, event4, event5, event6, reportEvent };
eventList.ForEach(eventObj =>
{
           factory.GetPipelineFactory(eventObj).GetPipeline(eventObj)
                                                  .Process(eventObj);
});
```

The first part of the code, where we are initializing the **ServiceCollection** instance and registering the required classes, is similar to what we have done in the preceding section.

We have added our **TokenFactory** as singleton to demonstrate different lifetime strategies for objects. For communicating with clients, we have used the possibility to customize class instance initialization and passed specific URLs to each of them. As you can notice in the customization method, developers have access to already registered objects, and they can be retrieved by using the **GetService<T>** method. Other classes are registered with the **AddScoped** method.

Then, we are using the received factory variable in this line:

```
var factory = provider.GetService<FactoryCreator>();
```

To process our events with initialized pipeline:

```
factory.GetPipelineFactory(eventObj).GetPipeline(eventObj).
Process(eventObj);
```

In the result of execution, this code will look as shown in the following *Figure 11.10*:

```
Microsoft Visual Studio Debug Console
DASHBOARD_CLIENT: Executing step: PROCESSING_STARTED for event: eda4fc01-3aa1-4fae-a329-26beb8dafeb2-IOT-TypeC
DASHBOARD_CLIENT: Executing step: SAVE_METADATA for event: eda4fc01-3aa1-4fae-a329-26beb8dafeb2-IOT-TypeC
DASHBOARD_CLIENT: Executing step: EVENT_PROCESSING for event: eda4fc01-3aa1-4fae-a329-26beb8dafeb2-IOT-TypeC
SYSTM_C_API_CLIENT: Sending message to http://systemC.processing.com/api. Message: {"Source":"IOT","Action":"TEMP_UPDATE
","Value":"92.2"}
DASHBOARD_CLIENT: Executing step: UPDATE_METADATA for event: eda4fc01-3aa1-4fae-a329-26beb8dafeb2-IOT-TypeC
DASHBOARD_CLIENT: Executing step: PROCESSING_FINISHED for event: eda4fc01-3aa1-4fae-a329-26beb8dafeb2-IOT-TypeC

DASHBOARD_CLIENT: Executing step: PROCESSING_STARTED for event: 87e80b4e-87bd-4846-a6ce-9708fbbc3afb-REPORT-TypeR
DASHBOARD_CLIENT: Executing step: EVENT_PREPROCESSING for event: 87e80b4e-87bd-4846-a6ce-9708fbbc3afb-REPORT-TypeR
DOWNLOAD_CLIENT: Downloading file from  http://typeA.file.url.
DASHBOARD_CLIENT: Executing step: EVENT_SEARCH for event: 87e80b4e-87bd-4846-a6ce-9708fbbc3afb-REPORT-TypeR
SYSTEM_A_API_CLIENT: Sending message to http://systemA.com/api/search. Message: TypeBFilename.jpg
DASHBOARD_CLIENT: Executing step: EVENT_PROCESSING for event: 87e80b4e-87bd-4846-a6ce-9708fbbc3afb-REPORT-TypeR
FILE_UPLOAD_CLIENT: Uploading file to http://file.storage.com/systemB/upload. File: {"FileName":"TypeBFilename.jpg","Con
tent":""}
DASHBOARD_CLIENT: Executing step: PROCESSING_FINISHED for event: 87e80b4e-87bd-4846-a6ce-9708fbbc3afb-REPORT-TypeR
DASHBOARD_CLIENT: Executing step: PROCESSING_STARTED for event: 87e80b4e-87bd-4846-a6ce-9708fbbc3afb-REPORT-TypeR
DASHBOARD_CLIENT: Executing step: SAVE_METADATA for event: 87e80b4e-87bd-4846-a6ce-9708fbbc3afb-REPORT-TypeR
DASHBOARD_CLIENT: Executing step: EVENT_PROCESSING for event: 87e80b4e-87bd-4846-a6ce-9708fbbc3afb-REPORT-TypeR
SYSTM_C_API_CLIENT: Sending message to http://systemC.processing.com/api. Message: {"Source":"REPORT","Action":"TEMP_UPD
ATE","Value":"92.2"}
DASHBOARD_CLIENT: Executing step: UPDATE_METADATA for event: 87e80b4e-87bd-4846-a6ce-9708fbbc3afb-REPORT-TypeR
DASHBOARD_CLIENT: Executing step: PROCESSING_FINISHED for event: 87e80b4e-87bd-4846-a6ce-9708fbbc3afb-REPORT-TypeR

MS ellapsed: 865
```

Figure 11.10: *Result of pipelines execution using IoC*

The code works as expected and has become more modular, robust, and testable.

At this moment, we have implemented most of the IoC approach, however, we have not fully applied the principle of DI. It is a crucial part of the IoC principle. Refer to the following *Figure 11.11*:

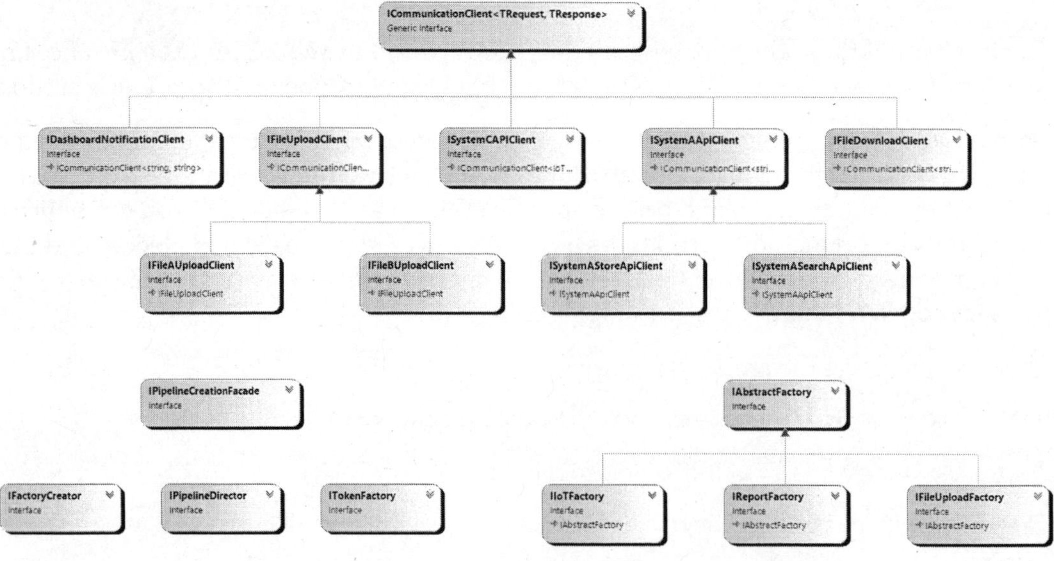

Figure 11.11: *Diagram of interfaces that should be created*

In the given figure, you can look at the interfaces that need to be created to apply DI on the classes registered in the IoC container at the current moment. Refer to the following *Figure 11.12*:

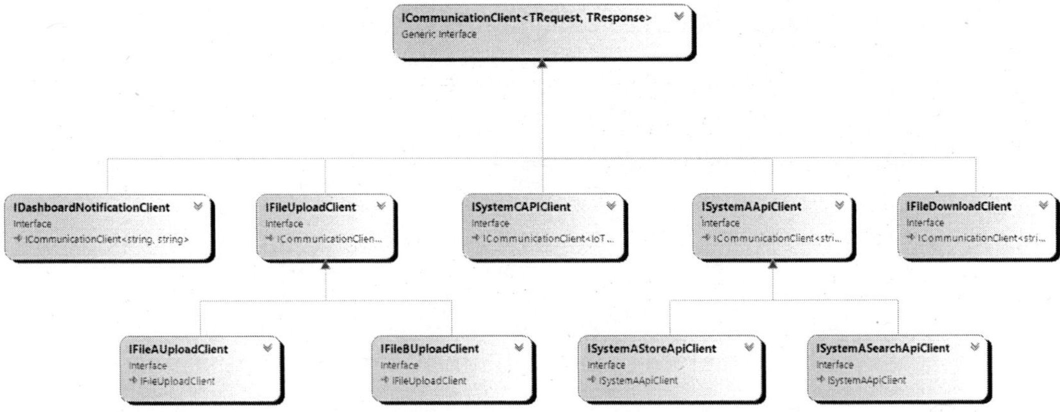

Figure 11.12: *Communication client's interfaces diagram*

The first part is about communication client. **`ICommunicationClient`** was used before, but we have created additional interfaces to separate our communication clients more precisely by the functionality they provide or by the endpoint they use to execute a request. Refer to the following *Figure 11.13*:

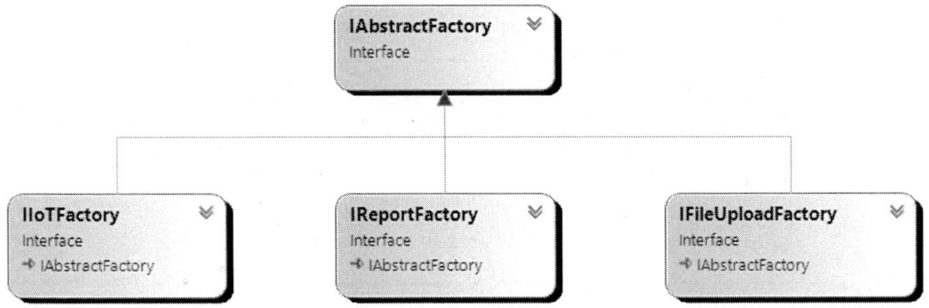

Figure 11.13: *Factory interfaces diagram*

For the next step, we need to convert **`AbstractFactory`** into an interface and create additional interfaces for each concrete factory class. Refer to the following *Figure 11.14*:

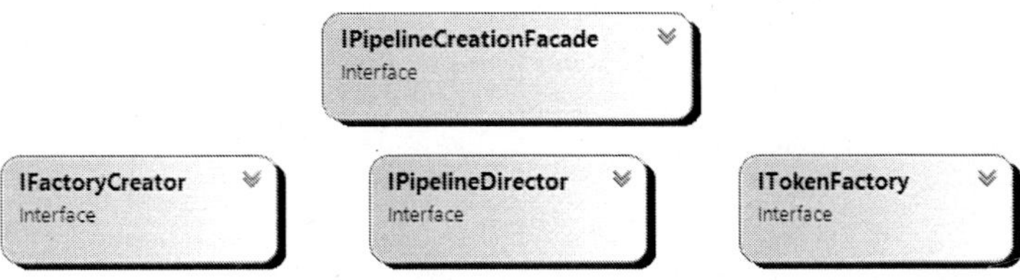

Figure 11.14: *Pipeline creation support classes interfaces diagram*

These interfaces should be created for helper classes responsible for **AbstractPipeline** instance creation.

Let us define these interfaces.

We will start with Communication clients and **ITokenFactory**:

```
public interface ICommunicationClient<TRequest, TResponse>
{
        TResponse ExecuteRequest(TRequest request);
}
public interface IDashboardNotificationClient : ICommunicationClient<string, string>
{
}
public interface IFileDownloadClient : ICommunicationClient<string, byte[]>
{
}
public interface IFileUploadClient : ICommunicationClient<UploadFileInfo,
int>
{
}
public interface IFileAUploadClient : IFileUploadClient
{
}
public interface IFileBUploadClient : IFileUploadClient
{
}
public interface ISystemASearchApiClient : ISystemAApiClient
{
}
public interface ISystemAApiClient : ICommunicationClient<string, string>
{
}
public interface ISystemAStoreApiClient : ISystemAApiClient
{
}
public interface ISystemCAPIClient : ICommunicationClient<IoTData, string>
{
}
public interface ITokenFactory
```

```
{
      Token GetToken(SystemType system);
}
```

First, we define **ICommunicationClient<TRequest, TResponse>** as a base interface for all communication clients. Then, we define interfaces whose names are inferred from their usage context and target endpoints. This is needed to separate them from each other and to provide the IoC framework with a clear indicator using which it can inject a correct instance of the classes.

Next, we are going to create interfaces for factory classes. We have three of them and the **AbstractFactory** class, which we will convert into an interface:

```
public interface IAbstractFactory
{
       AbstractPipeline GetPipeline(BasicEvent basicEvent);
}
public interface IFileUploadFactory : IAbstractFactory
{
}
public interface IIoTFactory : IAbstractFactory
{
}
public interface IReportFactory : IAbstractFactory
{
}
```

The same reason goes here: we need to separate them for IoC to be able to inject the correct instance into the correct constructor.

The last part is interfaces for support classes, which are responsible for pipelines creation:

```
public interface IFactoryCreator
{
       IAbstractFactory GetPipelineFactory(BasicEvent basicEvent);
    }
    public interface IPipelineCreationFacade
    {
       AbstractPipeline BuildFileUploadPipeline(bool shouldBeFileProcessed,
            bool shouldEventBeStored, bool shouldSaveMetadata,
```

```
            IFileUploadClient fileUploadClient,
            IFileDownloadClient fileDownloadClient,
            ISystemASearchApiClient searchApiClient,
            ISystemAStoreApiClient storeApiClient);
AbstractPipeline BuildIoTPipeline(bool shouldSaveMetadata,
            ISystemCAPIClient apiClient);

AbstractPipeline BuildReportPipeline(bool shouldBeFileProcessed,
            bool shouldEventBeStored, bool shouldSaveMetadata,
           IFileUploadClient fileUploadClient,
           IFileDownloadClient fileDownloadClient,
           ISystemASearchApiClient searchApiClient,
           ISystemAStoreApiClient storeApiClient,
           bool shouldSaveIoTMetadata,
           ISystemCAPIClient apiClient);
}

public interface IPipelineDirector
{
        AbstractPipeline BuildTypeAPipeline();
        AbstractPipeline BuildTypeBPipeline();
        AbstractPipeline BuildTypeCPipeline();
        AbstractPipeline BuildReportPipeline();
}
```

In the **IPipelineCreationFacade** interface, you can notice that we are using already-defined interfaces for our communication clients instead of the generic **ICommunicationClient<TRequest, TResponse>** interface.

With such separation on interfaces and concrete classes, our initialization code of IoC will look like:

```
private static IServiceProvider Configure()
{
           var container = new ServiceCollection();
           Configuration config = Configuration.Instance;
           container.AddSingleton<ITokenFactory, TokenFactory>();
          container.AddScoped<ISystemASearchApiClient, SystemASearchApiClient>
               (x => new SystemASearchApiClient(config.ASystemSearchApi,
                                x.GetService<ITokenFactory>()));
           container.AddScoped<ISystemAStoreApiClient,
```

```
            SystemAStoreApiClient>
                (x => new SystemAStoreApiClient(config.ASystemStoreApi,
                 x.GetService<ITokenFactory>()));
            container.AddScoped<IFileAUploadClient, FileAUploadClient>
                (x => new FileAUploadClient(config.ASystemUploadUrl,
                 x.GetService<ITokenFactory>()));
            container.AddScoped<IFileBUploadClient, FileBUploadClient>
                (x => new FileBUploadClient(config.BSystemUploadUrl,
                 x.GetService<ITokenFactory>()));
            container.AddScoped<IFileDownloadClient, FileDownloadClient>();
            container.AddScoped<ISystemCAPIClient, SystemCApiClient>
                (x => new SystemCApiClient(config.CSystemApi,
                 x.GetService<ITokenFactory>()));


           container.AddScoped<IDashboardNotificationClient,
                        DashboardNotificationClient>
                        (x => new DashboardNotificationClient(
                         config.DashboardLoggingUrl,
                         x.GetService<ITokenFactory>()));
           container.AddScoped<IPipelineCreationFacade,
                        PipelineCreationFacade>();
           container.AddScoped<IPipelineDirector, PipelineDirector>();
           container.AddScoped<IIoTFactory, IoTFactory>();
           container.AddScoped<IFileUploadFactory, FileUploadFactory>();
           container.AddScoped<IReportFactory, ReportFactory>();
           container.AddScoped<IFactoryCreator, FactoryCreator>();

           // Build the IoC and get a provider
           var provider = container.BuildServiceProvider();
           return provider;
}
```

Each registered class is paired with an appropriate interface. We can look at some of the classes by implementing their interfaces to see what has changed:

For example, look at some of the Communication clients:

```
public class FileUploadClient : IFileUploadClient
{
        private string baseUrl = string.Empty;
        private readonly ITokenFactory tokenFactory;
```

```
        public FileUploadClient(string baseUrl, ITokenFactory tokenFactory)
        {
            this.baseUrl = baseUrl;
            this.tokenFactory = tokenFactory;
        }
        public int ExecuteRequest(UploadFileInfo data)
        {
            var token = tokenFactory.GetToken(SystemType.SystemUpload);
            string jsonString = JsonSerializer.Serialize(data);
            Console.WriteLine($"FILE_UPLOAD_CLIENT: Uploading file to {this.
                                  baseUrl}. File: {jsonString}");
            return 0;
        }
}
public class FileAUploadClient: FileUploadClient, IFileAUploadClient
{
        public FileAUploadClient(string baseUrl, ITokenFactory
                         tokenFactory): base(baseUrl, tokenFactory)
        {
        }
}
public class FileBUploadClient : FileUploadClient, IFileBUploadClient
{
        public FileBUploadClient(string baseUrl, ITokenFactory
                   tokenFactory) : base(baseUrl, tokenFactory)
        {
        }
}
```

Right now, we have three different classes. One of them is a base class: **FileUploadClient**. The other two represent different endpoints against which they will be used: **FileAUploadClient** and **FileBUploadClient**. Each class is derived from an appropriate interface.

Let us take a look at them in more detail:

```
public interface IFileUploadClient : ICommunicationClient<UploadFileInfo, int>
{
}
public interface IFileAUploadClient : IFileUploadClient
{
}
public interface IFileBUploadClient : IFileUploadClient
{
}
```

The base interface **IFileDownloadClient** creates a bridge between **ICommunicationClient** interface and business functionality. It decouples the infrastructure contract from the business contract. In this case, business logic and infrastructure logic can be modified independently from each other. Such decoupling helps us build more modular and robust code that is not directly dependent on technical details.

We derive the concrete business interfaces from our base interface, **IFileUploadClient**, and then use them on concrete classes:

```
public class FileUploadClient : IFileUploadClient
{
        private string baseUrl = string.Empty;
        private readonly ITokenFactory tokenFactory;

        public FileUploadClient(string baseUrl, ITokenFactory tokenFactory)
        {
            this.baseUrl = baseUrl;
            this.tokenFactory = tokenFactory;
        }
        public int ExecuteRequest(UploadFileInfo data)
        {
            var token = tokenFactory.GetToken(SystemType.SystemUpload);

            string jsonString = JsonSerializer.Serialize(data);
            Console.WriteLine($"FILE_UPLOAD_CLIENT: Uploading file to {this.
                                      baseUrl}. File: {jsonString}");
            return 0;
        }
}
```

The base class derived from base interface provides all the needed functionality to execute the request.

Two additional (business) classes provide type definitions deriving from different interfaces, which are later used at the IoC registration phase:

```
public class FileAUploadClient: FileUploadClient, IFileAUploadClient
{
        public FileAUploadClient(string baseUrl, ITokenFactory
                              tokenFactory): base(baseUrl, tokenFactory)
        {
        }
}

public class FileBUploadClient : FileUploadClient, IFileBUploadClient
{
        public FileBUploadClient(string baseUrl, ITokenFactory
                              tokenFactory) : base(baseUrl, tokenFactory)
        {
        }
}
```

To register in IoC in these classes, we have used the following code:

```
container.AddScoped<IFileAUploadClient, FileAUploadClient>(x => new
FileAUploadClient(config.ASystemUploadUrl, x.GetService<ITokenFactory>()));
container.AddScoped<IFileBUploadClient, FileBUploadClient>(x => new
FileBUploadClient(config.BSystemUploadUrl, x.GetService<ITokenFactory>()));
```

After this, we can use these interfaces in other classes to receive instances through injection. As an example, we can look at **`PipelineDirector`**:

```
public class PipelineDirector: IPipelineDirector
{
        private ISystemASearchApiClient systemASearchClient;
        private ISystemAStoreApiClient systemAStoreClient;
        private IFileAUploadClient fileUploadAClient;
        private IFileBUploadClient fileUploadBClient;
        private IFileDownloadClient fileDownloadClient;
        private ISystemCAPIClient systemCApiClient;
        private IPipelineCreationFacade pipelineCreationFacade;
        public PipelineDirector(ISystemASearchApiClient systemASearchClient,
            ISystemAStoreApiClient systemAStoreClient, IFileAUploadClient
```

```
        fileUploadAClient, IFileBUploadClient fileUploadBClient,
        IFileDownloadClient fileDownloadClient,ISystemCAPIClient
        systemCApiClient,IPipelineCreationFacade
        pipelineCreationFacade)
    {
        this.systemASearchClient = systemASearchClient;
        this.systemAStoreClient = systemAStoreClient;
        this.fileUploadAClient = fileUploadAClient;
        this.fileUploadBClient = fileUploadBClient;
        this.fileDownloadClient = fileDownloadClient;
        this.systemCApiClient = systemCApiClient;
        this.pipelineCreationFacade = pipelineCreationFacade;
    }

    public AbstractPipeline BuildTypeAPipeline()
    {
        return pipelineCreationFacade.BuildFileUploadPipeline(true,
                                                    true, true,
            fileUploadAClient, fileDownloadClient, systemASearchClient,
                                                systemAStoreClient);
    }
    public AbstractPipeline BuildTypeBPipeline()
    {
           return pipelineCreationFacade.BuildFileUploadPipeline(true,
                  false, false, fileUploadBClient, fileDownloadClient,
                  systemASearchClient, null);
    }
    // Other methods
}
```

Now, this class accepts only interfaces through a constructor. These interfaces are fully business-specific. There are no **ICommunicationClient** instances.

In this case, we decouple this class from:

- Technical part of the project
- Implementation of the concrete functionality

It is also derived from the interface **IPipelineDirector**, which gives us an opportunity to inject it into other classes and use it through the interface.

As a result of such a transformation, we have received more clean, modular, and robust code, which is relatively easy to change and support. It works in the same way as non-transformed code, which you can see in *Figure 11.15:*

```
Microsoft Visual Studio Debug Console
DASHBOARD_CLIENT: Executing step: PROCESSING_STARTED for event: e6b99f81-7052-4922-8eab-31c27de7a628-IOT-TypeC
DASHBOARD_CLIENT: Executing step: SAVE_METADATA for event: e6b99f81-7052-4922-8eab-31c27de7a628-IOT-TypeC
DASHBOARD_CLIENT: Executing step: EVENT_PROCESSING for event: e6b99f81-7052-4922-8eab-31c27de7a628-IOT-TypeC
SYSTM_C_API_CLIENT: Sending message to http://systemC.processing.com/api. Message: {"Source":"IOT","Action":"TEMP_UPDATE
","Value":"92.2"}
DASHBOARD_CLIENT: Executing step: UPDATE_METADATA for event: e6b99f81-7052-4922-8eab-31c27de7a628-IOT-TypeC
DASHBOARD_CLIENT: Executing step: PROCESSING_FINISHED for event: e6b99f81-7052-4922-8eab-31c27de7a628-IOT-TypeC

DASHBOARD_CLIENT: Executing step: PROCESSING_STARTED for event: 511c73cd-df53-4684-9519-685d0869670c-REPORT-TypeR
DASHBOARD_CLIENT: Executing step: EVENT_PREPROCESSING for event: 511c73cd-df53-4684-9519-685d0869670c-REPORT-TypeR
DOWNLOAD_CLIENT: Downloading file from  http://typeA.file.url.
DASHBOARD_CLIENT: Executing step: EVENT_SEARCH for event: 511c73cd-df53-4684-9519-685d0869670c-REPORT-TypeR
SYSTEM_A_API_CLIENT: Sending message to http://systemA.com/api/search. Message: TypeBFilename.jpg
DASHBOARD_CLIENT: Executing step: EVENT_PROCESSING for event: 511c73cd-df53-4684-9519-685d0869670c-REPORT-TypeR
FILE_UPLOAD_CLIENT: Uploading file to http://file.storage.com/systemB/upload. File: {"FileName":"TypeBFilename.jpg","Con
tent":""}
DASHBOARD_CLIENT: Executing step: PROCESSING_FINISHED for event: 511c73cd-df53-4684-9519-685d0869670c-REPORT-TypeR
DASHBOARD_CLIENT: Executing step: PROCESSING_STARTED for event: 511c73cd-df53-4684-9519-685d0869670c-REPORT-TypeR
DASHBOARD_CLIENT: Executing step: SAVE_METADATA for event: 511c73cd-df53-4684-9519-685d0869670c-REPORT-TypeR
DASHBOARD_CLIENT: Executing step: EVENT_PROCESSING for event: 511c73cd-df53-4684-9519-685d0869670c-REPORT-TypeR
SYSTM_C_API_CLIENT: Sending message to http://systemC.processing.com/api. Message: {"Source":"REPORT","Action":"TEMP_UPD
ATE","Value":"92.2"}
DASHBOARD_CLIENT: Executing step: UPDATE_METADATA for event: 511c73cd-df53-4684-9519-685d0869670c-REPORT-TypeR
DASHBOARD_CLIENT: Executing step: PROCESSING_FINISHED for event: 511c73cd-df53-4684-9519-685d0869670c-REPORT-TypeR

MS ellapsed: 922
```

Figure 11.15: *The result of refactored code execution*

Introducing an additional framework will add some performance impact. However, as we used a compact library, this impact is not big. It takes an additional **`~30ms`** to register and initialize all objects in the IoC Container. It is not a high cost for the possibility of decoupling initialization and injection to a single startup class.

Conclusion

It is the last chapter of this book. We only took a quick look at the complexity hidden under the UI of most popular projects. In this small project, we have about ~30 entities. The real-world project contains millions of lines of code and thousands of entities, algorithms, and business rules. To manage the complexity, our predecessors already invented useful methods to deal, hide, and simplify it: GoF, SOLID principles, and many other patterns, practices, and principles software developers use in everyday work. However, principles like KISS, DRY, and SoC plus OOP methodology are crucial in applying more advanced techniques to your codebase. Always start with the simplest because it is a way to build complex. Overengineering and premature optimization are the bases of failure in the software development field.

You can notice that in this chapter, we did not touch **`AbstractPipeline`** class, and we have not moved its initialization to the IoC container. If you are interested enough, you can try to do it yourself. This is your possibility to take a practice lesson and improvise!

Good Luck, and Have Fun!

Index

O

P

R

S